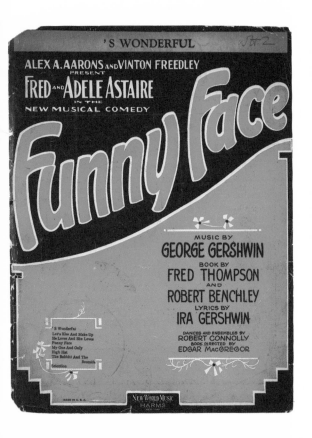

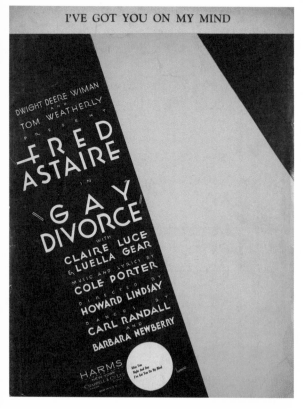

Easy to Remember

EASY

TO

REMEMBER

*The Great American Songwriters
and Their Songs*

WILLIAM ZINSSER

DAVID R. GODINE, PUBLISHER, INC.

First published in 2001 by
David R. Godine, Publisher
Post Office Box 450
Jaffrey, New Hampshire 03452
www.godine.com

Library of Congress Cataloging-in-Publication Data

Zinsser, William Knowlton.
Easy to remember: the great American songwriters and their songs / William Zinsser.
        p.cm.
ISBN 1-56792-325-9 (softcover: alk. paper)
1. popular music—United States—History and criticism I. Title.
ML3477.Z57 2000
782.421640973—dc21

Design by Katy Homans and Christine N. Moog

This book was set in Scala.

FIRST SOFTCOVER PRINTING, 2006

Printed in the United States of America

Contents

Easy to Remember

Introduction

I had the good luck to be born at the dawn of the golden age of American popular song, which began with the musical *Show Boat* in 1927 and lasted until the rise of rock in the mid-1960s. The thousands of songs written during that 40-year period—songs from Broadway shows, songs from Hollywood movies and songs that became hits on their own—were part of America's domestic landscape; everybody knew them. Today those songs are still in the air, still the standard literature and point of departure for jazz singers and musicians and cabaret artists. Frank Sinatra sang almost nothing else.

The America of my boyhood was a self-entertaining nation. Every home seemed to have a piano and at least one member of the family who could play it, and every five-and-ten-cent store sold sheet music of the latest hits; many stores employed a pianist to demonstrate the songs. My parents would bring home the sheet music from Broadway shows, and those songs worked their way into my ear. (It was my further good luck to be born with a musical ear—a gift I would later put to use as a part-time pianist.) The words appealed to me as much as the music; I already knew I wanted to grow up to be a newspaperman. I began to keep track of who had written the songs and to recognize the different composers and lyricists by their distinctive voice.

Harold Arlen and Ted Koehler were the first ones to hook me, with "Stormy Weather" (it was so emotional), and then Arthur Schwartz and Howard Dietz, with "Dancing in the Dark" (it was so suave), and then Cole Porter, with "You're the Top" (it was so clever), and then Irving Berlin, Jerome Kern, Dorothy Fields, and George Gershwin and Ira Gershwin with their brilliant scores for the Fred Astaire-Ginger Rogers movies. Those were my first giants, and I studied how they had constructed their songs, marveling that so

An immigrant kid named Irving Berlin wrote a song that sold a million copies in 1917, "Alexander's Ragtime Band," and he was still writing hits half a century later. Two of them, "White Christmas" and "God Bless America," became American anthems. No other songwriter so personifies the golden age of American song.

9

much originality and wit could be achieved in so small a space. It dawned on me that I was growing up along with an evolving body of American *lieder*, a cultural form as characteristic of the 1930s as the screwball comedies of Hollywood and the radio hours of Fred Allen and Jack Benny.

When I became a teenager I was deemed old enough to be exposed to Cole Porter's risqué lyrics, and my parents began taking me to Broadway shows. The pit orchestra was the most galvanizing of sounds, the musical theater the most wonderful of art forms. To hear the latest songs by Cole Porter and Irving Berlin and Rodgers & Hart (two new giants) actually delivered from a stage—belted out by some force of nature like Ethel Merman—was a thrill as potent as the one when I first saw the immaculate grass infield of the Polo Grounds. Musicals elbowed their way into my brain next to baseball as a life addiction.

But I wasn't a theater snob. I was just as addicted to movies, especially movie musicals, especially bad ones, the kind that starred people like Don Ameche and Betty Grable and Carmen Miranda, because many of the best new songs were being written for those movies by Harry Warren, Harold Arlen, Johnny Mercer, Jimmy Van Heusen, Frank Loesser and other Hollywood contract composers and lyricists. I wanted to hear their latest work as much as I wanted to hear the latest Cole Porter.

That quest whiled away many nights during World War II. I can still picture the army bases in North Africa and Italy where I saw *Iceland*, with Sonja Henie, in order to hear Warren's "There Will Never Be Another You," and saw *And the Angels Sing* and *Belle of the Yukon* to hear Van Heusen's "It Could Happen to You" and "Like Someone in Love," and saw *Here Come the Waves* and *The Sky's the Limit* to hear Arlen and Mercer's "Let's Take the Long Way Home" and "My Shining Hour." Songs were the sentimental glue of the war years—a whole subspecies of ballads of separation and longing and loss. Jule Styne and Frank Loesser and Sammy Cahn said it all with "I Don't Want to Walk Without You" and "I'll Walk Alone" and "Saturday Night Is the Loneliest Night of the Week."

Home from the war, I began my real occupation, as a writer and editor with the *New York Herald Tribune*. One day in 1948 the paper's venerable drama editor was gently retired and younger blood was sought. The managing editor remembered that I was a musical theater fan, and I found myself in charge of the Sunday section devoted to the theater, movies, music, dance and art. Two seats on the aisle for every Broadway opening came with the job of drama editor and with my subsequent job as movie critic—

a ten-year sojourn in the journalistic crannies of show business. Dozens of musicals arrived during that decade, including *South Pacific*, *Guys and Dolls*, *The King and I*, *The Music Man*, *West Side Story* and *My Fair Lady*. I saw them all and put their songs in my memory bank.

Only one gap remained in the bank: all the songs from all the shows that had come to Broadway before the first original-cast album—Decca's *Oklahoma!*—in 1943. That black hole was filled by Goddard Lieberson of Columbia Records with his impeccably pro-duced LPs reconstructing the scores of bygone musicals. I already knew the hit ballads from shows like the Gershwins' *Oh, Kay!* and Rodgers & Hart's *The Boys From Syracuse* and *Pal Joey*; they had long been standards. But what about all the *other* songs: the opening numbers and funny songs and situation songs? I consumed Lieb-erson's LPs and other archeological albums and retroactively filled in the blanks.

★   ★   ★

This book is the story of my lifelong romance with American popu-lar song—the Broadway songs, the Hollywood songs, the individual hits by composers like Hoagy Carmichael, and all the great one-shots that came from out of nowhere: "Moon River," "You Go to My Head," "I'll Never Smile Again." My book doesn't claim to be definitive; it's just one man's tour of his collection, as idiosyncratic as another man's collection of stamps or coins or butterflies. Nor am I unusual in the number of songs I know; jazz musicians have much of the literature somewhere in their fingertips, and many collectors—true fanatics—regard their knowledge as "encyclopedic."

I've organized the book around the lives of the great song-writers, more or less chronologically, explaining where their talent came from, how their songs got written, and why I think the songs are good—matters of construction and craft. Because so many of the songs originated on Broadway, my book is also a partial history of the American musical theater, especially where new ground was broken: *Show Boat*, *Of Thee I Sing*, *Porgy and Bess*, *Lady in the Dark*, *Pal Joey*, *Oklahoma!*, *Guys and Dolls*, *West Side Story*, *My Fair Lady*. But I'm not a theater historian; my emphasis is on the songs and the songwriters.

Nor am I a nostalgist, pining for a vanished age. "They don't write songs like that anymore," the mourners say. I think 40 years is a good run, and I'm grateful for what we got. My book is a cele-bration, not a funeral, and one of the miracles I'm celebrating is how powerfully the songs have become lodged in the nation's collective memory. I feel their power every time I play them and look at the faces in the room. I try to phrase the melody with the lyric in mind, as a jazz singer would—to play Hart more than Rodgers, Ira Gershwin more than George—because the songs first engage their listeners with what they say. People connect with the familiar story that the lyrics tell ("If they asked me I could write a book") or with the familiar curve of the melody that carries the words ("Somewhere, over the rainbow"). But the songs are even stronger in their associations. Like smells, they are an instant mechanism for recovering the past. "Pat and I first danced to that song," people tell me, or "That takes me back to Naples during the war," or "That was the big number at my high school prom."

Often I know the people in the room and know of some of their pains and disappointments. If I don't, I can often guess. But something happens when they listen to an old Gershwin tune, or an old Cole Porter or Rodgers & Hart song. Their faces change; the aches and worries drop away. Watching them, I'm reminded that pianists who play this literature end up doing more than they signed up to do. The songs themselves take over the keyboard, providing solace and release and joy and the consolations of memory.

Sigmund Romberg and the Europeans

The golden age of American popular song was born on December 27, 1927, when *Show Boat* opened on Broadway. The musical play by Jerome Kern and Oscar Hammerstein II was set in the heart of America—on the Mississippi River itself—and it dealt with social and racial themes that American songwriters hadn't previously aspired to touch. It thereby served notice that musicals could be a serious art form and could tell serious stories.

Until then they had made no such higher claims. Their plots were familiar fluff—coeds and college boys, flappers and millionaires—and many of them weren't even American in their origins. They were derived from a Viennese tradition of operetta, their scores written by composers like Rudolph Friml (*Rose Marie, The Vagabond King*) and Sigmund Romberg (*Blossom Time, The Desert Song*) who were born in the Austro-Hungarian empire. When those composers emigrated to the United States they continued to write European-style "light operas," and nobody seemed to mind. Romberg's *The Student Prince*, a musical about a German prince who falls in love with a waitress in Old Heidelberg, opened on Broadway in 1924 and ran for 608 performances.

Today it's hard to believe that audiences in the Jazz Age were willing to put up with waitresses in old Heidelberg for so long; F. Scott Fitzgerald told us the twenties were sophisticated. Perhaps World War I had given Americans their fill of reality; they knew they could attend a Romberg musical without being exposed to any new ideas. But probably the main reason was that Romberg and Friml, like their foreign-born predecessors Franz Lehar (*The Merry Widow*) and Victor Herbert (*Babes in Toyland*), wrote glorious melodies, evocative of string trios in the grand hotels of Europe. Just to sit in

ONE ALONE

LAWRENCE SCHWAB & FRANK MANDEL
PRESENT THE ROMANTIC OPERETTA

The Desert Song

BOOK & LYRICS BY
OTTO HARBACH
OSCAR HAMMERSTEIN 2ND
AND FRANK MANDEL
MUSIC BY
SIGMUND ROMBERG

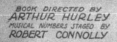

BOOK DIRECTED BY
ARTHUR HURLEY
MUSICAL NUMBERS STAGED BY
ROBERT CONNOLLY

Romance
The Riff Song
Let's Have A Love - Affair
Love's Dear Yearning
"It"
One Alone
The Desert Song
One Flower Grows Alone In Your Garden
Selection

HARMS
INCORPORATED
BY ARRANGEMENT WITH
M. WITMARK & SONS
NEW YORK

the warm bubble bath of all those notes was a luxury. To this day the tunes that Romberg composed for his operettas—"Deep in My Heart, Dear," "The Desert Song," "One Alone"—have an inevitability of line that is the mark of a born melodist. Once heard, they are never forgotten. The lyrics, on the other hand, are frozen in yesteryear:

> *One alone*
> *To be my own,*
> *I alone*
> *To know her caresses;*
> *One to be*
> *Eternally*
> *The one my worshipping soul possesses . . .*

Nobody has wanted to sing stuff like that for a long time—if they ever did. Caresses are out, and so are worshipping souls that possess. Actually the European composers didn't much care what the words said. When Oscar Hammerstein finished his hard-wrought lyric for "Lover Come Back to Me" he brought it to Romberg. The composer propped the words on his piano and perfunctorily mumbled them as he played the accompanying notes: "The sky was blue and high above the moon was new and so was love . . ." At the end he said: "It fits."

Not until the mid-1920s would a new generation of American-born songwriters turn their backs on Europe and insist that American musicals and American popular songs reflect the rhythms and the realities—and the language—of the new world. *Show Boat* was the opening salvo in that revolution.

Jerome Kern, Oscar Hammerstein and "Show Boat"

When Jerome Kern bought the dramatic and musical rights to Edna Ferber's best-selling new novel *Show Boat* in 1926, he was forty years old, half a generation older than George Gershwin, Richard Rodgers and the other young pups who were about to bring a new sound to Broadway.

He was the dean of the craft they were trying to learn. Gershwin recalled attending a family wedding reception as a teenager and hearing two songs so fresh that he ran over to the bandleader to ask what they were. Jerome Kern, he was told, had written them both— "You're Here and I'm Here" and "They Didn't Believe Me"—for an English import called *The Girl From Utah* that needed some modernizing. "Kern was the first composer who made me conscious that most popular music was of inferior quality," Gershwin said. "I followed his work and studied each song he composed."

In photographs Kern looks professorial; I don't picture him taking off his jacket when he sat down at the piano. The son of middle-class Jewish parents, he grew up in a musical home, attended the New York College of Music, and was sent abroad to study in Germany. There he came under the influence of European operetta and its long melodic line. That line became the hallmark of his own style when he returned to New York in 1905 and began contributing songs to Broadway shows—songs that still sound youthful, like "Look for the Silver Lining." One of them, "Till the Clouds Roll By," became the title song for MGM's 1946 movie biography of Kern, starring Robert Walker, who, as I recall, also kept his jacket on.

Dressed more like bankers than songwriters, the young Oscar Hammerstein II and the 40-year old Jerome Kern work on "Show Boat," which redefined the musical theater in 1927 by dealing with social themes such as racial oppression and intermarriage. Until then Broadway musicals had shown little inclination to get serious.

Of Kern's many lyricists in those early years, the best was P. G. Wodehouse. The English humorist so fondly remembered for creating Bertie Wooster and his butler Jeeves is little remembered for his influential work with Kern and the librettist Guy Bolton on a series of intimate musicals at the Princess Theater, which, judging by their titles (*Leave It to Jane*, *Oh, Boy!*, *Oh, Lady! Lady!*), didn't concern themselves with the big issues. Wodehouse's lyrics foreshadowed the lyrics of Ira Gershwin and Lorenz Hart in their conversational ease—a relief from the poetic striving of the day. One unused Kern-Wodehouse song, "Bill" ("you'd meet him on the street and never notice him"), would later achieve torch song immortality when it was dropped into the score of *Show Boat* and sung by Helen Morgan.

But for Kern it was mainly piecework: writing songs to be interpolated into lighthearted revues or writing musicals tailored to the whims of imperious stars. For *Sunny*, in 1925, the producer Charles Dillingham hired Cliff Edwards, better known as Ukulele Ike, whose contract specified that his vocal and ukulele act be performed between 10 and 10:15 p.m. Fitting the ukulele man into that slot without derailing the show, Oscar Hammerstein said, was one of his early challenges as a librettist. Hammerstein also recalled presenting *Sunny* to its principal star, Marilyn Miller, before it went into rehearsal. "She returned from Europe," he said, "and met us in the producer's office to listen to the story and the score Jerome Kern and I had written. We went through the whole plot and sang whatever numbers we had written up to that point. She seemed to be listening very attentively. When we were all finished there was a pause, and then Marilyn said, 'When do I do my tap specialty?'"

Show Boat would put an end to such indignities, raising Kern to gianthood. Edna Ferber thought Kern was crazy to try to wrest a musical out of her novel. It was a typical Ferber bouillabaisse of grand passions, spanning 50 years of life on Cap'n Andy's show boat, the "Cotton Blossom," and involving a huge cast of white and African-American characters. But Kern had faith that Oscar Hammerstein could tame Ferber's unruly saga. Scion of a theatrical family, grandson of the first Oscar Hammerstein, an impresario who built theaters and opera houses, he was 33 years old and just beginning what would be a prodigious career as a librettist and lyricist in the musical theater.

Hammerstein adapted Ferber's novel without dodging its darker themes of miscegenation and racial inequality—the marriage of the mulatto girl Julie and the white man she can't help lovin', the oppression of the colored folks who work on the Mississippi while the white folks play—and Kern wrote a score that often approached opera in its scope and texture. Today that score is mainly remembered for its six popular standards: "Can't Help Lovin' Dat Man," "Why Do I Love You?", "Bill," "You Are Love," "Make Believe" and "Ol' Man River." Most of them have a European lilt; "Make Believe" soars and swoops in intervals as long as a seventh, an octave and a tenth.

But music also ran through *Show Boat* as an organizing whole—an undercurrent of leitmotifs for the various characters and of uniquely American musical forms: marches and banjo numbers and snippets of ragtime and blues. As Richard Rodgers said, Kern was "the first man to break with European tradition in theater music, in much the same sense that Beethoven was the last of the classicists and the first of the romanticists."

Overnight, *Show Boat* elevated the musical from a grab bag of unrelated songs into a drama with musical numbers that established character and anchored the story in its social context. "Ol' Man River" is still a bombshell of a song, seeming to have sprung out of the Southern soil. Kern's melody is as majestic as the Mississippi in its flow, and Hammerstein's lyric has the plain eloquence of a spiritual. Five years later, when a political satire, the Gershwins' *Of Thee I Sing*, became the first musical to win a Pulitzer Prize, the groundwork had been done by *Show Boat*. Hammerstein must have had a wry laugh in 1943 over the acclaim that hailed his and Richard Rodgers' *Oklahoma!* for the pioneering integration of book, music and lyrics. Sixteen years earlier he had been there and done that.

Such was the sumptuousness of the *Show Boat* score that at its out-of-town premiere, in Washington, D.C., on November 15, 1927, the curtain didn't come down until 12:40 a.m. Severe cuts had to be made, and those cuts removed much of the emotional fabric of Kern's score, especially the dolorous Negro chorale, "Misery's Comin' Aroun'." Since then Humpty Dumpty has never quite been put back together. Three Broadway revivals, three Hollywood movies and three London productions have been relatively prim and pretty, conveying only a glimmer of the musical and racial turmoil of the show Kern and Hammerstein originally wrote. In 1978 the original orchestral parts were found in a warehouse, and the Houston Grand Opera used them in a 1983 production that largely restored the original script and score. Full restoration, with all the dialogue and underscoring—an archeological labor of love—was finally achieved in 1988 by John McGlinn in a remarkable 3-hour-and-42-minute recording for EMI/Angel.

Of the various movie versions, Universal's 1936 film comes closest to taking us back to the first Broadway performance. Three of its stars—Helen Morgan, Charles Winninger and Sammy White—

repeated their original roles, and the movie's main star, Irene Dunne, played Magnolia on *Show Boat*'s first national tour. Paul Robeson, for whom the role of Joe was written, didn't get to play it until the London production in 1928, but his powerful rendition of "Ol' Man River" in the Universal film identified him with the song for the rest of his life.

After *Show Boat*, Kern seemed to erase all memory of having created the theater's breakthrough musical. He went right back to composing Viennese-style musicals, like *The Cat and the Fiddle* and *Music in the Air*, with inane plots and turgid lyrics, mostly by Hammerstein and Otto Harbach, of the kind they once supplied for Sigmund Romberg—lyrics in which the breeze kisses the heroine's hair and the trees do a lot of talking. But the melodies continued to soar: "Don't Ever Leave Me," "Why Was I Born?", "I've Told Every Little Star," "The Song Is You," "The Touch of Your Hand," "Yesterdays," "Lovely to Look At," "Smoke Gets in Your Eyes."

Not until Kern went to Hollywood in the mid-1930s and began to team with lyricists who were hip—Dorothy Fields, Johnny Mercer and Ira Gershwin—would he again begin to sound more American than European. Meanwhile, a new breed of sophisticated young songwriters took up where *Show Boat* left off.

For Ed Jablonski
With best wishes
Ira Gershwin
March 12, 1941.

George and Ira Gershwin

George Gershwin was the brightest of all the meteors who shot across the sky of the twenties, lighting up the decade with his dynamic music and personality. Unlike other prodigies, he displayed no interest in music until the advanced age of ten, when, one day—the story is part of the folklore of American popular music—a second-hand upright piano was hoisted into the window of his parents' apartment on New York's Lower East Side. Rose Gershwin had bought it because she thought her older son, Ira, should take lessons. Ira was the studious one; George was a street kid, always outside and often in trouble.

As soon as George saw the piano, Ira later recalled, "he twirled the stool down to size, sat, lifted the keyboard cover, and played an accomplished version of a then-popular song. I was particularly impressed by harmonic and rhythmic effects I thought as proficient as those of most pianists I had heard in vaudeville." George explained that he had been fooling around on the player piano of a neighborhood friend. Ira was duly excused from keyboard duties, and the lessons went to George. Actually, he said, his interest had been piqued at the age of six, when "I stood outside a penny arcade listening to Rubinstein's 'Melody in F' on a player piano. The peculiar jumps in the music held me rooted. To this very day I can't hear that tune without picturing myself outside that arcade, barefoot and in overalls, drinking it all in avidly."

After two years of piano lessons Gershwin graduated to a master teacher, the pianist and avant-garde composer Charles Hambitzer, who immersed him in Debussy and Ravel and in the dazzling piano literature of Chopin and Liszt. By then Gershwin himself had begun to dazzle, and he gave some thought to becoming a concert pianist.

The composer George Gershwin and his lyricist brother Ira brought a revolutionary freshness of melody, rhythm and language to the songs they wrote for Broadway musicals in the 1920s. Today, many of those songs are still around, part of the standard repertory of singers and jazz musicians, including "Someone to Watch Over Me," "Embraceable You," "The Man I Love," "But Not for Me" and "How Long Has This Been Going On?"

Sheet music covers were a vibrant form of American poster art in the 1920s, capturing the flamboyance of the musical theater. (This one was bright red.) They also included a lot of information about who created the show. Here the humorist Robert Benchley turns up as one of the writers of the Gershwins' "Funny Face" (1927).

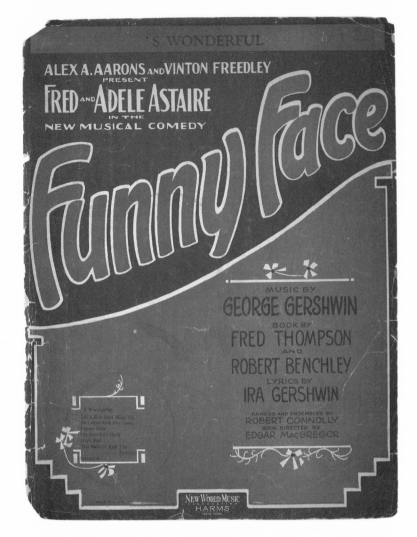

Instead he dropped out of school at 16 to become a songplugger on Tin Pan Alley, where he was in steady demand; nobody else could put over a new song so contagiously.

From plugging the songs of other writers to writing songs of his own was the inevitable next step, and one of his first efforts, "Swanee," a faux ode to Dixie, was sung in a show called *Sinbad* with such maudlin gusto by Al Jolson ("My Mammy's waiting for me") that it became the biggest single hit Gershwin would ever have. The lyric was by Irving Caesar, another Jewish kid who hadn't been south of Canal Street. Such nuances of geography never troubled the bards of Tin Pan Alley or stanched their flow of songs pining for a train that would take them back to Mammy in the South. Irving Berlin's choo-choo to Alabam' left at midnight.

Famous at 19 because of "Swanee," Gershwin began to place songs in various Broadway revues of the early 1920s, such as *George*

White's Scandals. Those songs, like "I'll Build a Stairway to Paradise," were something new in the American air. The child of immigrant Jews from Russia, Gershwin grew up hearing the jagged rhythms of urban and industrial America. He also loved the early ragtime tunes of Irving Berlin and the vibrant jazz of the black pianists he kept going to Harlem to hear.

All those American and African rhythms came together in his own music, combined with melodies that had a blue flavor because of their flatted (minor) notes—the Russian-Jewish heritage. Jerome Kern would never have flatted the two notes that punctuate Gershwin's climb to paradise: "I'll build a stairway to PAR-adise/ With a new step every DAY." Or the climaxing note in the fourth bar of "Somebody Loves Me": "Somebody loves me, I wonder WHO." Or the recurring flatted notes in "The Man I Love" that give the song its yearning: "Some day he'll come a-LONG/ The man I LOVE/ And he'll be big and STRONG . . . " Try it without flatting those notes. No yearning.

But what brought Gershwin instant celebrity, landing him on the cover of *Time* when he was only 26, was *Rhapsody in Blue.* Commissioned by the bandleader Paul Whiteman for his "Experiment in Modern Music" at Aeolian Hall, in New York, on February 24, 1924, one of the most famous concerts of the 20th century, Gershwin's piano concerto, which he composed in three weeks, electrified the audience—Gershwin himself was the soloist—with its interplay of plaintive themes and syncopated tempos, starting with the 17-note clarinet *glissando* that people could hardly believe they were hearing. (The title came from Ira Gershwin, who borrowed it from a Whistler painting he had admired in a gallery.) A year later, George's ambitious *Concerto in F* proved that the *Rhapsody* was no fluke. Both works have remained in the repertory of symphony orchestras ever since.

The other major event of 1924—though nobody could have known how major it would be—was that Ira Gershwin became his brother's lyricist. Until then Ira had been writing occasional lyrics for other composers under the name of Arthur Francis, not wanting to ride on George's fame. The deeply intuitive collaboration between the two brothers lasted for the rest of George's life, perfectly meshing what was new in American popular music with what was new in the American language—all the short-hand ways of saying "I love you":

> *'S wonderful!*
> *'S marvelous!*
> *You should care*
> *For me!*

Ira was lucky in the time and place of his birth and his education. New York's Townsend Harris high school had a required course in classical poetics, and on his own Ira experimented with French verse forms such as the rondeau, the triolet and the villanelle. His classmate, the future lyricist E. Y. (Yip) Harburg, was similarly addicted, and the two friends started a column of humorous topical verse for the school newspaper, signed "Gersh" and "Yip," that they would continue when they went on to City College in 1914.

"We were living in a time of literate revelry in the New York daily press," Harburg recalled, "and we wanted to be a part of it." All the local newspapers ran columns of light verse, most famously Franklin P. Adams' "The Conning Tower," in the *World*, and Don Marquis' "The Sun Dial," in the *Sun*. Contributions from readers were encouraged, and it was in those hospitable oases that many later luminaries and wits—Robert Benchley, Russel Crouse, Dorothy Parker, Alexander Woollcott, Dorothy Fields—saw some of their first writing in print.

Ira Gershwin soaked up everything that rhymed, keeping scrapbooks of favorite poems and studying earlier masters of playful verse, especially W. S. Gilbert. But his best tip came from a British playwright who told him to "learn especially your American slang." Heeding that advice, he made his lyrics conversational and idiomatic. "Oh, lady, be good to me!" he said, and "I've got a crush on you," and "Little wow, tell me now, how long has this been going on?" "I got rhythm," he said. Not "I've got rhythm."

George's music matched with its energy the pleasure Ira conveyed with his words. Much of that energy came from repeated notes:

> THAT CERTAIN FEEL-*ing*,
> *(beat)* THE-FIRST TIME I MET *you*,
> I HIT THE CEIL-*ing*,
> *(beat)* I-COULD NOT FORGET *you*.

The repeated notes are punched out, full of life. Together with the syncopated (skipped) beat and the squashed-together words ("the-first," "I-could"), they are an intravenous drip into our veins from the Jazz Age; hearing those repeated notes today, I also can't help feeling that certain feeling. Where Gershwin's notes aren't repeated, they are at least in near proximity, unlike the long intervals of a Jerome Kern song. The first 22 notes of "Fascinating Rhythm" are within four notes of each other:

> *Fascinating rhythm,*
> *You've got me on the go!*

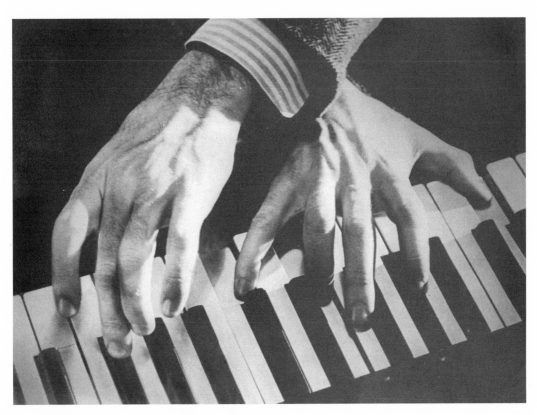

George Gershwin, a classically trained pianist (these are his hands), played his songs with dazzling skill and pure enjoyment. That faraway sound in all its youthful energy can still be heard in the piano rolls he recorded at the time.

Fascinating rhythm,
I'm all a-quiver.

Only the final low note breaks the song open. Then the pattern is repeated, four notes higher, the composer cranking up our metabolism:

What a mess you're making!
The neighbors want to know
Why I'm always shaking
Just like a flivver.

In "Sweet and Low-Down" the opening bars grab us with their insistence as they climb a ladder of notes that are never more than two whole tones apart:

Grab a cab and go down
To where the band is playing,
Where milk and honey flow down,
Where ev'ryone is saying
Blow that sweet and low-down!

These songs are *moving*. The melody and the words propel each other with their enjoyment—all the more enjoyable, in this case, because "sweet and low-down" was a brand-new idiom. Ira

The stunning success of "Rhapsody in Blue" propelled George Gershwin onto the cover of "Time" on July 28, 1925, at the age of 26. He was the first American-born musician to achieve that honor. He would continue to write ambitious classical scores, including the "Concerto in F," the tone poem "An American in Paris" and the opera "Porgy and Bess."

coined it by combining Tennyson's lullaby about the Western wind ("sweet and low") with the low-down American adjective. Though he would deprecate it as "small philological honor," he was pleased when his portmanteau word later made it into the *The American Thesaurus of Slang.*

The brothers hit full stride just when the American musical theater and the Roaring Twenties were at their roaringest, between 1925 and 1930. Times were good, and Broadway producers pressed the Gershwins and other hot young songwriters—Vincent Youmans, Rodgers & Hart, DeSylva, Brown & Henderson—for a new score at least once a year. Glamorous new stars were hatched in those Gershwin shows. Fred Astaire starred in *Funny Face*, and both Ethel Merman (singing "I Got Rhythm") and Ginger Rogers made their debut in *Girl Crazy*—a show whose pit orchestra, incidentally, included Benny Goodman, Gene Krupa, Glenn Miller, Jack Teagarden and Jimmy Dorsey.

The party ended with a crash in October of 1929, and the Depression put a lid on lavish new musicals. But by then the Gershwins' songs had entered the permanent vocabulary of American popular music, constantly played ever since and lovingly revived in all-Gershwin movies like *An American in Paris* and *Funny Face*: "Embraceable You," "But Not For Me," "I've Got a Crush on You," "How Long Has This Been Going On?", "Isn't It a Pity?", "Lady, Be Good!", "The Man I Love," "My One and Only," "Soon," "Maybe," "Bidin' My Time," "Someone to Watch Over Me," "I Got Rhythm," "He Loves and She Loves," "Liza," "Strike Up the Band," "Of Thee I Sing," "Who Cares," and many more.

George and Ira Gershwin were as different as a major and a minor chord. George was the Jazz Age personified: tall, handsome, dapper, magnetic, a bachelor man-about-Manhattan who played his music at parties all night long with unabashed pleasure in his brilliant talents, lionized wherever he went. (We can still hear that boyish zest in his pyrotechnical piano recordings.) Ira was short, stout, rumpled, bookish, married, reticent and pathologically modest. Far from resenting the intense light of George's fame, which eclipsed his own role in the partnership, he held his younger brother in amazed adoration and wanted it no other way.

But Ira's lyrics are what give Gershwin songs their lasting identity and emotion. "'S Wonderful!" wouldn't be remembered for its melody. The notes of "Embraceable You" forever say "embraceable you." When we picture Fred Astaire and Audrey Hepburn dancing beside the Seine in the movie *Funny Face*, what we hear is "He loves, and she loves…" To this day Ira Gershwin's lyrics seem exactly

right, disarming us with their urbanity and humor, their outer and inner rhymes, their conversational freshness and circumvention of cliché. By combining the wit and literacy of light verse with the colloquial speech of the moment, he created a new model for a new era of songwriting, one that only Lorenz Hart and Johnny Mercer would equal.

By 1937 George Gershwin would be dead, having composed his masterpiece *Porgy and Bess* and some of his finest songs for three Hollywood movies. Ira would start over with new collaborators, creating a distinguished musical with Kurt Weill and writing his all-time hit song with Jerome Kern and his best torch song with Harold Arlen. But that's another story.

Early Rodgers & Hart

When *The Garrick Gaieties* was performed on Broadway on Sunday evening, June 8, 1925, it was supposed to run for just one night— as a showcase for young Theatre Guild actors and for the unknown songwriting team of Richard Rodgers and Lorenz Hart. Instead the revue was such a winning infusion of fresh talent that it was resuscitated by popular demand and kept alive for 211 performances. The brightest ornament in Rodgers & Hart's score was "Manhattan," the anthem of every girl and boy who can hardly believe the wonder of being young and in love in New York:

We'll have Manhattan,
The Bronx and Staten
Island too.
It's lovely going through
The zoo . . .

The score had a youthfulness that was new in American musicals, and over the course of almost 30 more shows and movies Rodgers and Hart never sounded even slightly old, endlessly inventing new ways to move the ear and touch the heart.

Except in the writing of songs they were oddly matched. When they met, Dick Rodgers was still in high school, a serious 16-year-old who had started composing melodies on the family Steinway at the age of nine; his father was a Manhattan doctor, his mother a good amateur pianist. Larry Hart was a 23-year-old cosmopolite: urbane, cynical and witty, devoted to drink and cigars, a lover of books and poetry, Columbia-educated. On his father's side—his father was a businessman—he was descended from the poet Heinrich Heine, and he used that gene to write lyrics as a hobby and to support himself translating German operettas for the Shuberts. Hart was abnormally short, less than five feet tall. Mary Rodgers, Richard

The methodical young Richard Rodgers and the mercurial Lorenz Hart were temperamental opposites, but as composer and lyricist they were ideally paired. The songs they wrote for a series of vivacious musicals in the late 1920s had a youthful buoyancy and wit that were a new sound in the musical theater.

"The Girl Friend" (1926) and "A Connecticut Yankee" (1927) were the first of many Rodgers and Hart musicals that had a book by Herbert Fields, one of Broadway's most productive librettists. Two other children of that prolific theater dynasty were his sister and brother, the lyricist Dorothy Fields and the playwright Joseph Fields. Their father was the comedian Lew Fields of Weber and Fields.

Rodgers' daughter, once recalled that when she was a child she thought Hart was also a child because he was so small; the only anomaly was the cigar.

Brought together in 1918 by a mutual friend who knew that Rodgers needed a lyricist and Hart needed a composer, the kid and the cosmopolite found that they shared a passion for theater songs, especially the scores for the Princess Theater musicals that Jerome Kern and P. G. Wodehouse were then writing, which Hart seemed to have memorized. He had no patience, he said, with the trite and slipshod lyrics of the day. Why, he wondered, couldn't lyrics be written with the same precision, sensitivity and taste that went into a good poem?

Suddenly, as Rodgers later recalled the moment, "I was hearing for the first time about interior rhymes, feminine rhymes and false rhymes. I listened with astonishment as Larry launched a diatribe against songwriters who had small intellectual equipment and less courage, who failed to take advantage of every opportunity to inch a

The score of "A Connecticut Yankee" contained not only the infectious "Thou Swell" but the first of the grand melodies ("My Heart Stood Still") that would be a hallmark of Richard Rodgers' long career. The dances were by Busby Berkeley, later famous for his kaleidoscopic dances in "Forty-Second Street" and other Warner Brothers musicals.

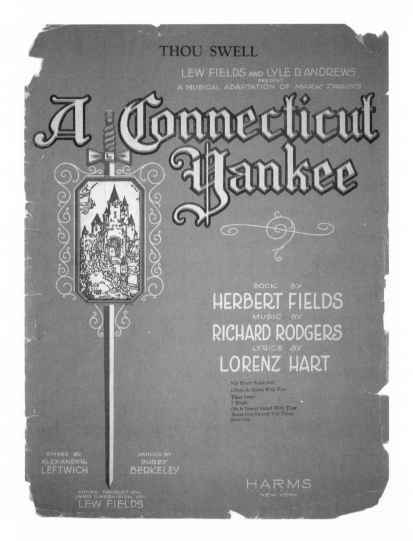

little farther into unexplored territory." Rodgers played some of his melodies, which Hart liked, and by the end of the afternoon they had agreed to work together. One song Rodgers probably didn't play was the one that had actually been performed: "Campfire Days," written when he was a 14-year-old at Camp Wigwam, in Maine.

But the new team proved not to be what the world was waiting for. Publishers repeatedly turned down Rodgers and Hart's songs, and the scores they wrote for amateur musicals and Columbia University varsity shows—Rodgers had since entered Columbia—brought no offers of professional work. Success struck only once, in 1919, when their "Any Old Place With You" was interpolated in a Broadway show called *A Lonely Romeo*. It was their first published song and the first time a melody by Richard Rodgers was heard in a professional theater. Like so many that were to follow, it was a lighthearted tune, ideal for Hart's lighthearted itinerary:

I'll go to hell for ya,
Or Philadelphia,
Any old place with you . . .

But otherwise it was five years of rejection, and both men began to lose faith in their talent. Discouraged and depressed, they talked about breaking up and finding some other line of work, Rodgers going so far as to accept a job as a salesman of children's underwear. It is piquant to think that the world came that close to having one more underwear salesman and not having *Oklahoma!* But Rodgers never reported for work. Fate put in a phone call from a man who was assembling the 1925 revue that would be called *The Garrick Gaieties*, and Rodgers and Hart never looked back. Show after show poured out of them.

If the young George Gershwin caught the energy of the Jazz Age, the young Rodgers and Hart caught its softer side, the innocence and credulity of first love. Sometimes love ended badly: "He Was Too Good to Me," "Ship Without a Sail." But mostly the news of the heart was good, and Rodgers set it to irresistible music: "Sentimental Me" ("and poor romantic you"); "A Tree in the Park" ("just five minutes from your doorstep/ I'll wait for your step/ to come along"); "You Took Advantage of Me" ("so lock the doors/ and call me yours"); "Blue Room" ("we'll have a blue room/ a new room/ for two room"); "Mountain Greenery" ("where God paints the scenery/ just two crazy people together"); "Thou Swell" ("Thou witty! Thou sweet! Thou grand!"); "I've Got Five Dollars" ("take my heart that hollers/ ev'rything I've got belongs to you"). Rodgers was more lyrical than Gershwin, his melodies less angular, his rhythms less brittle, and when he opened the throttle for a full-bodied romantic ballad—"My Heart Stood Still," "With a Song in My Heart"— he served notice that a composer of unusual spaciousness had arrived.

That gift for the grand melody went with Rodgers in the early 1930s when the team answered the call of Hollywood, where they wrote some memorable songs—"Isn't It Romantic?", "You Are Too Beautiful," "Lover," "Blue Moon," "It's Easy to Remember (and So Hard to Forget)"—for unmemorable movies, such as Maurice Chevalier's *Love Me Tonight*. But the work was sporadic and the glory meager; the adored songwriters of Broadway were just hired help in Movieland. The phone stopped ringing, and one day Rodgers saw an item in O. O. McIntyre's newspaper column that said, "Whatever became of Rodgers and Hart?" He sat down and wrote McIntyre a letter thanking him for the wake-up call. "The day our contract was up," he later recalled, "we climbed aboard the Chief and came back to

Who knew that Barbara Stanwyck ever looked like this? Rodgers and Hart were among the first New York song-writers to take their talent to Hollywood in the early 1930s as the Broadway musical the-ater withered for lack of money. They wrote a few memorable songs ("Blue Moon," "Isn't It Romantic?") but were dispirited by the ano-nymity of their toil and came back east.

the United States. I felt as if I had just been given my pardon."

At that low moment, probably even he didn't dare to dream how far he would ultimately stretch his gift—first with Hart, com-posing ten brilliant Broadway scores in eight years, and then with Oscar Hammerstein, pushing the musical theater into terrain it had never explored before. He was just getting started.

ALL THE THINGS YOU ARE

MAX GORDON presents

VERY WARM FOR MAY

A MUSICAL COMEDY

music by
JEROME KERN
book and lyrics by
OSCAR HAMMERSTEIN, 2ND

production by
VINCENT MINNELLI

ALL IN FUN
HEAVEN IN MY ARMS
IN OTHER WORDS, SEVENTEEN
THAT LUCKY FELLOW
ALL THE THINGS YOU ARE
IN THE HEART OF THE DARK

CHAPPELL
& CO · INC ·
RKO BUILDING
ROCKEFELLER
CENTER · N · Y · C
MADE IN U S A
CHAPPELL
& CO · LTD · LONDON

Anatomy of the Popular Song

I. The Verse

One of George and Ira Gershwin's best gifts to songwriting was to bring freshness and charm to the "verse," the introduction that precedes the "chorus." The verse and the chorus are two of the three structural components of the American popular song, the third being the lyric. This chapter takes a look at those three elements. Consider it a brief anatomy lesson.

The verse has always been an orphan, sung in the original Broadway show or Hollywood musical and then abandoned on the commercial record. The 32-bar chorus was the melody that record producers wanted to insinuate into the public's ear on the radio and on jukeboxes, and the verse usually got dropped. Our collective memory is stored with choruses.

Yet the verse is an organic element of the song—the appetizer that prepares us for the main course—and in expert hands it's a delicacy. If you like oysters, the verse is oysters. I'm grateful to the preservationists—Ella Fitzgerald in her "Song Books," cabaret singers in their acts—who begin the song where the composer and lyricist began it, reminding us of these lost jewels. Some of George Gershwin's most exploratory melodies went into his verses, joined to some of Ira's most affecting lyrics as he sneaked up on the song's main idea.

Unlike the chorus, which adheres to a fixed tempo, the verse is often played and sung "ad lib," not in a strict rhythm, its mood relaxed and explanatory. "I'm about to tell you a story," the verse says, "but first there are a few things you ought to know." It then explains the existing mood or situation.

Jerome Kern's last Broadway musical, "Very Warm for May" (1939), was a five-week flop, but its score contained the most perfectly constructed of all popular standards, "All the Things You Are." Kern effortlessly moves his Bach-like theme through five keys in 32 bars—the textbook illustration of how songwriters achieve freshness within the form's tight limits.

"I was always the self-sufficient type," a typical (hypothetical) verse might begin, proceeding to enumerate the joys of the single life. You don't have to be a psychic to know where that verse is going. It will build to a chance encounter ("Then one day I saw you") and a blinding revelation ("Suddenly I knew")—whereupon the tempo will quicken to 4/4 time and the chorus will start spreading the main news ("I never want to be alone again"). The verse is where hopes and dreams are stated. The chorus is where they get ratified ("At last"), deferred ("Wouldn't it be loverly?"), frustrated ("I can't get started") or dashed ("Here's that rainy day").

Nobody was better than Ira Gershwin at describing the state of mind that will be either developed or subverted by the chorus. In the following verse a girl tells us she is tired of receiving upbeat advice:

> *Old man Sunshine, listen, you,*
> *Never tell me dreams come true,*
> *Just try it*
> *And I'll start a riot.*
> *Beatrice Fairfax, don't you dare*
> *Ever tell me he will care,*
> *I'm certain*
> *It's the final curtain.*
> *I never want to hear*
> *From any cheer/ful Pollyannas*
> *Who tell you fate*
> *Supplies a mate,*
> *It's all bananas!*

Why is she so melancholy? The chorus explains: "They're writing songs of love, but not for me."

That verse took much of its appeal from Ira's topical allusions and idioms, and George's music matched the wistfulness of the words. It has the unhurried quality that verses need, with none of the urgency of a George Gershwin chorus. Like all his verses—a form he would superbly refine in his final songs, written for the Fred Astaire movies *Shall We Dance?* and *Damsel in Distress*—it's just right.

Cole Porter was another master, writing extended verses that reflected the world-weariness of high-society folk:

> *My story is much too sad to be told,*
> *But practically everything leaves me totally cold.*
> *The only exception I know is the case*
> *When I'm out on a quiet spree,*

Fighting vainly the old ennui
And I suddenly turn and see
Your fabulous face.

That's just about perfect, and the chorus completes the job. "I get no kick from champagne," it says, or from cocaine, or from *flying* too *high* with some *guy* in the *sky*, but "I get a kick out of you."

Porter's language ideally suited his jaded characters and their studied boredom; you won't find anyone fighting ennui in the songs of Irving Berlin or Yip Harburg and the other populists. Porter was also adept at the last-minute switch or ironic twist that can give the verse a touch of humor, like the punch line of a standup comic:

Times have changed
And we've often rewound the clock
Since the Puritans got a shock
When they landed on Plymouth Rock.
If today
Any shock they should try to stem,
'Stead of landing on Plymouth Rock,
Plymouth Rock would land on them.

The tempo picks up, and the chorus sails forth exuberantly:

In olden days a glimpse of stocking
Was looked on as something shocking,
Now, heaven knows,
Anything goes . . .

Here's another example, delightful in its originality, from Hugh Martin and Ralph Blane's "The Boy Next Door," beginning halfway through the verse:

. . . But he doesn't know I exist,
No matter how I may persist.
So it's clear to me
There's no hope for me
Though I live at Fifty-one Thirty-five Kensington Avenue
And he lives at Fifty-one Thirty-three.
[chorus]
How can I ignore
The boy next door
I love him more/ than I can say . . .

Irving Berlin was also a whiz at getting his choruses launched. The verses he wrote for the numbers in *Top Hat* are some of the best Fred Astaire ever got: "Top Hat" ("I just got an invitation in the mails . . . "); "No Strings" ("I wake up every morning with a smile on my face . . . "); "Isn't This a Lovely Day to Be Caught in the Rain?" ("The thunder and lightning/ seemed to be fright'ning . . . "). Both musically and lyrically they convey pleasure in the situation that is about to be made specific by the chorus, which, thus primed for the race, gallops out of the starting gate.

II. The Chorus

The chorus is the essence of the American popular song; in effect, it *is* the American popular song. Seemingly artless, it's a highly stylized form that imposes strict rules on the composer.

Brevity is the biggest limitation. Ninety-nine percent of popular songs are 32 bars long—no more, no less. Occasionally a composer will break out of that straitjacket. "Day In, Day Out" requires 56 bars for the composer, Rube Bloom, to develop his musical idea, but if you follow his trail you'll see that there isn't a note he could have left out; the song found its proper length. Harold Arlen needed 64 bars for "That Old Black Magic." Cole Porter's "Begin the Beguine" runs to 104 bars; the beguine, once begun, takes an eternity to end.

But those are exceptions; we expect our songwriters to say what they have to say in 32 bars, or "measures." Because traditional western music is mathematical in its notation, it insists on order—which means, among other things, even numbers. A 31-bar song would leave us vaguely uneasy. So would a 7-bar opening statement; our metabolism has been conditioned to need the full eight.

Sequence is another restriction. Almost all popular songs fall into one of two formats. The most common one is A-A-B-A. Here the composer states the main melody (A) in the first 8 bars, which usually also contain the title, either at the beginning ("I'm in the mood for love") or at the end ("That's why the lady is a tramp"). Then the A section is repeated. Then comes the 8-bar "bridge," or "release" (B), which introduces a new musical idea. Then the first 8 bars (A) are repeated one last time, often varying near the end to build to a proper conclusion. A classic A-A-B-A song is Harold Arlen's "Over the Rainbow." The first two A sections are identical; the bridge (B) provides contrast, and the final A section varies only in the last 2 bars as it climbs to the poignant "Why, oh, why can't I?" Pure as a nursery song, it's satisfying in its symmetry.

The other common format is A-B-A-B, or its variant, which could be called A-B-A-B^I or (if you prefer) A-B-A-C. Here the main musical theme (A) is stated in the first 8 bars:

Embrace me, my sweet embraceable you,
Embrace me, you irreplaceable you.

Then comes a different musical theme (B), which amplifies or answers the first theme for 8 bars:

Just one look at you my heart grows tipsy in me,
You and you alone bring out the gypsy in me.

Then A is repeated for 8 bars, and the song concludes with another B or with a variant (B^I or C), which builds to a heightened climax. The variant melody, however, is so true to what has gone before that we hardly notice that it's a departure. Think of songs like "White Christmas," "My Romance," "A Foggy Day" and "Moon River." The final 8 bars break fresh ground but are musically and emotionally consistent with the whole composition; Irving Berlin, Richard Rodgers, George Gershwin and Henry Mancini knew just what kind of wrap-up would seem to have been inevitable. That inevitability is at the heart of every song that people remember.

Occasionally the format will be broken, or at least enjoyably bent. The best of the benders was Jerome Kern. In "Long Ago and Far Away," a typical Kern mutation, he states the melody in the first 8 bars (A). The song is in the key of F, and it begins on that note:

Long ago and far away
I dreamed a dream one day
And now that dream is here beside me.

Then Kern restates the melody, but this time he starts on the higher note of A-flat:

Long the skies were overcast,
But now the clouds have passed,
You're here at last.

That upward jump into the key of A-flat gives the song a shot of adrenaline because it takes us by surprise, after which Kern modulates back down to the home key of F. There he restates A one more time ("Chills run up and down my spine . . . ") and ends with a new 8-bar finale ("Just one look and then I knew . . . ").

Another seamless journey in and out of various keys is Kern's "I'm Old-Fashioned." It's one of his finest songs, particularly pleasing because of the recurring use of the four-beat metrical motif that states the title. Every time we hear those four beats ("this year's fancies," "passing fancies," "I don't mind it," "stay old-fashioned"), we're reminded that we're in the hands of a craftsman.

Which brings me to the "bridge," the middle section of every A-A-B-A song. Only 8 bars long, this interloper is crucial to the song's success. Its other name, the "release," perfectly expresses its function: to break the sameness of the two successive A sections by altering the song's mood or direction. Martin and Blane's "Have Yourself a Merry Little Christmas" takes its amazing purity from the opening 8-bar melody (A), which makes three separate ascents on the notes of the major triad: C, E, G, C:

Have yourself a merry little Christmas,
Let your heart be light,
Next year all our troubles will be out of sight.

Then the melody (A) is repeated, with only a slight variation near the end. At that point we crave something different, and the bridge provides it, reversing the upward motion and slipping back down the scale:

Once again as in olden days,
Happy golden days of yore...

Thus released, we are ready for one last statement of the main theme and for the wistful coda, or "tag," that sends us on our way.

But the surest way to announce a change of mood at the start of the bridge is to move into another key. Every piece of Western tonal music is grounded in a home key, to which it must periodically and ultimately return. There are 12 keys, one for each note contained in an octave. (Picture the 12 successive black and white notes on the piano: C, D-flat, D, E-flat, E, F, etc.) Every key has its own emotional color. The "flat" keys, such as D-flat, E-flat and B-flat, have a warm and mellow feeling, prized by jazz musicians. The "sharp" keys, such as E-major and A-major, sound earnest and reliable; I associate them with Protestant hymns and Sunday morning rectitude.

Therefore a song in the key of C that jumps to E-flat for the bridge will get an instant emotional lift. Some keys are more compatible than others—a matter of shared notes or shared harmonic terrain. For example, the keys of C and E-flat are compatible because G is an important note in both scales—it's a fifth in the key of C and a third in the key of E-flat; a composer can modulate easily between the two. Certain other keys can't be entered without a wrench that's not worth the discomfort.

Once in his new key, the composer has only 8 bars to do his leavening work and get back out. He makes his return to the home key by using certain chords, mainly sevenths, that the Western ear recognizes as leading to certain destinations. (Sevenths must be resolved; a song can't end on a seventh.) This movement toward resolution, inexorable as a law of physics, occurs in the bridge of countless standards ("Imagination," "Easy to Remember," "It Might As Well Be Spring," "A Nightingale Sang in Berkeley Square"). Subconsciously we are pleased to hear the composer navigate his way home, often at the last moment, on those familiar chord progressions.

Sometimes, however, the bridge begins and we think: "Hey! What's he *doing*? How is he going to get back out of this one in eight bars?" Two of my favorite key-changing bridges—gems of unexpectedness—are Richard Rodgers' "Have You Met Miss Jones?" ("Then all at once I lost my breath . . . ") and Hoagy Carmichael's "Skylark" ("And in your lonely flight . . . "). But the champion, by common agreement, is Johnny Green's "Body and Soul," a bridge unlike any other. The first 4 bars are in the key that's a half-tone above the home key ("I can't believe it, it's hard to conceive it . . ."); the next 4 bars are a half-tone *below* the home key ("Are you pretending, it looks like the ending . . . "), and all the harmonic changes required to bring off this feat of acrobatics, including the safe landing on the final chord, are so logical as to seem foreordained.

For total 32-bar construction the prize goes—also by general consent—to Jerome Kern's "All the Things You Are," a Bach-like melody that progresses through five keys in 32 bars without breaking a sweat. Written in the key of A-flat, it stays in that key for the first 8 bars ("You are the promised kiss of springtime . . . "), finally descending to the note of E (" . . . makes the lonely winter seem LONG"). Then it slides down to E-flat ("You are the breathless hush of evening . . . ") and stays in *that* key for 8 bars, ending on the note of B (" . . . brink of a lovely SONG"). B is the major third in the key of G, which allows Kern to enter *that* key compatibly and to zoom upward for 4 bars ("You are the angel glow that lights a STAR")—a tremendous lift—and to land on a high B. B is the fifth note in the key of E-major, enabling Kern to slip compatibly into *that* key for 4 bars, ending on G-sharp ("the dearest things I know are what you ARE").

G-sharp is the same note as A-flat, the note on which the song began—and on which it now starts over ("Some day . . . "), back in its home key of A-flat, Kern using the final 8 bars to compose a soaring finale. What gives that final transition its elegance is what Kern does beneath the pivotal words "are" and "some." Under "are" he changes from an E major chord to an augmented (raised) A-flat chord, which leads automatically to an F-minor chord under "some." That's the chord that began the song in bar 1 and that he had to return to in bar 25. This "enharmonic" change is Kern's last master touch in putting his jewel box together.

The miracle about the construction of melodies is that no two are alike. Thousands of popular songs have been written, their composers limited to 32 bars and only 12 notes—or, in the case of predominantly major-scale composers like Frederick Loewe of *My Fair Lady*, who seldom use flatted notes, seven. Now and then, inevitably, a song comes along that reminds us of some other song. But the remarkable thing is how often we're *not* reminded of some other song. The great composers never run out of ways to put the notes together in a pattern that makes us say, "Isn't that wonderful! I've never heard anything like that before."

III. The Lyric

Of all forms of writing, the lyric of a popular song might appear to be the simplest: just a few strains of poetry set to a few recurring strains of music. Actually it isn't simple and it isn't poetry. A lyric and a poem are very different forms. The lyricist is bound by strict rules of length and order and musicality that the poet doesn't have to worry about. Poems are self-sufficient; they are written to be spoken and they look tidy on the printed page. Most lyrics sound banal when they are spoken, and they look inept on the page:

> *I've got the world on a string,*
> *Sittin' on a rainbow,*
> *Got the string around my finger.*
> *What a world, what a life,*
> *I'm in love!*

Speak that lyric and not much happens. But sing it—add the music—and the lyric springs to life. We hear how intuitively the lyricist Ted Koehler caught the exuberance of Harold Arlen's melody: the joy of sitting on a rainbow. Arlen's melody is like a jazz riff—it spans an octave and a half in the first two bars—but we wouldn't know that from reading the lyric. Here's another:

Moon River, wider than a mile,
I'm crossing you in style,
Some day.
Old dream-maker,
You heart-breaker,
Wherever you're goin', I'm goin' your way . . .

Also not so great to look at or to read aloud. But sing Johnny Mercer's down-home words to Henry Mancini's easygoing waltz and the lyric goes waltzing. We recognize the musicianship that makes it work—Mercer's sensitivity to the contour of the melody. Here's one more:

Just in time,
I found you just in time,
Before you came my time
Was running low . . .

Pretty dull. But sing Betty Comden and Adolph Green's blunt lyric to Jule Styne's pulsing melody and we hear a perfect marriage of words and music. The words couldn't exist on their own—and weren't meant to.

Poets, on the other hand, operate only in the service of poetry—which is why they generally don't make good lyricists. Over the years quite a few have tried their hand at Broadway musicals, but I'm never quite comfortable with the result; the rhymes are a little humpbacked, the stresses a little off. I get the feeling that people are singing poetry to each other, not talking to each other in music.

Good lyric writers never give a singer a moment's discomfort with an awkward meter or cadence. You can sing the entire vast literature of Johnny Mercer's work and never think, "That doesn't quite work." Mercer, of course, was a swinging singer himself. But even when the great lyricists weren't musicians, they were deeply musical. Men like Ira Gershwin, Lorenz Hart and Alan Jay Lerner grew up listening to music and paying attention to how it functions with words and with the ups and downs of the human voice.

The question all songwriters get asked is: "Which comes first: the words or the music?" Collaboration being a skittish process, the question has many answers. It's most easily answered in the case of people who write both the words and the music: Irving Berlin, Cole Porter, Frank Loesser, Jerry Herman, Stephen Sondheim. They usually start with a title, or with a first line, or with a situation, and let the song grow organically. As they scribble some words they are likely to be visited by an accompanying melody, or as they compose a melody they are visited by some possible words, and gradually they tinker the song to completion.

In the case of the great partnerships—the Gershwin brothers, Rodgers and Hart, Harold Arlen and Johnny Mercer, Frederick Loewe and Alan Jay Lerner, John Kander and Fred Ebb—the process is most often collaborative, starting at the piano. The lyricist throws some titles and phrases at the composer, the composer throws some melodic ideas at the lyricist, and, God willing, one of those ideas will sound promising. The lyricist then takes it home for further work and comes back the next day for another session.

That process drew out of Richard Rodgers some of his most buoyant melodies and also drove him almost crazy. The problem was that Lorenz Hart was hard to find. A much-loved man but a drinker and a night owl, he would turn up tardily at Rodgers' apartment, if at all, and would empty his pockets of scraps of paper on which he had jotted fragments of lyrics. Those scraps got converted into some of the most tender songs in the American literature. But Rodgers was a methodical man. He looked and talked and dressed like a businessman and even composed like a businessman; stunning melodies poured out of him with businesslike speed and efficiency. In Hart he was hitched to his metabolic opposite. Once, recalling the day when he and Hart met and decided to work together, Rodgers said: "In one afternoon I acquired a career, a partner, a best friend and a source of permanent irritation."

That changed when Rodgers teamed with Oscar Hammerstein in 1942 to write *Oklahoma!*—and seven subsequent musicals. Hammerstein was as orderly as Rodgers, and his method was to write the lyrics first. Rodgers therefore reversed his lifelong process and composed melodies to fit Hammerstein's words. From the start those melodies had a different color—they didn't sound as spontaneous as Rodgers & Hart melodies. But they were beautiful melodies. Where genius is involved, it doesn't matter which comes first.

Still another constraint on the lyricist is that his words must "sing." Some vowels and consonants sing better than others. Open vowels sing best of all, especially at the end of a line—which is why so many lines end with a me or a you, or a blanket of blue, or a pie in the sky or a man that got away.

> *It's quarter to three,*
> *There's no one in the place except you and me.*
> *So set 'em up, Joe,*
> *I've got a little story you ought to know.*

Johnny Mercer's ear told him not to close the bar at quarter to twelve or to name the bartender Bob.

Not all consonants are bad for singers—"l" is mellifluous, "r" is resonant, and "v" is forever good for "love." But the harsh consonants tighten the throat, and lyricists try to avoid them. Oscar Hammerstein never stopped chastising himself for concluding "What's the Use of Wonderin'," in *Carousel*, with "and all the rest is talk." By making the singer end on a "k," which definitely doesn't sing, he thought he killed the song's chances of becoming a hit.

Finally, the lyricist must tell a story. It's not enough to merely state a romantic condition ("Night and day, you are the one"). Some kind of consummation—some moment of pleasure or enlightenment—is expected in the final 8 bars ("And my torment won't be through/ till you let me spend my life making love to you"). Pleasure was preferred. Publishers in the Brill Building, mother church of Tin Pan Alley, enjoined their songwriters to "get 'em in bed by the last eight."

Such actual romps weren't allowed in popular songs of the golden age, but savvy lyricists like Dorothy Fields and Frank Loesser never forgot that bed was the destination of choice, however allusively it was reached. "Oh, is it any wonder? I'm in the mood for love," asks Fields' singer at the end of bar 16, already considerably aroused, and by the last 8 she might as well be in bed:

> *If it should rain, we'll let it.*
> *But for tonight, forget it!*
> *I'm in the mood for love.*

Loesser's "Baby, It's Cold Outside" is more direct. In the final bars of that antiphonal duet the long-resisting girl finally agrees with her boyfriend that it really *is* too cold for her to go home.

So exacting is the lyricist's trade that only a few people master it in any generation, and none are born overnight. Ira Gershwin summed up the specifications and the timetable: "Given a fondness for music, a feeling for rhyme, a sense of whimsy and humor, an eye for the balanced sentence, an ear for the current phrase, and the ability to imagine oneself as a performer trying to put over the number in progress—given all this, I still would say it takes four or five years collaborating with knowledgeable composers to become a well-rounded lyricist."

Vincent Youmans

Only one other composer in the new generation of American song-writers, Vincent Youmans, achieved the same kind of celebrity during the 1920s as George Gershwin and Richard Rodgers. Today his name has lost the instant recognition it had in the Jazz Age; his career flickered out too soon and his legacy of songs was too small. But at his peak he brought a sound of unusual vitality to the musical theater, and he left a half-dozen melodies that are among our most durable standards—most famously, "Tea for Two."

A Christian in a predominantly Jewish field, Youmans was born to capitalist affluence, the son of a prosperous New York hatter ("Gentlemen's silk hats and derbies," "Ladies' bonnets and walking hats") who wanted his son to go into the family business. But the son demurred, preferring to try his luck at writing songs. He had shown an aptitude for music since the age of four, when he began playing chords on the family piano in suburban Westchester. (Where would American popular music be if all those parents hadn't bought all those pianos?)

The hat business's loss was show business's gain. Like George Gershwin, his exact contemporary, Youmans would become a prominent figure along the Great White Way in his twenties, a handsome young blade, composing dynamic scores for a succession of Broadway hits—*No, No, Nanette* (1925), *Oh, Please* (1926), *Hit the Deck* (1927), *Rainbow* (1928), *Great Day!* (1929), *Smiles* (1930)—and for the movie *Flying Down to Rio* in 1933. But at that point his health was sapped by tuberculosis, and he spent his remaining dozen years as a semi-invalid, dying young, as Gershwin also had. He was a pure specimen of the Prohibition era, a bright candle that burned out.

His talent was first professionally recognized during World War I by another high-voltage composer, John Philip Sousa, who was bandmaster at the Great Lakes naval training base where Youmans was stationed. Youmans submitted a lively march to Sousa, who

Of the few pictures of Vincent Youmans that survive, the one that turns up most often is this snapshot of the composer at his favorite pastime. Fishing was the last way of spending an afternoon that would have occurred to his fellow songwriters—urban men, mostly the sons of immigrants, whose shoes didn't stray far from the sidewalks of New York.

Vincent Youmans gets the biggest type on the stylish sheet music cover for "Flying Down to Rio"—and he should. His songs for "the aerial musical picture" had the trademark Youmans energy, especially the title song, which accompanied a scene in which bevies of chorus girls dance on the wings of a plane bound for South America.

Vincent Youmans gets the biggest type on the stylish sheet music cover for "Flying Down to Rio"—and he should. His songs for "the aerial musical picture" had the trademark Youmans energy, especially the title song, which accompanied a scene in which bevies of chorus girls dance on the wings of a plane bound for South America.

liked it so much that he had it played by navy bands all over the country. Ten years later, remembering its success with America's sailors, Youmans resurrected it on Broadway for *Hit the Deck*. Titled "Hallelujah!" and given a suitably exultant lyric by Leo Robin and Clifford Grey, it turned out to be no less popular with civilians and has been around ever since, its call to meeting hard to resist:

> *Sing "Hal-le-lu-jah! Hal-le-lu-jah!"*
> *And you'll shoo the*
> *Blues away . . .*

What gives Youmans' songs their tremendous energy is their small range. Unlike Jerome Kern and other composers whose melodies rise and fall over a long trajectory, Youmans generally uses only a few adjacent notes. Even in the bridge he feels no compulsion to seek variety. "Tea for Two" doesn't have a bridge at all—it merely restates the theme in a higher key and then returns to the original key—and the bridge of "I Want to Be Happy" continues the same metrical pattern as the first 16 bars. Notice how little motion Youmans requires to tell his story:

Tea For Two

```
C  Pic-              -on
B        you       knee, tea        two
A    -ture  up-  my          two          tea . . .
G                     just  for  and  for
```

I Want To Be Happy

```
G  want  be  -py,  I   be  -py  I   you
F             but won't hap- till make  hap . . .
E  I   to  hap-
```

Sometimes I'm Happy

```
F                   -py,                    -tion
E      -times I'm hap-     -times I'm blu-  dis-po-si-
E♭ Some-           Some-            My
D                          -ue,
```

I Know That You Know

```
A                I'll go   you go,
G                    where    I
F
E  I know  you know          choose you,  lose you
D     that      that              won't
```

Great Day

```
E  When  down  out,      head  shout,      be
D    you're and  lift  your  and  There's -na  great
C                 up               gon-  a  day
```

The biggest hit in Vincent Youmans' intense but brief career was "Tea for Two," in "No, No, Nanette" (1925). Its repetitive bursts of melody overcame with their energy—as Youmans' melodies often did—lyrics so inane as almost to be cause for arrest. This one, as Irving Caesar cheerfully admitted, didn't take him long.

Time On My Hands

```
E                                                    view . . .
C       on              in                      in
B  Time      hands, you     arms,     -ing
A       my              my        noth-      love
G                                          but
```

Flying Down To Rio

```
C              by              down
B         o    the        ing      to
A  Ri-  Ri-        see-  Fly-       Ri-
G  My   o,              o,              o . . .
```

By all the laws of music those songs should be monotonous. But they're full of life. Their very repetitiveness propels them forward, giving them a nervous momentum that's as characteristic of the 1920s as Gershwin's early numbers from the same period, like "That Certain Feeling." The enjoyment that these songs convey is no accident; with Youmans I'm always aware of a craftsman at work, of choices thoughtfully made, both melodically and harmonically, and when he allows himself to slow down and enjoy the scenery, as in his best ballads, like "More Than You Know," which have some leisure in them, the result can be very affecting.

The fatal impediment in Youmans' work was his lyricists. His career is a case study in the importance of that underestimated man or woman. While other major composers of his era were teamed with writers of originality and wit—George Gershwin had Ira, Rodgers had Hart, Harold Arlen had Ted Koehler—Youmans never took a regular partner, hitching his destiny to various lyricists who were merely adequate. His songs contain none of the verbal pleasures that elevate the work of his fellow composers: the surprises of rhyme and wordplay, of image and allusion. "Without a Song" and "Orchids in the Moonlight" are strong melodies struggling under a heavy load of pretension. "Tea for Two" is a triumph of music over words that are little short of hilarious. Irving Caesar, who claimed that the lyric took him only five minutes, died in 1996 at the age of 101 and was quoted in his obituary as saying, "Sometimes I write lousy, but always fast."

Vincent Youmans deserved better. He was a major American songwriter who let enduring fame slip away.

TEA FOR TWO

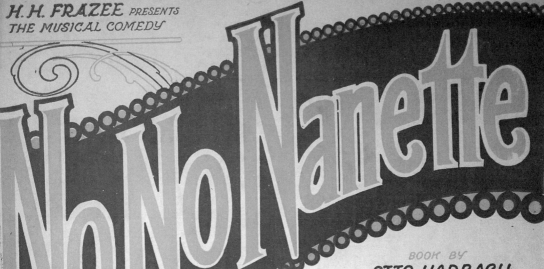

H. H. FRAZEE PRESENTS
THE MUSICAL COMEDY

No No Nanette

BOOK BY
OTTO HARBACH
AND
FRANK MANDEL
LYRICS BY
OTTO HARBACH
AND
IRVING CAESAR
MUSIC BY
VINCENT YOUMANS

Entire production staged
under the direction of
Edward Royce

HARMS
INCORPORATED
NEW YORK

MADE IN
U.S.A.

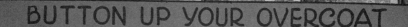

BUTTON UP YOUR OVERCOAT

LAURENCE SCHWAB
AND FRANK MANDEL
PRESENT
A MUSICAL SLICE OF COUNTRY CLUB LIFE

FOLLOW THRU

WITH
DESYLVA, BROWN AND HENDERSON SONGS

BOOK BY
LAURENCE SCHWAB
AND
B. G. DeSYLVA
BOOK DIRECTED BY
EDGAR MacGREGOR
MUSICAL NUMBERS STAGED BY
ROBERT CONNOLLY

YOU WOULDN'T FOOL ME, WOULD YOU
BUTTON UP YOUR OVERCOAT
NO MORE YOU
MY LUCKY STAR
I WANT TO BE BAD
FOLLOW THRU
I COULD GIVE UP ANYTHING BUT YOU
THEN I'LL HAVE TIME FOR YOU
SELECTION

DE SYLVA, BROWN AND HENDERSON, INC.
Music Publishers
DE SYLVA, BROWN AND HENDERSON BUILDING   745 SEVENTH AVENUE, NEW YORK

DeSylva, Brown and Henderson

The mindless optimism of the twenties had its perfect symbol in the songs written by the lyricists Buddy DeSylva and Lew Brown and the composer Ray Henderson for a half-dozen hit musicals between 1926 and 1930: shows like *Good News!* ("the collegiate musical comedy") and *Follow Thru* ("a musical slice of country club life"). "DeSylva, Brown & Henderson" was a household name, and no wonder—just the titles of the songs written by that trio made people feel better: "The Best Things in Life Are Free," "You're the Cream in My Coffee," "Life Is Just a Bowl of Cherries," "Just Imagine," "Button Up Your Overcoat," "I'm a Dreamer (Aren't We All?)," "(Keep Your) Sunny Side Up," "(This Is My) Lucky Day," "Together," "Lucky in Love," "You Are My Lucky Star," "The Varsity Drag," "Good News." Even their classic "Birth of the Blues" bubbles with major notes, blue only in its account of what got born.

Those amiable songs are gems of economy: not many words and not many notes, but all of them just right—easy to sing and easy to remember. Henderson once described the team's working methods: "We usually roughed out the show in New York and then went to Atlantic City, where we took a suite at the Ritz for ten days and finished the score. We tried to write a balanced score—love songs, rhythm songs, comedy, low down or torch numbers, and ensembles." And they succeeded. Their sheet-music artists also got it just right. All those golf balls! Everybody understood that the country hadn't turned serious. Life really was a bowl of cherries.

Not until the 1930s would the cream in the coffee turn to powdered milk.

The songwriting team of DeSylva, Brown and Henderson didn't break any new ground with their resolutely cheerful musicals, but the sunny songs and sheet music covers (also on the next two pages) are nothing but a pleasure. Janet Gaynor, of "Sunny Side Up," would later become a major movie star, best remembered for her role in the 1937 version of "A Star Is Born," opposite Fredric March as the alcoholic actor who memorably walks out to sea.

THE BEST THINGS IN LIFE ARE FREE

LAURENCE SCHWAB AND FRANK MANDEL
PRESENT
THE COLLEGIATE MUSICAL COMEDY

GOOD NEWS!

WORDS AND MUSIC BY
B.G. De SYLVA, LEW BROWN AND RAY HENDERSON

BOOK BY
LAURENCE SCHWAB
AND
B. G. De SYLVA

BOOK STAGED BY
EDGAR MacGREGOR

MUSICAL NUMBERS
STAGED BY
ROB'T. CONNOLLY

WITH
GEORGE OLSEN
(HIMSELF)
AND HIS MUSIC

GOOD NEWS
THE VARSITY DRAG
HAPPY DAYS
LUCKY IN LOVE
THE BEST THINGS
    IN LIFE ARE FREE
JUST IMAGINE
A GIRL OF THE
        PI BETA PHI
HE'S A LADIES' MAN

DE SYLVA, BROWN AND HENDERSON, INC.
Music Publishers
DE SYLVA, BROWN AND HENDERSON BUILDING   745 SEVENTH AVENUE NEW YORK

MADE IN U.S.A.

(I'M A DREAMER)
AREN'T WE ALL
WILLIAM FOX PRESENTS
JANET GAYNOR
AND
CHARLES FARRELL
IN
SUNNY SIDE UP
STORY, DIALOG, LYRICS & MUSIC BY
B.G. DE SYLVA, LEW BROWN AND RAY HENDERSON
DIRECTED BY
DAVID BUTLER
DANCES STAGED BY
SEYMOUR FELIX
SUNNY SIDE UP
(I'M A DREAMER) AREN'T WE ALL
TURN ON THE HEAT
IF I HAD A TALKING PICTURE OF YOU
YOU'VE GOT ME PICKIN' PETALS OFF O' DAISIES
YOU FIND THE TIME I'LL FIND THE PLACE
DE SYLVA, BROWN AND HENDERSON, INC.
Music Publishers
DE SYLVA, BROWN AND HENDERSON BUILDING 745 SEVENTH AVENUE, NEW YORK
MADE IN U. S. A.

Harold Arlen
(and Ted Koehler)

It was "Stormy Weather," from the *Cotton Club Parade* of 1933, that first got me hooked on American popular song, and Harold Arlen has been my favorite popular composer ever since. My parents brought home the hit record of the song, with Arlen himself doing the vocal. His voice was as high as a schoolboy's, but plaintive beyond a schoolboy's years, and his melody had a faraway sadness—the stormiest kind of weather for someone in love.

I learned that Arlen was from Buffalo, the son of a cantor who improvised beautiful melodies for texts that had no music. He quit school at 15 to form a group called "The Snappy Trio," which grew into a quintet called "The Southbound Shufflers," playing on lake steamers out of Buffalo, which later grew into an 11-man band called "The Buffalodians." (Someone in the band had a talent for nomenclature.) Arlen was the singer, pianist and arranger. "I could always improvise," he said, "and I loved to invent unconventional turns for the men in the band who couldn't do anything but follow the melody."

That gift opened the door to his life work when he came to New York in the late 1920s. Until then he had never thought of writing songs. Hired as a singer for Vincent Youmans' musical, *Great Day*, he filled in one afternoon when the rehearsal pianist got sick. Improvising a vamp for the dancers, he hit upon a tune so catchy that it caught the ear of everyone in the house. Somebody paired him with the lyricist Ted Koehler, who put words to the vamp. Sung by Ruth Etting as the finale of her *9:15 Revue*, in 1930, it became Arlen's first hit: "Get Happy."

From there Arlen and Koehler went on to write the score for eight of the Cotton Club's semi-annual revues between 1930 and 1934, creating a string of instant standards that included "Stormy

Even as a young man, Harold Arlen, newly arrived in New York to try his luck as a singer and an arranger in 1929, wore a boutonniere. He fell into songwriting by chance and went on to compose many of America's most deeply felt popular songs, including "Over the Rainbow," "Stormy Weather," "Blues in the Night" and "The Man That Got Away."

Ted Koehler was Harold Arlen's too-little-known lyricist for a string of hits written for the semi-annual revues at Harlem's legendary Cotton Club. Here he and Arlen show their newest song, "Let's Fall in Love," to the torch singer Ruth Etting. Etting had introduced their first hit, "Get Happy," in a Broadway musical. In 1955 her tear-stained career would be the subject of the film biography "Love Me or Leave Me."

Weather" (Koehler's lyric is as much a classic as the melody), "Ill Wind," "I've Got the World on a String," "Between the Devil and the Deep Blue Sea," "I Love a Parade" and "As Long As I Live." Harlem's legendary Cotton Club was then presenting the best black singers, dancers and musicians—giants like Bill Robinson, Duke Ellington and Ethel Waters—and they responded to Arlen's affinity for the Negro sensibility. He had absorbed the idioms of African-American jazz by hanging out in Harlem clubs with George Gershwin, and he fused those rhythms with the Jewish melancholy that was his birthright.

Thus was born what the world would come to know as the Arlen sound: blue melodic line ("Blues in the Night"), jauntiness of rhythm ("Let's Take a Walk Around the Block"), strong jazz flavoring ("Hit the Road to Dreamland") and infectious humor ("Accentuate the Positive"). Over his long career, many of his finest songs would be introduced by black singers in movies—"Happiness Is a Thing Called Joe" (*Cabin in the Sky*)—and in Broadway shows: "The Eagle and Me" (*Bloomer Girl*), "Come Rain or Come Shine" (*St. Louis Woman*) and "Sleepin' Bee" (*House of Flowers*).

What moved me most when I first heard "Stormy Weather"

was the blue melodic line—the sorrowful arc of flatted notes—and when "Ill Wind" came along a year later I was addicted to the Arlen sound. There was something ancient and mysterious about the melody. It sounded as old as Jerusalem:

Branching out from the Cotton Club, Arlen composed two more standards with Koehler ("I Gotta Right to Sing the Blues" and "Let's Fall in Love"), wrote another one with E. Y. (Yip) Harburg ("It's Only a Paper Moon"), and teamed with Harburg and Ira Gershwin on the Broadway revue *Life Begins at 8:40*. But theater money was drying up, and in the mid-1930s he moved to Hollywood. There, mostly with Johnny Mercer, he spent a decade composing superb songs—"Blues in the Night," "This Time the Dream's on Me," "My Shining Hour," "One for My Baby," "That Old Black Magic," "Out of This World," "Let's Take the Long Way Home" —for mediocre movies. I saw them all, often two or three times, always marveling at the originality of Arlen's melodies amid the Hollywood sludge.

As a movie, only *The Wizard of Oz* matched the high standards of its composer. Arlen and Harburg's amiable songs ("We're Off to See the Wizard," "If I Only Had a Brain," "Ding-Dong! The Witch Is Dead") were the glue that held together the first movie musical in which the songs and the story were integrated—now one of America's national myths. One of those songs, "Over the Rainbow," launched another national myth, Judy Garland. Thus inoculated, Garland sang a high proportion of Arlen ballads for the rest of her life, including his last great torch song, "The Man That Got Away," in *A Star Is Born*.

Returning to Broadway in the 1940s, Arlen composed three scores of unusual richness. *Bloomer Girl*, written with Harburg, had 14 sunny numbers ("Right As the Rain," "Evelina"), including three waltzes—seemingly the work of a happy man. But his own favorite song was the rueful "Last Night When We Were Young," and in his next two shows, both of which had Negro casts—*St. Louis Woman* (with Johnny Mercer) and *House of Flowers* (with Truman Capote)— he was back in the familiar mode of heartbreak: the flatted notes and straining seventh chords ("I Had Myself a True Love," "Don't Like Goodbyes"). *St. Louis Woman* put it all together for me. It was my favorite Broadway score, an exuberance of ballads and blues, lullabies and cakewalks and chorales.

I got to know Harold Arlen when I interviewed him for a newspaper article in connection with *House of Flowers* and wasn't surprised to find him a gentle and modest man, quick to laugh. Later, for *Harper's*, I wrote the only long magazine piece that was ever published about him; such was his lifelong anonymity. His face could have been his fortune if his songs hadn't been—a vertical face, interestingly lined by the struggles of composition, with coal black hair and deep blue eyes. His clothes were as elegant as his songs—he wore a fresh boutonniere every day—and he was generous in his affections. For many years he sent my two young children a book or a record every Christmas, though he had never met them. The inscription would say: "For Amy and John. Merry Xmas. Friend Harold."

For my *Harper's* article I talked with four of Arlen's lyricists. Here are some of the things they told me:

JOHNNY MERCER: "Harold's melodies are way out because Jewish melodies are way out—they take unexpected twists and turns. He's more inventive than Gershwin in trying to find new forms for his songs. The rhythm of both men is wonderful, but George's often strikes me as mathematical—listen to the precision of 'Sweet and Low-Down' or 'Fascinatin' Rhythm'—while Harold's comes from the bottom of his feet."

IRA GERSHWIN: "To me the Hebraic influence is the big one in Harold's music, and it's something my brother George didn't have. Our parents, like Harold's, came from Eastern Russia, but there was no Jewish religious music in our family. Harold is always original, always himself. His songs are, well, *peculiarly* constructed, so that I never know what to expect. I remember thinking 'The Man That Got Away' was too long and unorthodox to be a hit, but it grew on people. Harold's songs always do."

E. Y. HARBURG: "He leads you into situations that are unanticipated. I often have to wait a day or two to let the melody work on me, to see what he's really doing. A lot of people can write songs, but only an artist can make other people feel the music deeply. Harold touches something in all of us that responds, but what he has above all is individuality."

Two of Harold Arlen's bluest songs, "Ill Wind" and "Stormy Weather" (this page and next page), were introduced in revues at the Cotton Club, where "Duke Ellington and His Famous Orchestra" were in long-term residence. Ethel Waters, aggrieved by a recent divorce, was coaxed out of retirement to sing "Stormy Weather," which, duly forlorn, became her signature song.

TRUMAN CAPOTE: "The sadness, the echo of loneliness that wails through Arlen's music seemed to me the foundation of his sensibility, for he is a man obsessed with the tragic view of life. At the same time, amid the sighs, the long sad looks, laughter was always ready to run rampant. He has one of the most distinctive laughs I've ever heard—a wild, high-pitched chuckling that reddens his face and fills his eyes with tears. For him, music is the entire story. There, inside a world of sound, he is always courageous, intelligent, incapable of cliché."

My favorite Arlen story came from Robert Breen, director of the *Porgy and Bess* company that toured the world in 1955. When the troupe was in Cairo, Breen told me, he went to a symphony concert that featured works by Mozart and Beethoven and concluded with a

STORMY WEATHER

Cotton Club
presents

ETHEL WATERS
GEORGE DEWEY WASHINGTON

in

COTTON CLUB
PARADE

22nd EDITION

with

DUKE ELLINGTON
AND HIS FAMOUS ORCHESTRA

STORMY WEATHER
HAPPY AS THE DAY IS LONG
RAISIN' THE RENT
GET YOURSELF A NEW BROOM
AND SWEEP THE BLUES AWAY
CALICO DAYS
MUGGIN' LIGHTLY

lyrics and music by
TED KOEHLER
HAROLD ARLEN

STAGED BY
DAN HEALY

DANCES BY
ELIDA WEBB • LEONARD HARPER

MILLS MUSIC
INC.
Music Publishers
1619 Broadway—New York, N.Y.

Returning to New York in the 1940s after a long stint in Hollywood, Harold Arlen wrote elegant scores for three Broadway musicals: "Bloomer Girl," "St. Louis Woman" and "House of Flowers." The last two had all-black casts. African-American singers were strongly drawn to Arlen's music—an emotional mixture of his Jewish heritage and the jazz he and George Gershwin kept going to Harlem to hear.

suite called "American Folk Music." Breen gradually realized that the suite consisted entirely of songs by Harold Arlen: "Stormy Weather," "Ill Wind," "I Gotta Right to Sing the Blues," "Blues in the Night" and "Accentuate the Positive." Afterward he asked the conductor if he knew who wrote the suite. "But sir," the conductor said, "nobody wrote it. They are just old folk ballads that we made into a medley." He assumed that they were from Stephen Foster's day. Breen looked at the score and saw a tiny handwritten scrawl that said H. ARLENE. "When I told the conductor that 'H. Arlene' was still alive," Breen said, "he couldn't believe it."

Arthur Schwartz
and Howard Dietz

I've always been sorry that Arthur Schwartz wrote so few songs—far fewer than Kern, Gershwin, Rodgers, Arlen and the other great composers. He brought a sound of unusual elegance to the Broadway theater and left a half-dozen standards that still evoke the svelte era that replaced the raucous twenties. "Dancing in the Dark" is the perfect emblem of the new decade.

A cultivated man with an M.A. and a law degree from Columbia, Schwartz taught English and practiced law in New York before giving up his legal practice in 1929 to be a full-time composer, and in Howard Dietz he had a literate and urbane lyricist. The label "Dietz & Schwartz," attached to a string of "smart" revues in the early 1930s—*The Second Little Show, Three's a Crowd, The Band Wagon, Flying Colors, Revenge With Music*—was a guarantee of sophisticated taste.

Nobody wrote melodies as sensuous as "Alone Together" and "You and the Night and the Music," with their rich minor-key coloring, or "Dancing in the Dark" and "I See Your Face Before Me." They are grandly constructed songs, soaring at exactly the moment when they need to take flight and then returning to earth, all musical issues resolved. "By Myself" needs only 24 bars to tell its lovelorn story—a minimalist gem. It was definitively sung by Fred Astaire in MGM's 1953 movie *The Band Wagon*, a Dietz & Schwartz retrospective that brought back from the team's heyday such ingratiating songs as "A Shine on My Shoes," "I Guess I'll Have to Change My Plan," "New Sun in the Sky," "I Love Louisa" and "Louisiana Hayride."

One song newly written for that movie, "That's Entertainment," a bouquet in the same class as Irving Berlin's "There's No Business

The composer Arthur Schwartz and the lyricist Howard Dietz with Cyd Charisse in Hollywood during the filming of "The Band Wagon," the movie built around the songs they wrote for a half-dozen popular Broadway revues in the 1930s. Theatergoers attending a "Dietz & Schwartz" show knew they were in for evening of sinuous melodies and debonair lyrics, typically "Dancing in the Dark" and "Alone Together."

Like Show Business," finds Dietz reveling in the infinite varieties of fare that mummers have always provided:

> *The plot/ may be hot/ simply teeming with sex,*
> *A gay/ divorcee/ who is after her ex,*
> *It could be Oedipus Rex,*
> *Where a chap kills his father*
> *And causes a lot of bother . . .*

After Arthur Schwartz's prolific early years he composed only in spurts for the rest of his long life. Dietz found regular employment as publicity director of MGM, where, among other achievements, he devised the studio's lion trademark. But whenever Schwartz did write for Hollywood or Broadway the songs were of high quality: "A Gal in Calico," "They're Either Too Young or Too Old," "Haunted Heart," "Rhode Island Is Famous for You." I partic-

"Flying Colors" (1932) was "lighted" by Norman Bel Geddes, later a pioneer industrial designer, and had dances by Agnes De Mille, later the pioneering choreographer of "Oklahoma!" Jack Buchanan, star of "Between the Devil" (1937), later starred in the movie of "The Band Wagon," memorably singing such Dietz & Schwartz songs as the regretful "I Guess I'll Have to Change My Plan."

ularly remember the musical *A Tree Grows in Brooklyn* (1951). With lyrics by Dorothy Fields ("Make the Man Love Me," "I'll Buy You a Star"), it was one of the most beautiful of all Broadway scores. The man couldn't help being a class act.

Andy Razaf and the African Connection

African-Americans have been credited with writing so few popular standards that anyone might think they were writing a different kind of music. But the music composed by American blacks in the early years of the 20th century is one of the cornerstones of American popular song. Theirs was the jazz and ragtime sensibility that George Gershwin, Harold Arlen and many other white songwriters went to Harlem to draw inspiration from.

It was the black songwriters' fate, however, to be born too soon. The white establishment shut them out. Broadway producers wouldn't use their songs in white musicals, and music publishers treated them degradingly, buying their songs for $25 or $50 and publishing them as the work of the firm's white writers. Only a few born-in-Harlem hits achieved national fame on their own—mainly songs of the late 1920s and early 1930s, such as "Memories of You," by Andy Razaf and Eubie Blake, and "Ain't Misbehavin,'" "Honeysuckle Rose" and "Keeping Out of Mischief Now," by Razaf and Fats Waller.

But black composers had long been helping to shape the modern era of song. One of the best was Shelton Brooks, whose "Some of These Days," written in 1910, is still a standard and whose "Darktown Strutters' Ball" (1917) is still irresistible. Another was W. C. Handy, who composed the landmark "Memphis Blues" in 1911. Although Handy was known as the father of the blues, he was actually their midwife, the first musician to notate the melancholy fragments with which Negro slaves had sung their sorrows since plantation days. He also composed some blues of his own, such as "Yellow Dog Blues," "Beale Street Blues" and "St. Louis Blues." With those songs Handy codified the blues in the 12-bar format,

Andreamenentania Razafinkeriefo, the son of a Madagascar prince, who simplified his name to Andy Razaf, was the best black American lyricist, teaming with the composers Eubie Blake and Fats Waller to write such enduring standards as "Memories of You," "Ain't Misbehavin'" and "Honeysuckle Rose." Black performers also strongly influenced American popular song, especially jazz pianists like James P. Johnson and Art Tatum and singers like Billie Holiday and Ella Fitzgerald.

with standard repetitions and chord patterns, that jazzmen have obeyed ever since. He made the blues part of America's vocabulary, both as subject matter—the language of lament—and as a melodic line with blue (flatted) notes. "I hate to see that evening sun go down," his "St. Louis Blues" mournfully begins, and no song begins any better. Harold Arlen's three-part "Blues in the Night" ("My mama done tol' me") is its direct descendant.

But the biggest contribution that blacks made to American popular song was through their tremendous pianists, especially James P. Johnson, Eubie Blake and Art Tatum, who played with a technical brilliance beyond what had been imagined possible with only ten fingers. They were the first in a long line of black pianists—Willie "The Lion" Smith, Jelly Roll Morton, Earl Hines, Teddy Wilson, Fats Waller, Count Basie, Erroll Garner, Oscar Peterson, Ellis Larkins and many more—who pumped new energy into popular song, forever connecting it in the public mind with jazz and with the pleasures of improvisation. Later a long line of great black women singers would make the same connection, from Ethel Waters and Billie Holiday through Ella Fitzgerald, Carmen McRae and Sarah Vaughan.

While the black pianists played to adoring white audiences, the black songwriters labored in a ghetto, their songs confined to Harlem revues and occasional all-black Broadway shows like Eubie Blake and Noble Sissle's *Shuffle Along* ("I'm Just Wild About Harry"). The one man who made it his mission to win dignity for African-American songwriters, the lyricist Andy Razaf, got his revolutionary zeal from the circumstances of his birth. Born Andreamenentania Razafinkeriefo, the son of a Madagascar prince, he was the product of a curious fling in American foreign policy. His grandfather, a black American politician named John Waller, was appointed United States consul to Madagascar in 1895, the idea being that a man of African descent could work with the local population to thwart French designs on the island. His 16-year-old daughter Jennie married a prince of the royal family, and Waller agitated for American blacks to settle there. This so agitated the French that they invaded Madagascar and annexed it as a colony. During the turmoil the prince was killed, John Waller was put in prison, and his pregnant daughter fled to the United States, where the future lyricist was born.

Andrea Razafkeriefo (as he then called himself) was a handsome boy with poetic dreams, who dropped out of high school in New York to support his mother. Working as an elevator operator in a building that housed some music publishers, he persuaded one

SAY IT WITH YOUR FEET

CONNIE'S HOT CHOCOLATES

Lyrics by
ANDY RAZAF

Music by
THOMAS WALLER
and
HARRY BROOKS

Staged by
LEONARD HARPER

AIN'T MISBEHAVIN'
OFF TIME
THAT RHYTHM MAN
DIXIE CINDERELLA
GODDESS OF RAIN
THAT SNAKE HIP DANCE
SWEET SAVANNAH SUE
THAT JUNGLE JAMBOREE
WALTZ DIVINE
CAN'T WE GET TOGETHER?

 MILLS MUSIC
Music Publishers
Mills Building
148-150 West 46 St. New York

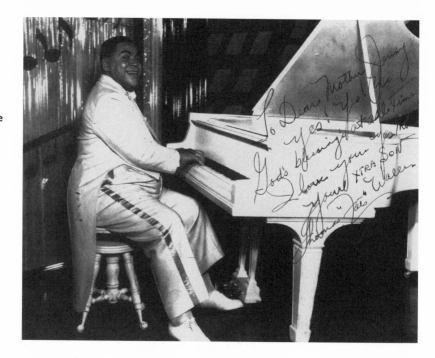

The man in the white suit and white shoes at the white piano is the ebullient Fats Waller. "Dear Mother Jenny," to whom this picture is fervently inscribed, was Andy Razaf's mother. He regarded her as a surrogate mother and signs himself "your xtra son."

captive passenger to interpolate a song of his called "Baltimo'" in *The Passing Show* of 1913. But that remarkable first sale was also his last, and after seven years of menial employment he took a job in a different line of work—as a pitcher with a new semipro Negro baseball league in Cleveland. Meanwhile, he had also become known in Harlem as a gadfly poet of social protest in Negro newspapers.

Returning to New York in 1921, Andy Razaf finally found composers who kept him busy writing lyrics, especially the Englishman Paul Denniker ("S'posin'"), Eubie Blake, and Thomas "Fats" Waller. Waller, still in his teens, was a prodigious pianist and entertainer ("Your Feet's Too Big") and was also endlessly fertile as a composer; songs of high exuberance tumbled out of him almost as fast as his hands touched the keys ("Squeeze Me," "The Joint Is Jumpin'"). He could match Razaf's playful side ("Honeysuckle Rose") and also his serious concerns, as in the poignant race song "Black and Blue" ("What did I do to be so black and blue?").

But Waller was also endlessly truant—an obsessive eater, drinker and womanizer, impossible for Razaf to pin down, jailed several times for nonpayment of wife support, and so besieged for money that he would sell all the rights to his and Razaf's songs to pay whatever creditor was at the door. The Madagascar prince must have found it ironic that two of their biggest hits were hymns to domestic fidelity: "Ain't Misbehavin'" and "Keeping Out of Mischief Now."

Sheet Music

I grew up in a house full of sheet music. My father and mother would go to Broadway musicals and bring home the songs from the score, which were sold in the theater's lobby. Those gaudy covers, a striking form of American poster art, have been part of the landscape of my life ever since. Eventually I took over my parents' collection, and I've also never been able to resist buying the stuff on my own; the covers call out to me from cardboard bins at antique shows and flea markets and garage sales. Heaped on my piano, they are ghosts from an era when years of piano lessons had paid off in some member of every family's being able to play the latest songs for everyone in the family to sing.

I loved all the information on those covers: who starred in the musical; who wrote the music and the lyrics and the book; who directed and choreographed the show; who designed the costumes and the sets, and, best of all, what other songs were in the score— they were always listed near the bottom of the page. Much of what I know about the musical theater was first absorbed from those covers, long before I was old enough to see an actual show.

It was obviously a world of high glamour. Those three hoofers on the cover of "Body and Soul" (*next page*)—Fred Allen, Libby Holman and Clifton Webb—struck me as impossibly suave. They were so fully in motion, gliding across the stage as if propelled, and the men were so elegantly dressed, especially Allen: the subtly cross-hatched suit and double-breasted vest, the pleats and pointed shoes and spats. The composer of the song, who would later become the protean arranger, pianist, Hollywood Bowl conductor and MGM musical director Johnny Green, was still John W. Green, a young Harvard economics graduate who had worked on Wall Street, when he made his reputation by writing what would become one of the most frequently recorded American popular songs. Inserted into the revue *Three's a Crowd*, "Body and Soul" upstaged

"Music by John W. Green" says the line at the top of the sheet music of "Body and Soul," one of the all-time biggest hit songs. Not long out of Harvard, John W. would soon become Johnny, Hollywood's jack of all musical trades. The two covers on the next two pages illustrate the ability of sheet music artists to catch the spirit not only of a particular show but of its historic period. "Garrick Gaieties" is pure Jazz Age in its warmth, "Roberta" pure 1930s in its cold lines.

a Dietz & Schwartz score that included "Something to Remember You By." Libby Holman, queen of the torch singers, famous for her rendition of "Moanin' Low," was just the thrush to extract the last drop of aggrieved abandonment from Edward Heyman and Robert Sour's lyric. The eagerness of the singer to offer more than her soul to her ungrateful man gave the song a sexual edge it has never lost.

The illustration for "Body and Soul" freezes in historical time—as sheet music covers often do—the earlier career of performers we know only in some later incarnation. Today I can hardly imagine that Fred Allen and Clifton Webb were ever song-and-dance men. I associate Webb with the silky movie roles he subsequently played—stalking Gene Tierney in *Laura*—and I only remember Allen as the writer-star of the Sunday night show that was the crown jewel of American radio during my boyhood, an hour of literate humor. Allen's persona was so owlish, his use of the English language so fastidious, that he seemed to be a latter-day H. L. Mencken in our midst. To picture him dancing with Libby Holman is unthinkable.

But mainly I enjoyed the sheet music covers as art: commercial art of a surprisingly high order, especially because it only used two-color printing. The artists' achievement was to capture not only the spirit of the show but the cultural climate of the moment. The cover of *The Garrick Gaieties* (*next page*) instantly tells us it's an artifact of the 1920s: warm tone, mauve palette, playful lettering, high-kicking flappers. The adjacent cover of *Roberta* is pure 1930s: cool and unsentimental. The sans-serif letters are the typographical equivalent of the new "modernistic" furniture; the black is boldly deployed, and the intervening green is as icy as key-lime pie. So is the lady, seen only in silhouette, her back turned.

Another cool cucumber from that period is Duke Ellington's "sophisticated lady," a creature of long lines and long fingers (*page 82*). She typifies the covers of songs that were stand-alone ballads, not part of a Broadway or Hollywood score. There, the artists' job was to convey the emotional nature of the song itself, and they proved to be deft psychiatrists, needing only a few brushstrokes to suggest the feelings of a girl venturing into new romantic terrain ("This my first affair") or a boy all alone by the telephone.

But by the mid-1930s the artists' long reign was coming to an end. Broadway musicals continued to use original art, but songs from Hollywood movies were illustrated by a scene from the movie, and individual ballads went strictly promotional, using a photograph of the "vocalist" who made a hit record of the song or the band-leader who "featured" it in a nightclub or on the air. Often those bandleaders are wearing a fedora and a topcoat, as if photographed a long way from the bandstand—perhaps out at the track. The reso-nant names of their bands still echo down the decades: Harry Reser and his Clicquot Club Eskimoes, Harry Horlick and his A & P Gypsies. Tie-ins with performers were suddenly important to the music publishers as the upstart medium of radio cut into sheet music sales. Families now sat around the Philco instead of standing around the piano.

Today all that pictorial pleasure and all that information is gone. After World War II, music publishers stopped issuing the standards with their original covers, replacing them with generic covers, mostly white, that only use type. Displayed in music stores,

APRIL FOOL

GARRICK GAIETIES
AS PRESENTED BY
THE THEATRE GUILD Jr. PLAYERS
AT THE GARRICK THEATRE, NEW YORK

LYRICS BY
LORENZ HART
MUSIC BY
RICHARD RODGERS

VOCAL

MANHATTAN

SENTIMENTAL ME

ON WITH THE DANCE

APRIL FOOL

DO YOU LOVE ME
(I Wonder)

OLD FASHIONED GIRL

___

ORCHESTRA

Fox-Trot Dance
Arrangements by
ARTHUR LANGE

MADE IN U.S.A

STAGED BY
PHILIP LOEB

EDWARD B. MARKS MUSIC CO.,
223-225 WEST FORTY-SIXTH STREET.
NEW YORK

YOU'RE DEVASTATING

MAX GORDON PRESENTS

ROBERTA

ADAPTED FROM
THE NOVEL BY
ALICE DUER MILLER

BY
JEROME KERN
AND
OTTO HARBACH

(When Your Heart's On Fire)
Smoke Gets In Your Eyes
Let's Begin
The Touch Of Your Hand
Yesterdays
Something Had To Happen
You're Devastating
I'll Be Hard To Handle

T.B. HARMS
COMPANY
NEW YORK

MADE IN U.S.A.

BETWEEN THE DEVIL AND THE DEEP BLUE SEA

The COTTON CLUB
presents

RHYTH·MANIA

STAGED BY
DAN HEALY

DANCES BY
CLARENCE ROBINSON

LYRICS BY
TED KOEHLER

MUSIC BY
HAROLD ARLEN

GET UP, GET OUT,
GET UNDER THE SUN

BREAKFAST DANCE

NEATH THE PALE CUBAN MOON

WITHOUT RHYTHM

BETWEEN THE DEVIL
AND THE DEEP BLUE SEA

KICKIN' THE GONG AROUND

MADE
IN
U.S.A.

MILLS MUSIC
Music Publishers
Mills Building
148-150 West 46th St. New York

The name "Leff" at the bottom of "Between the Devil and the Deep Blue Sea"—and on "Sophisticated Lady" (next page), "Ill Wind" (page 63) and "Stormy Weather" (page 64)—is the signature of Sydney Leff, one of the most sought-after sheet music artists of the 1920s and '30s, who sometimes drew as many as four covers a day. Recently he licensed six of them for use on coffee mugs.

they look almost identical, shorn of their connection to a musical or a movie, a singer or a band. Sheet music as a historical document and as an art form has become extinct, surviving only as a "collectible" in the American home, framed on the wall or papering the bathroom.

But the images that look out at us are still strong, and one question they ask across the years is: Who were the artists who drew those covers? Very few of the covers were signed; evidently it was just free-lance contract work. Only one signature—LEFF— caught my eye with some regularity when I was growing up. I first saw Leff's signature on the Arlen-Koehler songs for the Cotton Club—"Ill Wind," "Stormy Weather" and "Between the Devil and the Deep Blue Sea" (*pages 63, 64, 80*)—and on Irving Berlin's "Blue Skies" and "How Deep Is the Ocean." I liked the artist's bold sense of design, which had an Art Deco feeling. I also liked his sense of self; in that vast sea of anonymous toil he put his name on his work.

One day in 1997 I happened to meet an artist in New York named Joan Miller. Somehow we got to talking about the old songs, and I mentioned my hoard of sheet music. She said her father had illustrated many of the early covers. I asked her what his name was. She said it was Sydney Leff. I could hardly believe the coincidence. I told Mrs. Miller how I used to study her father's Cotton Club covers, more than 60 years ago. I said I was only sorry I never got to ask him about his work.

"Would you like to meet him?" Mrs. Miller asked. She said her father had just flown in from Florida for a family celebration that night. It was his 95th birthday. He was staying with his other daughter, Gail Raab, who was also an artist. Their mother, Rita Leff, had also been a prominent New York artist.

The next day at Mrs. Raab's apartment I found a tall, vigorous man with curly white hair and amused eyes who didn't look a day over eighty. Sydney Leff told me he was still active as a free-lance illustrator. Recently he had been interviewed by a television station in West Palm Beach, and six of his covers had just been issued on a set of coffee mugs: "Stormy Weather," "Ain't Misbehavin'," "Sophisticated Lady," "Are You Lonesome Tonight?", "Five Foot Two, Eyes of Blue" and "Yes, Sir, That's My Baby."

Leff said he grew up in Brooklyn and commuted by subway to East Harlem to attend the only New York City high school that taught advertising art. One of his classmates was Al Hirschfeld, the equally durable theater caricaturist of the *New York Times*. One day in 1923 he answered a help-wanted ad—"artist to design sheet music cover"—placed by the composer Sam Coslow ("Cocktails for

SOPHISTICATED LADY

Vocal

Music by
Duke Ellington

Words by
Irving Mills
and
Mitchell Parish

WE DO OUR PART

Gotham Music Service INC
1619 Broadway,
New York City

SOLE SELLING AGENTS

MILLS MUSIC INC
Music Publishers
1619 Broadway–New York, N.Y.

Two," "My Old Flame"). Coslow liked the kid's sketch and bought it for $15—the first of two thousand covers Leff would sell in the next two decades to every publisher on Tin Pan Alley.

"The proportion of songs that became real hits was very small," Sydney Leff told me. "They were ground out by the dozens." Nobody ground them out faster than Irving Berlin, and he became one of Leff's biggest patrons. "There were only four or five of us doing this work," he said, "and we didn't worry about the competition—there were plenty of jobs to go around. I'd drop in on the offices of the different music publishers. They all had song-pluggers sitting in little cubicles, playing their new numbers for bandleaders and singers, trying to get them to promote those songs.

"I would get the lyrics and a professional copy of any song that needed a cover, and the next day I'd bring the publisher a rough thumbnail sketch. Sometimes I drew as many as four a day. If the publisher liked it I would make a finished illustration. You could accomplish a lot with only two colors, using Benday screens to get different tones of black and gray. Type wasn't used; I did all my own lettering—it was an integral part of the design. I had certain formulas, depending on the song. Reflections on the water, for romance. Top hats. Chorus girls. Palm trees. Silhouettes of beautiful women. The moon. I always knew where to put the moon. Life was simple."

Because sheet music was in such demand for home entertainment in the 1920s and 1930s, and because it was affordable, costing only 25 cents a copy, Sydney Leff and the other stars of the field sailed through those decades making good money—non-starving artists, even in the Depression. They rode the high tide of popular affection for American popular song and matched it with an affection of their own.

"It was a great era," Leff told me. "During the flapper period, the only thing those people thought about was having fun."

Cole Porter

It was from Cole Porter, in 1934, that I first glimpsed what it might mean to be "sophisticated." I was a small and sheltered boy with three older sisters; whatever sophistication existed in our family ended with them. When my father brought home the songs from Porter's *Anything Goes*—especially "You're the Top" and "I Get a Kick Out of You" and "Anything Goes"—I could hardly believe that such a clever body of work was attainable by man. It wasn't just the wordplay that dazzled me: "I'm sure that if/ I took even one sniff/ That would bore me terrif/ic'ly too . . ." It was the universe that the words described—a continental playground where people stayed at the Ritz and played on the Riviera, where to be rich and privileged was to be a little weary of it all.

"You're the Top" was my first "list song." Over the years I would hear many others—songs that used some kind of enumerating device to catalogue affairs of the heart: "These Foolish Things," "They Can't Take That Away From Me," "I Wish I Were in Love Again." But there was never such a list as Porter's:

> You're the top, you're Mahatma Gandhi,
> You're the top, you're Napoleon brandy . . .
> You're the nimble tread/ of the feet of Fred/ Astaire,
> You're an O'Neill drama/ you're Whistler's mama,
> You're Camembert . . .

Cole Porter, a rich boy from Indiana, came east to Yale and kept going east to Paris and the Riviera, where he found his lifelong subject: the world-weary folk of high society. Songs like "I Get a Kick Out of You" were a catalogue of expensive tastes and rarefied pleasures: sipping Champagne, sniffing cocaine, and flying too high with some guy in the sky.

I had never heard of Napoleon brandy or Camembert. I knew who Gandhi was—his picture was often in the newspapers—and I had probably heard of the Colosseum and the Louvre Museum, the Tower of Pisa and the Mona Lisa, Inferno's Dante and the nose on the great Durante. But I know I wasn't up on my brandies and cheeses. After "You're the Top" I knew that Napoleon was the best brandy, Camembert the best cheese, Bendel's the best bonnet. I knew because Porter told me so. I became his slavish fan, memorizing his

lyrics and relishing his allusions, even when I had no idea what
they meant:

> *Here I sit above the town*
> *In my pet/ paillet/ted gown,*
> *Down in the depths on the ninetieth floor . . .*

What the hell were paillettes?

> *If I invite*
> *A boy some night*
> *To dine on my fine finnan haddie,*
> *I just adore*
> *His asking for more,*
> *But my heart belongs to Daddy . . .*

What the hell was finnan haddie?

> *Farming, that's the fashion,*
> *Farming, that's the passion*
> *Of our great celebrities of today.*
> *Kit Cornell is shellin' peas,*
> *Lady Mendl's climbing trees,*
> *Dear Mae West/ is at her best*
> *In the hay . . .*

Who the hell was Lady Mendl?

Of all the songs written for Broadway musicals in the 1930s,
Porter's were the most insistent on being heard again as soon as
possible. They had gone by so fast on the stage, a Perseid shower
of brilliant rhymes and references, that people could hardly wait to
take the sheet music home and reconstruct the songs at their own
piano.

Cole Porter was born into the moneyed world he wrote about.
The son of a druggist in Peru (pronounced Pee-ru), Indiana, he was,
more pertinently, the grandson of the millionaire financier J. O.
Cole. His strong-willed mother, Katie Cole Porter, sensitive to the
artistic temperament of her boy, who played the piano at an early
age, sent him East to boarding school and then to Yale, thereby
alienating the financier. J. O. Cole wanted his grandson to carry
on the family's agricultural interests and threatened to cut off his
inheritance.

But Cole Porter never looked back to his Midwestern roots, nor
did anyone at Yale take him for a farmer. A homosexual dandy, he
kept his classmates entertained for four years with his amusing

Irene Bordoni made a career of playing coquettish French girls in musicals that dabbled in the Gallic game of love. (The bangs helped.) Those qualifications made her the perfect flirt to introduce "Let's Do It," the first of Cole Porter's great list songs, in the 1928 musical "Paris."

songs and his lively participation in campus musical and dramatic groups, abetted by Monty Woolley, who, half a lifetime later, would star in Porter's Broadway musical *Jubilee*. Two serious songs, "Bingo, Eli Yale!" and "Bull Dog," written in 1910 and 1911, became instant Yale anthems and have echoed through Yale Bowl on fall afternoons ever since. Academically, Porter was drawn to the Romantic poets, one of whom, Robert Browning, had been a boyhood favorite. "I suppose Browning started me writing lyrics," he once said.

After Yale, Porter continued east—to Europe, where he became a habitué of Paris and the Riviera and the Lido, discovering the *haut monde* that he would make his lifelong subject. His metamorphosis into a boulevardier was smoothed by his marriage in 1919 to Linda Lee Thomas, an older woman with a million-dollar divorce

"You're the Top," Porter's other great list song, was sung by Ethel Merman in "Anything Goes" (1934) with such trumpet-like clarity, every syllable reaching the last row of the balcony, that Porter wrote four other musicals for her: "Red, Hot and Blue," "DuBarry Was a Lady," "Panama Hattie" and "Something for the Boys." Two songs that she belted into submission in those shows were "It's De-Lovely" and "Friendship."

settlement and a coterie of admirers, and their sexless but not loveless union was one of the grand alliances of the Jazz Age—a glittering non-stop party. Everybody who was anybody knew "les Colporteurs."

Beneath the glitter, however, Porter was struggling to find his songwriting voice; for two years he studied harmony and counterpoint at a school founded by the French composer Vincent d'Indy. Finally a decade of experiment and self-doubt ended with two hit musicals: *Paris* (1928) and *Fifty Million Frenchmen* (1929). In subject matter they didn't stray far from Porter's adopted playground or from the game of sex that the French seemed to have patented. All the songs listed on the sheet music of *Paris* are vaguely "naughty": "You Do Something to Me," "What Did You Do to Me?", "Let's Misbehave," "Please Don't Make Me Be Good," "Quelque Chose" and "Let's Do It," Porter's first great list song, which put to ultimate use the songwriter's equivalent of everybody else's four-letter word—the two-letter word "do." "Doing" was infinitely suggestive, as Ira Gershwin would also prove with "Do, Do, Do (What You Done Done Done Before)" and "Aren't You Kind of Glad We Did?" As for "Quelque Chose," I won't even try to guess what that was about.

Not until Porter wrote "Night and Day" for Fred Astaire's Broadway musical *Gay Divorce*, in 1932, did he find his mature touch. (When the musical was made into a movie its title was changed to *The Gay Divorcée*; divorce was not a laughing matter in the movies, but divorcees were evidently allowed to laugh.) The A-flat major chord that opens "Night and Day" gives the song an unexpected jumpstart, and the beguine beat adds a sultry pulse—more night than day—that would become Porter's trademark sound as he began to write strong romantic ballads for a series of musicals like *Jubilee* ("Just One of Those Things") and *Leave It to Me* ("Get Out of Town") and for films like *Born to Dance* ("I've Got You Under My Skin") and *Broadway Melody of 1940* ("I Concentrate on You"). These are big songs—sinuous, fully developed, and, it would seem, deeply felt.

As a teenager being taken to Porter's Broadway musicals—shows like *DuBarry Was a Lady* and *Panama Hattie*—I was still under his spell as the most clever of lyricists. The world-weary plaints like "Make It Another Old-Fashioned, Please," sung by Ethel Merman, were ultrasophisticated ("Make it for one who's due/To join the disillusioned few/Make it for one of love's new/refugees"), and the frequent double entendres, sung by leering clowns like Bert Lahr, appealed to my adolescent humor. Only when I went off to World War II did I put away my own WASP boyhood and my infatuation with Porter's rhymes about shallow

YOU'RE THE TOP
VINTON FREEDLEY INC.
PRESENTS
WILLIAM GAXTON ETHEL MERMAN VICTOR MOORE
IN
"anything GOES"
A NEW MUSICAL COMEDY
WITH
BETTINA HALL
MUSIC BY
COLE PORTER
STORY BY
GUY BOLTON
AND
P.G. WODEHOUSE
STAGED BY
HOWARD LINDSAY
DANCES AND ENSEMBLES BY
ROBERT ALTON
ANYTHING GOES
BUDDIE BEWARE
YOU'RE THE TOP
ALL THROUGH THE NIGHT
GYPSY IN ME
BLOW, GABRIEL, BLOW
I GET A KICK OUT OF YOU
MADE IN U. S. A.
harris
HARMS
INCORPORATED
NEW YORK
CHAPPELL & Co LTD
LONDON SYDNEY

society people and give my heart to lyricists like Lorenz Hart, who wrote about ordinary folk facing ordinary emotional travails.

But Porter's music has never gone out of my metabolism. The great society-beat standards—"What Is This Thing Called Love?", "Night and Day," "Anything Goes," "I Get a Kick Out of You," "All Through the Night," "Just One of Those Things," "I've Got You Under My Skin," "Begin the Beguine," "In the Still of the Night," "Why Shouldn't I?", "Easy to Love," "It's De-Lovely," "Do I Love You, Do I?", "Rosalie," "Dream Dancing," "Ev'rything I Love," "Every Time We Say Goodbye," "I Love You," "All of You"—are still all around us, still the bread and butter of upscale dance bands, their propulsive energy pulling couples out onto the dance floor as invincibly they did at debutante parties half a century ago. No other American songwriter left behind such a residue of energy, not even George Gershwin.

Where did that energy come from? Unlike Jerome Kern, whose melodies had their roots in Viennese operetta, or Gershwin and Harold Arlen, whose music grew out of their Jewish heritage and the black jazz they grafted onto it, Porter seems to be self-invented, an American original. Most of his songs are built of short bursts of melody, which almost demand a beguine accompaniment, and many have the further exoticism of being in a minor key, nearer to Russia than Indiana: "Love for Sale," "Just One of Those Things," "My Heart Belongs to Daddy," "I Concentrate on You," "You'd Be So Nice to Come Home To," "So in Love," "From This Moment On," "Were Thine That Special Face," "I Love Paris," "It's All Right With Me." How those Slavic tonalities and south-of-the-border rhythms found their way into the bloodstream of a Protestant boy from the Midwest I'll leave to some ethnomusicologist. But the resulting sound is unlike anybody else's—the sound of wedding receptions and dancing till dawn. Cole Porter's eternal gift to us is the illusion of eternal youth.

That he could continue to generate that gaiety was an act of high courage; he was invalided and in constant pain from a riding accident in 1937 that shattered both his legs and required 35 operations. In 1948, rebounding from nine years of flops and of reviews suggesting that he was washed up, Porter wrote his richest and most integrated Broadway score, *Kiss Me, Kate*. Never had he written so many songs that were so finely crafted, including the ballads "So In Love" and "Were Thine That Special Face," the torrid "Too Darn Hot," and one of the funniest of all Porter numbers, "Always True to You in My Fashion":

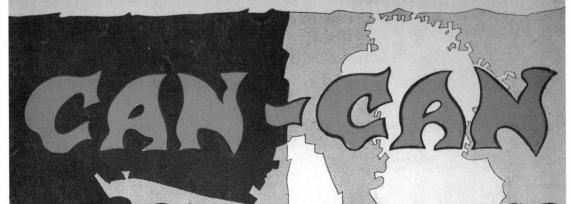

IT'S ALL RIGHT WITH ME

CAN-CAN

words and music by **COLE PORTER**

50¢

FEUER and MARTIN present
COLE PORTER'S
CAN-CAN
book and direction by
ABE BURROWS
dances and musical numbers staged by
MICHAEL KIDD
settings and lighting by
JO MIELZINER
costumes by
MOTLEY

CAN-CAN • C'EST MAGNIFIQUE
NEVER GIVE ANYTHING AWAY
ALLEZ-VOUS-EN GO AWAY
I LOVE PARIS • I AM IN LOVE
IT'S ALL RIGHT WITH ME • MONTMART'
COME ALONG WITH ME
IF YOU LOVED ME TRULY

BUXTON HILL MUSIC CORPORATION
RKO BUILDING • Rockefeller Center • NEW YORK
Sole Selling Agent
CHAPPELL & CO., INC.

Mr. Harris, plutocrat
Loves to give my hand a pat,
If the Harris pat means a Paris hat, Bébé! . . .
But I'm always true . . .

Porter's final triumph, in 1956, was the movie *High Society*,
its debonair songs ("You're Sensational," "I Love You, Samantha,"
"True Love") a perfect vehicle for those relaxed charmers Bing
Crosby and Frank Sinatra.

In the last three decades of his life Cole Porter lived at New
York's Waldorf-Astoria Hotel, in a luxurious tower suite furnished
with Oriental rugs and parquet floors brought from a French
chateau. But Paris was still his spiritual home town. His last two
musicals, *Can-Can* and *Silk Stockings*, were set there, and three of
the songs in *Can-Can* had French titles. Another, "I Love Paris,"
didn't say much more than that—and didn't need to. Written when
Porter was old and ill, it still sounds young and enamored of the city
in every season and every kind of weather, from drizzle to sizzle.
Most unusually—perhaps symbolic of how Paris continued to
enchant him—the song starts in a minor key but can't help going
major in the seventeenth bar.

"Porgy and Bess"

Porgy and Bess is the Mount Everest of the American musical theater. The "folk opera" by George Gershwin, Du Bose Heyward and Ira Gershwin opened on Broadway in 1935 to somewhat patronizing reviews—the drama critics said it wasn't quite a musical and the music critics said it wasn't quite an opera—and closed after only 124 performances, losing all the money the Theatre Guild invested in it. Not until 1942 was it revalued as a major modern opera and given the first of the many revivals and restorations that have taken it all over the world, one of America's most admired cultural exports.

For George Gershwin it was a hugely ambitious achievement. By the end of the 1920s he had become impatient with the Broadway musical's simplicities—the same old boy-meets-girl plots, the same old 32-bar format. He wanted to take the musical theater into new territory, and in his last three shows—*Strike Up the Band* (second version, 1930), *Of Thee I Sing* (1931) and *Let 'Em Eat Cake* (1933)—he and Ira and their librettists George S. Kaufman and Morrie Ryskind turned to social satire. The shows lampooned, among other sacred institutions, war, the League of Nations, foreign affairs, the president, the vice-president, government, politics, the Far Right and the Far Left, and the scores used recitatives and other extended operetta forms. In their seriousness of purpose those three musicals were a bridge between *Show Boat* (1927) and *Lady in the Dark* (1941), the high point being *Of Thee I Sing*'s winning of the Pulitzer Prize for 1931. Until then musicals had been regarded as frivolous, unworthy of drama's highest award.

But *Porgy and Bess* was a quantum leap to greatness, its score a marvel. Many of the songs are breathtakingly beautiful ("Bess You Is My Woman Now," "I Loves You, Porgy," "My Man's Gone Now," "Oh Bess, Oh Where's My Bess?"); many are enormously infectious ("I Got Plenty o' Nothin'," "It Ain't Necessarily So," "There's a Boat Dat's Leaving Soon for New York," "A Woman Is a Sometime

George Gershwin orchestrating "Porgy and Bess," his opera about the community called Catfish Row near Charleston, South Carolina, in the summer of 1935. During the previous summer he had moved to Folly Island, one of the "Sea Islands" off the Carolina coast, to immerse himself in the culture of the Gullah Negroes and their distinctive forms of singing and "shouting."

Thing," "Oh, I Can't Sit Down"), and "Summertime" is the classic American lullaby. Gershwin's whole, however, is greater than the individual parts. With his densely textured scoring and often violent undercurrent of rhythm, his connective use of Negro street cries and shouts and chants and chorales, he aspired to portray the everyday life of an entire Negro community near Charleston, South Carolina.

That community, called Catfish Row, had first been the subject of a novel, *Porgy*, by the Charleston writer and poet Du Bose Heyward, in 1924, and of a subsequent Theatre Guild play, also called *Porgy*, by Heyward and his wife Dorothy Heyward. Gershwin had wanted to make an opera of *Porgy* since first reading the book. But it was 1933 before legal clearances and production details with the Theatre Guild fell into place and he could commit himself to the 11 months of composition and nine months of orchestration that the project would require.

Gershwin welcomed Heyward as his librettist and co-lyricist. The other lyricist was Ira Gershwin. It was an ideal pairing of two writers who loved the play of words, each bringing strengths to the task that the other didn't possess. Heyward's are the "poetic" songs like "Summertime," rich in Southern imagery. Few American lyrics are so fondly remembered:

> *Summertime, and the livin' is easy,*
> *Fish are jumping, and the cotton is high . . .*

Ira Gershwin couldn't have written that lyric—fish and cotton weren't his domain—and Heyward couldn't have written Ira's "It Ain't Necessarily So," Sportin' Life's sardonic reminder that the things that you're li'ble to read in the Bible aren't necessarily to be believed. But most of the lyrics were a collaboration, the novice Heyward grateful for Ira's vast experience and skill, Ira grateful for Heyward's knowledge of the Negro community and its vernacular. The result is a body of lyrics that are alive with humanity, one of the ornaments of American popular literature.

Meanwhile George Gershwin was composing "as quickly as someone might type a letter," as his cousin, the painter Henry Botkin, reported. (It was under Botkin's tutelage that Gershwin developed an avid interest in modern art and became an excellent painter himself.) At Heyward's urging, Gershwin moved for the summer of 1934 into a shack on Folly Island, off Charleston, to immerse himself in the Gullah culture. The Negroes living on the isolated "Sea Islands" off the Carolina coast still spoke their own Gullah dialect and used words and names and forms of singing, dancing and storytelling that could still be found in the West

On the occasion of the
first public performance
of "Porgy and Bess," on
September 30, 1935, in
Boston, its three creators
posed for a picture:
composer George
Gershwin; librettist
and co-lyricist Du Bose
Heyward, and co-lyricist
Ira Gershwin. Charac-
teristically, George's
hands are on the piano
and Ira's are on a cigar.
Heyward and Ira
Gershwin admiringly
inscribed the photo-
graph to George, whom
Heyward calls "my oper-
atic sponsor."

George Gershwin had been an early admirer of Du Bose Heyward's book *Porgy* and had spoken of wanting to adapt it to music. But his time and energy went into composing Broadway musicals, and not until 1932 did he write this letter to Heyward telling him of his interest.

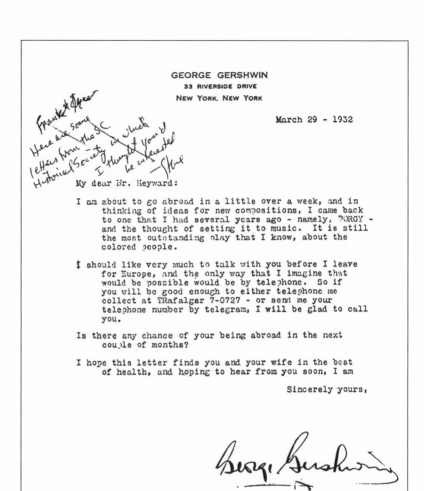

African countries from which their ancestors had been brought as slaves to work the rice, cotton and indigo plantations. They gave Gershwin what Heyward called "an inexhaustible source of folk material."

"But the most interesting discovery, as we sat listening to their spirituals," Heyward recalled, "was that to George it was more like a homecoming than an exploration. The Gullah Negro prides himself on what he calls 'shouting.' This is a complicated rhythmic pattern beaten out by the feet and the hands as an accompaniment to the spirituals and is indubitably an African survival. I shall never forget the night when, at a Negro meeting on a remote sea-island, George started 'shouting' with them. And eventually to their huge delight stole the show from their champion 'shouter.' I think he is probably the only white man in America who could have done it."

Because of that immersion it is often said that Gershwin wrote a Negro opera. Probably the truth is closer to what Jerome Kern told

98

Oscar Hammerstein when they were considering making a musical of *Messer Marco Polo*, by Donn Byrne. Hammerstein was worried because it was a book by an Irishman about an Italian who travels in the Orient, and he asked Kern what kind of music he would write. "It will be good Jewish music," Kern told him. Richard Rodgers could have told Hammerstein the same thing about their Siamese musical, *The King and I*. Composers compose out of who they are. Verdi's *Aïda* moves us because it's good Italian music, not good Egyptian music, and Puccini never set foot in Madam Butterfly's Japan.

Still, I like to think that *Porgy and Bess* has some authentic Negro strains. The only other score that moves me in the same way is Harold Arlen's all-Negro *St. Louis Woman*. Not only were Arlen and Gershwin strongly drawn to the black jazz they heard in Harlem; their parents came from regions of Russia and eastern Europe that had long been penetrated by African music, as Paul Robeson demonstrated in a famous concert at Carnegie Hall in 1958, noting that the folk music of widely disparate countries comes from a common source. Robeson sang an American Negro spiritual, an East African tribal chant, a 13th-century Slovakian plainchant and an ancient Jewish chant from Israel that were almost identical. He explained that the Abyssinian church and the church of the Sudan were once part of the church of Byzantium. Music from Africa thereby found its way into the liturgy of the early Byzantine church and subsequently filtered out into eastern Europe and parts of Russia.

Similar connections have been described to me by other black musicians. "American Negro spirituals were a source of wonder in Europe when they were first performed there by touring choirs like the Fisk Jubilee Singers from Nashville," the French-horn player Willie Ruff told me. "The spirituals were just close enough to the Europeans' own folk songs and their own religious music to be strangely familiar." When Ruff and the pianist Dwike Mitchell toured the Soviet Union in 1958, Mitchell was moved by many Russian songs that resembled spirituals he had heard as a boy in black Southern churches. "I felt a mysterious bond between their people and my people," he said. "I connected with their suffering."

That still doesn't mean George Gershwin wrote a Negro opera. But it's also no coincidence that the all-black casts of *Porgy and Bess*, singing good Jewish music, strike a resonance with audiences in so many parts of the world, or that Ella Fitzgerald seems to have come home when she sings a Gershwin song like "The Man I Love." Somewhere, it's all connected.

My first contact with Porgy and Bess *was the stylized black-and-white drawing on the cover of the sheet music. It's one of the great sheet music designs, seemingly childlike but highly complex in its dynamics. Porgy is in his goat cart, Catfish Row is in the background, Bess and Crown are in the foreground, and the potent finger—presumably of Sportin' Life— points toward the boat that's leaving soon for New York.*

I could just make out the tiny signature B. HARRIS in the lower left corner. I've since learned that the artist was Ben Harris, a native of Georgia and a relative of Joel Chandler Harris, who wrote the Uncle Remus stories. A prolific sheet music illustrator, he was an early advocate of the airbrush technique, along with his wife Georgette, who signed her own sheet music JORJ. Together, under the name BEN JORJ HARRIS, they wrote a textbook called Airbrush Illustration, *which describes their work for various music publishers.*

Almost no original art work for sheet music covers has survived. But in 1998 Ben Harris's illustration for Porgy and Bess, airbrushed in black ink on white cardboard, turned up at a New York auction gallery, where it was bought for $5,500 by the pianist, singer and popular-song scholar Michael Feinstein. "It's a perfect evocation of the period and of what Gershwin was trying to do with the music," Feinstein said. "The artist must have heard a good deal of the music before executing the cover, since it's a miniature encapsulation of the story."

But of all the design decisions that went into that cover, the boldest was the decision not to use color. Broadway musicals were colorful by nature, their flamboyance central to their appeal, and so, historically, were their sheet music covers. Porgy and Bess—so its sheet music proclaimed—would be something different.

SUMMERTIME

THE THEATRE GUILD PRESENTS

PORGY and BESS

MUSIC BY
GEORGE GERSHWIN
LIBRETTO BY
DuBose HEYWARD

LYRICS BY
DuBose HEYWARD and IRA GERSHWIN
PRODUCTION DIRECTED BY
ROUBEN MAMOULIAN

GERSHWIN PUBLISHING CORP.
RKO BLDG. NEW YORK N.Y.
CHAPPELL & CO. INC.
SOLE SELLING AGENT
MADE IN U.S.A.

Writing for Fred Astaire

1. *Irving Berlin*

Between 1935 and 1938, because of the influence of one man, five of America's best songwriters wrote 28 songs that collectively stand as a museum exhibit of the form. The writers were Irving Berlin, Jerome Kern, Dorothy Fields, George Gershwin and Ira Gershwin, and the man who elicited this body of work was Fred Astaire. The songs were written for six successive Astaire movies: *Top Hat, Follow the Fleet, Swing Time, Shall We Dance, A Damsel in Distress* and *Carefree*. His dancing partner in all but one was Ginger Rogers.

But it was Astaire the singer, not Astaire the dancer, that the songwriters wanted to write for. They knew that whatever they wrote, he would sing it *perfectly*, every note true, every syllable clear, every nuance of emotion and humor caught with natural elegance and timing and taste. Knowing this, they stretched their wings and reached a high level of freshness and artistry. As each of the movies came out, the songs from the soundtrack were released on Brunswick records, brightly backed by the orchestras of Johnny Green, Ray Noble and Leo Reisman and often including the rap-tap-tap of Astaire's dancing feet. Those recordings—now preserved on the album *Starring Fred Astaire*—are an education in the craft of the American popular song. To this day I wouldn't want a note or a word of those songs written or sung differently.

For Berlin, Kern, Fields and the Gershwins, Astaire's movies were salvation in the desert of the Depression. Broadway musicals were drying up for lack of money; George Gershwin would never write another, and Kern would write only one, *Very Warm for May*, a flop that yielded his only other theater hit, "All the Things You Are."

Ginger Rogers, Irving Berlin and Fred Astaire in Hollywood. No body of work created during Depression era is more fondly remembered than the movies of Fred and Ginger, and it was Berlin who set the standard, with "Top Hat," in 1935. His songs had so much charm that they pushed his fellow songwriters—Jerome Kern and Dorothy Fields, and George and Ira Gershwin —to new heights in their own subsequent scores for the two hoofers.

Hollywood was where the jobs were, and that's where the Broadway songwriters began to emigrate, colonizing themselves around Kern, the Gershwins, Harold Arlen, the tennis court, the golf course and the swimming pool. Photographs and home movies show them stripped to the waist, embracing the California sun.

But it was Irving Berlin who set the standard for the Astaire-Rogers movies that Kern and Gershwin felt challenged to match. The songs Berlin wrote for *Top Hat* and *Follow the Fleet*, seen on television six decades later, tumble out with as much gaiety and charm as they did when they were new. "I . . . m/ Puttin' on my top hat/ Tyin' up my white tie/ Brushin' off my tails," sings Fred Astaire in *Top Hat*, exulting in the pleasure of having been given a song consummately tailored to who he was and what he did better than anyone else. His four other numbers—"Cheek to Cheek," "Isn't This a Lovely Day (to Be Caught in the Rain)?," "No Strings" and "The Piccolino"—are just as pleasing, their apparent simplicity masking their careful workmanship.

Follow the Fleet was more of the same: seven songs that exactly served the dramatic need of the moment and were wholly unlike each other. "We Saw the Sea" is funny ("We joined the Navy to see the world/ And what did we see?/ We saw the sea"); "But Where Are You?" is plaintive; "Let Yourself Go" is a flat-out summons to dance; "Get Thee Behind Me, Satan" is sultry; "I'm Putting All My Eggs in One Basket" is romantic; "I'd Rather Lead a Band" is jaunty, and the finale, "Let's Face the Music and Dance," alternately minor and major, dark and light, is one of those Irving Berlin melodies that come from out of nowhere. Just when we think the man has done it all, he throws us another surprise.

Carefree was still more of the same, memorably including "Change Partners" and "I Used to be Color Blind." Those three Hollywood scores are a brilliant body of work at the center of a life that has long been part of the mythology of American success. A boy named Israel Baline, born in Siberia in 1888, the son of a cantor, flees with his family at the age of five to New York, where they live in harsh poverty. The father dies three years later, forcing the boy to go to work at whatever odd jobs he can find or improvise, one of which is singing the popular hits of the day on the sidewalks of the Lower East Side. In his teens he gets a regular job as a singing waiter and begins writing songs himself, at prolific speed. In 1911 he writes a song that sells a million copies in seven months—"Alexander's Ragtime Band"—and makes him a household name. The name is now Irving Berlin.

Strictly speaking, "Alexander's Ragtime Band" wasn't a ragtime

Top Hat, White Tie and Tails
Music and Lyrics by
IRVING BERLIN
from
THE RKO RADIO PICTURE
TOP HAT
starring
FRED ASTAIRE
and
GINGER ROGERS
a PANDRO S. BERMAN production
directed by
MARK SANDRICH
CHEEK TO CHEEK
ISN'T THIS A LOVELY DAY
(To be caught in the rain?)
THE PICCOLINO
NO STRINGS (I'm fancy free)
Top hat, white tie and tails
IRVING BERLIN Inc.
Music Publishers
799 SEVENTH AVE., NEW YORK, N.Y.
MADE IN USA

The engineers who made the soundtrack recordings of the Astaire and Rogers movies never forgot that the movies were about dance. When Astaire broke into a dance they didn't edit out the rap-tap-tap of his feet just because people listening to the record couldn't see him. The sound of his shoes told them all they needed to know.

number, like the many ragtime tunes that Berlin actually did write when he was starting out—songs with a "ragged" or syncopated beat, which influenced the young George Gershwin. But the song did have a high-octane American energy, especially in its opening theme ("Come on and hear . . . ") and its radical jump into a higher key after four bars. Berlin had an immigrant's ear, tuned to every scrap of music and rhythm in the air of his adopted country. Ultimately he would transmute and serve back everything he heard. Ultimately he would also write "God Bless America."

Once switched on, Berlin just couldn't stop writing hits: "A Pretty Girl Is Like a Melody," "Always," "You Keep Coming Back Like a Song," "How Deep Is the Ocean," "Remember," "Blue Skies," "How About Me?", "What'll I Do?", "Russian Lullaby," "Lazy," "Say It Isn't So," "The Song Is Ended," "Let's Have Another Cup of Coffee," "Puttin' on the Ritz," "Now It Can Be Told," "I've

Got My Love to Keep Me Warm" . . . on and on and on. No two songs were alike, and all of them were instantly familiar. They had an inevitability of line, both musical and verbal—American simplicity at its best.

Among all the great songwriters, Irving Berlin's gift is the most mysterious. Although he had no musical education and could play the piano only in the key of F-sharp, he instinctively knew where he wanted to go with a melody, veering into other keys and safely back out without having learned the technical rules of the road. Unlike a Harold Arlen or a Richard Rodgers or a Cole Porter, he has no musical signature—he is nobody and everybody—and his lyrics are just as artless, seemingly without strain. His contemporaries who made a study of light verse—Ira Gershwin and Lorenz Hart and E. Y. Harburg—didn't say what they had to say any better than Berlin did:

> *Heaven . . . I'm in heaven . . .*
> *And the cares that hung about me through the week*
> *Seem to vanish like a gambler's lucky streak*
> *When we're out together dancing cheek to cheek.*

And who could improve "Change Partners," from his last Astaire film, *Carefree*:

> *Must you dance/ every dance*
> *With the same fortunate man?*
> *You have danced with him since the music began.*
> *Won't you change partners and dance with me?*

The song is still the point of reference for every man who came of age in the ballroom-dancing 1930s and learned from the edge of the dance floor that the girl he loved preferred to be in the arms of somebody else.

2. Dorothy Fields and Jerome Kern

Jerome Kern was once described by Richard Rodgers as "a giant with one foot in Europe and the other in America." By the mid-1930s, Kern's European foot was still dominant; after *Show Boat* he had gone back to composing operettas like *Music in the Air*, their Viennese melodies and trite lyrics almost untouched by the sounds and rhythms of the New World. What finally brought the other foot down was a Fred Astaire movie and a thoroughly modern lyricist. Thanks to Dorothy Fields, in *Swing Time* Kern actually learned to swing.

Jerome Kern and Dorothy Fields in Hollywood working on the score of "Swing Time." The young lyricist recalled that the formidable older composer kept a bust of Wagner on his piano. She didn't say anything about the lamp.

Fields was one of only three women songwriters who made a sizable contribution to the literature of American popular song. The others were Betty Comden, who, with Adolph Green, wrote the lyrics for many Broadway and movie musicals, and Carolyn Leigh, lyricist for a half-dozen Broadway hits, mainly with the composer Cy Coleman, in the 1950s and 1960s. Earlier, three gifted women composers left a small but exceptional legacy.

The best known was Kay Swift, whose "Can't We Be Friends?" is still a favorite. In 1930 her long-running Broadway hit, *Fine and Dandy*, with its energetic title song, was the first Broadway musical to have a score composed by a woman. (The lyricist, "Paul James," was her husband James P. Warburg.) A well-rounded musician, Swift worked with her close friend George Gershwin on various projects, including the orchestrations of *Porgy and Bess*. Later she composed the music for many Radio City Music Hall productions and was still composing in her nineties.

Ann Ronell, a girl from Omaha named Anna Rosenblatt until George Gershwin suggested a more marketable name, got her start as a Broadway rehearsal pianist in the 1920s. As a songwriter her output included two memorable songs that were as different as

black and white—specifically, as different as "Willow Weep for Me"
and "Who's Afraid of the Big Bad Wolf?" The first, an angular
melody suggestive of sadness and loss, with a weeping willow of
a lyric (her own), remains a staple of torch singers in the wee small
hours of the morning. The other, written for Walt Disney's 1933
cartoon *The Three Little Pigs*, swept the country as an antidote to the
Depression, a tonic in its irreverence and bounce.

Dana Suesse, another girl from the Midwest with big-town
dreams, started as a child vaudeville performer in Kansas City.
When she came to New York, also in the 1920s, Suesse began composing jazz suites, one of which, "Concerto in Three Rhythms," was
performed at Carnegie Hall by Paul Whiteman's orchestra in 1933.
Many of her hit songs, like "My Silent Love," were drawn from her
longer compositions. Her two other big hits were "You Oughta Be
in Pictures" and "The Night Is Young and You're So Beautiful."

But Swift, Ronell and Suesse are barely remembered; they were gallant also-rans in a man's race. Today that lopsided ratio seems hard to understand. Yet as far back as Gilbert & Sullivan we seldom hear of women writing music or lyrics for the theater. I can only guess that the exclusion was the result of an old cultural bias: a set of assumptions about the proper role of women in a world dominated by male producers, directors and music publishers.

Dorothy Fields had the good luck to be born into that favored lineage. She was the daughter of Lew Fields, half of the popular team of "German" vaudeville comics, Weber & Fields, and the sister of the Broadway playwrights and librettists Herbert and Joseph Fields. But she didn't need any nepotistic favors; from the beginning she was one of the best American songwriters, eventually writing the lyrics for more than 400 songs in a career that lasted four decades.

Like Ira Gershwin and E. Y. Harburg, Fields first tried her hand at writing light verse for F.P.A.'s newspaper column "The Conning Tower." Unlike them, she also tried her voice in amateur musicals at suburban country clubs. The voice was as amateur as the musicals, but it was noticed by the composer J. Fred Coots ("You Go to My Head," "For All We Know"). What caught Coots' attention was Fields' involvement with what each song was saying, and he urged her to try writing lyrics. She did, but everything she submitted was rejected. Finally, in 1928, with the composer Jimmy McHugh, for a show called *Blackbirds*, she wrote the unrejectable "I Can't Give You Anything but Love." It was the start of a partnership that also produced "Sunny Side of the Street," "Don't Blame Me" and "I'm in the Mood for Love"— three of the hardiest perennials in American popular song.

What gives Fields' lyrics their wallop is their directness. They say what someone in love would say—no inversion, no allusion, no poetic effects:

> *I can't give you anything but love, baby,*
> *That's the only thing I've plenty of, baby . . .*

> *Don't blame me*
> *For falling in love with you,*
> *I'm under your spell,*
> *So how I can I help it?*
> *Don't blame me.*

> *I'm in the mood for love,*
> *Simply because you're near me,*
> *Funny, but when you're near me*
> *I'm in the mood for love . . .*

This is the English language at its most declarative—a writer making her feelings available to us.

When the 50-year-old Jerome Kern was paired with the 30-year-old Dorothy Fields for RKO's *Swing Time*, in 1936, it was the best stroke of fortune that could have happened to them both. The young lyricist drew out of the famously intractable older composer a score of unusual zest. His spacious melodies in turn stretched her beyond the 32-bar orthodoxies. For "The Way You Look Tonight," which would win the Academy Award, Fields wrote an opening lyric that is in fact a 26-word sentence, typically coming right to the point:

> *Some day, when I'm awf'ly old,*
> *When the world is cold,*
> *I will get a glow just thinking of you*
> *And the way you look tonight.*

"A Fine Romance," from the same score, is perhaps the only successful sarcastic love song, avoiding sarcasm's usual tart residue and leaving us amused by the inertia of two people supposedly in love:

> *You're calmer than the seals in the Arctic ocean,*
> *At least they flap their fins to express emotion . . .*

It's also typical Fields, once again, as an assertion of feminine desire. When Ginger Rogers complains to Fred Astaire that he won't nestle and won't wrestle, she's telling him, "Hey, I could use a little more action."

The other four songs in *Swing Time* push Astaire hard, both as a singer and as a dancer—which is what he wanted and what always brought out his best. "Bojangles of Harlem" is a jazzy homage to the tap-dancing giant Bill Robinson, Kern repeatedly raising the key to heighten the singer's praise:

> *Oh . . . Bo . . . jangles of Harlem*
> *You dance . . . such . . . hot . . . stuff,*
> * Young . . . Bo's . . . love you in Harlem*
> * They say . . . you've . . . got . . . stuff,*
> *   Tough Guys rhumba out of poolrooms*
> *   And kids start trucking out of schoolrooms . . .*

But dragging Jerome Kern into the American mainstream wasn't easy. (Fields recalled that the composer kept a small bust of Wagner on the piano.) At one point she and Astaire tried to extract from Kern a number that would swing. They found him unsure of exactly what that verb meant. When Kern went to the bathroom, as Fields later reconstructed the moment, Astaire turned to her and said, "My God, how can I get a tune I can dance to?" When Kern came back they sat him down, she said, and Astaire "danced all over the room and gave him ideas, and finally Jerry came up with a very good tune, 'Bojangles of Harlem.'" Two other songs, no less vivacious, are "Pick Yourself Up," an up-tempo gavotte about a hoofer learning a tough step, and "Never Gonna Dance," a serpentine ballad, with three separate themes, in which Astaire renounces his dancing shoes for reasons of the heart. All three numbers are musically inventive, and Fields' lyrics are sophisticated—not a cliché in sight—and often funny. The concluding "Waltz in Swing Time" is Kern in high gear, launching Fred and Ginger on the most sumptuous of all their duets, swirling across shiny marble floors and up and down marble stairs. If one sequence sums up the elegance of all the Astaire-Rogers movies, this is it.

From that fine Hollywood score Fields would go on to a long and solid career, contributing to 19 Broadway musicals as the lyricist or as the co-librettist, often with her brother Herbert Fields (*Annie Get Your Gun*). For *A Tree Grows in Brooklyn* her lyrics perfectly caught the tenderness of Arthur Schwartz's melodies ("Make the Man Love Me"); for Sigmund Romberg's *Up in Central Park* she wrote the standard "Close as Pages in a Book," and for Cy Coleman's jazz-inflected *Sweet Charity* and *Seesaw* her hits included "Big Spender" and "If My Friends Could See Me Now." By then she was in her sixties, still writing with warmth and wit, and still learning. "Cy brought a new style of writing into her life and it just revitalized her," said her son, the pianist David Lahm.

Jerome Kern remained in Hollywood and sporadically composed for movies. *High, Wide and Handsome* reunited him with Oscar Hammerstein and resulted in two gems: "Can I Forget You?" and "The Folks Who Live on the Hill." In the 1940s he teamed with two other great lyricists, Johnny Mercer and Ira Gershwin, to write attractive scores for the films *You Were Never Lovelier* and *Cover Girl*, which produced, respectively, two of his best songs, "I'm Old-Fashioned" and "Long Ago and Far Away." For other movies, with other lyricists, he wrote "In Love in Vain" (Leo Robin) and "Can't Help Singing" (E. Y. Harburg). Melodically, he still had a lot to say.

In the fall of 1945 Kern visited New York to see the revival of *Show Boat* at the Ziegfeld Theater, where it had opened exactly 19 years earlier, and to discuss his next project, *Annie Get Your Gun*. His lyricist was to be Dorothy Fields; it had been her idea to create a musical for Ethel Merman as the sharpshooting Annie Oakley. Instead the assignment fell to Irving Berlin. Kern collapsed on Park Avenue and was taken to a city hospital on Welfare Island, where, in a ward for indigent patients, he was identified from a membership card of the American Society of Composers, Authors and Publishers (ASCAP) in his wallet. He was taken to a private hospital but died soon afterward, at the age of sixty, his fate not unlike that of his great melodic ancestor, Stephen Foster, who died a pauper in New York's Bellevue Hospital in 1864.

3. George and Ira Gershwin

Writing for Fred Astaire was the inducement that brought George and Ira Gershwin to Hollywood in 1936. George was somewhat adrift after the disappointing reception of *Porgy and Bess* and also somewhat broke; his total royalties from the opera almost exactly equaled the cost of copying the orchestral parts for the musicians. He was eager to get back to his original métier of writing popular songs. But the studio chiefs at RKO were nervous that *Porgy and Bess* had turned him highbrow, and the contractual marriage was delayed while Gershwin tried to reassure them. One of his telegrams said: RUMORS ABOUT HIGHBROW MUSIC RIDICULOUS. AM OUT TO WRITE HITS. The bosses needn't have worried. The songs that George and Ira created when they went to California were some of the best they ever wrote.

Their first movie score, for *Shall We Dance*, was every bit as rich and varied as the ones Berlin, Kern and Fields had written for Astaire; the challenge was met. Ira, in particular, with "They Can't Take That Away From Me," "They All Laughed," "Let's Call the Whole Thing Off" and "I've Got Beginner's Luck," achieved a sureness of reference ("The way you wear your hat, the way you sip your tea") and a romantic buoyancy that have kept the songs alive in popular affection ever since, and George's melodies, along with "Slap That Bass" and "Shall We Dance," had a lightness and a gaiety that turned Astaire on. He sang them with the insouciance he had brought to the earlier movies, and his dance to "Slap That Bass," taking his cues from the pistons in the engine room of an ocean liner, is one of his most dynamic solos.

George Gershwin wrote songs for only two more movies—*A Damsel in Distress*, starring Fred Astaire and Joan Fontaine, and *The Goldwyn Follies*, which he didn't live to finish, dying of an undiagnosed brain tumor in 1937 at the age of thirty-eight. The suddenness of that death still hovers over American music. Part of us rejoices at so huge an output in so short a life: the hundreds of songs, the *Rhapsody in Blue*, the *Concerto in F*, the *Cuban Overture*, *An American*

Harold Arlen and Ira Gershwin on the tennis court of the Gershwin house at 1019 Roxbury Drive in Beverly Hills, a gathering place for the New York songwriters who moved to Holly-wood during the Depres-sion. It also had a swimming pool. The émigrés had no trouble adapting to the Cali-fornia life.

The line on the sheet music of "The Goldwyn Follies" that says "Addi-tional Music by Vernon Duke" is George Gersh-win's obituary. Duke was called in to finish the score when Gershwin died. Fred Astaire is also nowhere to be seen in that bizarre cluster of Goldwyn talent—every-one from the upscale Vera Zorina to the down-market Ritz Brothers. Astaire's six hallmark musicals and their great scores were behind him.

in Paris, the piano preludes, *Porgy and Bess.* But we also mourn the music he didn't live to write and the new avenues he didn't live to explore. His next project was to have been a ballet for George Balanchine.

Gershwin's final songs—"A Foggy Day," "Nice Work If You Can Get It," "Things Are Looking Up," "Love Walked In," "(Our) Love Is Here to Stay"—come closer to being "art songs" than anything he wrote for Broadway when he was young. "A Foggy Day" disarms us with its simplicity and its serenity. The repeated notes echo the rep-etitions that gave an electric charge to his youthful hits like "That Certain Feeling," but the song is calm and mature, wise in its understatement. So is his last song, "Love Is Here to Stay." It's a ballad held in perfect equilibrium. The two B sections (it's in an A-B-A-B format) make us smile with their departure from a pre-dictable solution, especially the second "B," slightly different from the first. It's the parting musical statement of an American boy wonder who never grew old:

> *In time the Rockies may crumble,*
> *Gibraltar may tumble,*
> *They're only made of clay, but*
> *Our love is here to stay.*

LOVE WALKED IN

SAMUEL GOLDWYN presents

The Goldwyn Follies

IN TECHNICOLOR

Music by
GEORGE GERSHWIN
Lyrics by **IRA GERSHWIN**
Additional Music by VERNON DUKE

I WAS DOING ALL RIGHT
LOVE IS HERE TO STAY
LOVE WALKED IN
SPRING AGAIN
I LOVE TO RHYME
HERE PUSSY, PUSSY

with ADOLPHE MENJOU ★ The RITZ BROS. ★ ZORINA
KENNY BAKER ★ ANDREA LEEDS ★ HELEN JEPSON
PHIL BAKER ★ ELLA LOGAN ★ BOBBY CLARK
JEROME COWAN ★ THE AMERICAN BALLET ★ THE
GORGEOUS GOLDWYN GIRLS and introducing
EDGAR BERGEN and 'CHARLIE McCARTHY'
Story by BEN HECHT ● Released Thru United Artists

CHAPPELL
& CO · INC ·
RKO BUILDING
ROCKEFELLER
CENTER · NYC
CHAPPELL
& CO · LTD · LONDON
MADE IN U.S.A.

Duke Ellington
(and Billy Strayhorn)

The historical coincidence that brought George Gershwin and Duke Ellington into the world within seven months of each other—Gershwin in 1898, Ellington in 1899—was hard to miss when their centennials came around. Throughout the anniversary years of 1998 and 1999 the composers were honored with a blizzard of special concerts, tributes, records, books, articles and scholarly symposia. That linkage couldn't have been more appropriate. Gershwin and Ellington were the two colossi who bestrode the world of serious popular music.

Gershwin's genius and ambition took him well beyond Broadway and Tin Pan Alley: to *Porgy and Bess* and the concertos and tone poems and piano preludes. Ellington never wrote an opera, but that was one of the few genres that got away. No other 20th-century composer was so prolific, both in his output—almost 2,000 pieces—and in the variety of forms he worked in. At no time was he primarily a songwriter; he was a pianist, bandleader, arranger and jazz composer. But the melodies that poured out of him were so compelling that many of them became huge international hits when they were fitted with a lyric.

Lyrics, however, aren't finally the point of a Duke Ellington song. Only in a few cases is a story so strongly attached to his melody that we can't think of one without the other: "Don't Get Around Much Anymore," "I Got It Bad and That Ain't Good," "Do Nothing Till You Hear From Me." Otherwise the music is the engine that drives the song. We know what the song is supposed to be about from the title ("Sophisticated Lady," "Mood Indigo"), but we're not required to know the words. The melody of "Sophisticated Lady" is so striking and so suave—all those chromatically descending half-tones—that it says "sophisticated lady" to anyone who hears

Although Duke Ellington was a brilliant pianist, his real instrument was the orchestra. The instrumentals that he wrote for his musicians were a shifting sea of colors and moods. Many of his popular songs were first composed as instrumentals and later fitted with lyrics. Ellington kept his orchestra together from 1926 until his death in 1974, often using his own royalties to pay the bills.

it; ladies don't get any more sophisticated. "Mood Indigo" and "In My Solitude" are self-sufficiently sad and lonely. Why is the singer blue? Why is she alone? Who cares?

Edward Kennedy Ellington was born in Washington, D.C., to a middle-class African-American family that had strong cultural leanings. He was playing the family piano by the time he was eight and was also a gifted artist. A tall, athletic boy, he was a natural at baseball, football and track. His mother started him on piano lessons to deflect him from baseball after she saw him accidentally hit on the head with a bat. His first piano teacher, he claims, was named Miss Clinkscales.

"My mother used to play piano, pretty things like 'Meditation,' so pretty they'd make me cry," Ellington recalled in his autobiography, *Music Is My Mistress.* "My father used to play, too, but by ear, and all operatic stuff." One day when Ellington was a teenager, confined to the house with a bad cold, he said, "I started fiddling around on the piano, using what was left over from my piano lessons—mostly the fingering—and I came up with a piece I called 'Soda Fountain Rag,' because I had been working as a soda jerk at the Poodle Dog Cafe. I started playing this around, and it attracted quite a lot of attention."

In his senior year of high school, Ellington won an art scholarship to Pratt Institute, in Brooklyn. By then, however, people had begun to notice him as a pianist playing at parties and with dance bands in the Washington area, and he decided to devote his life to music. In 1923 he formed his own band, "The Washingtonians," and took it to New York, landing an engagement at the improbably named Kentucky Club, at Broadway and 49th Street. The gig lasted four years. "It was a good place for us to be," Ellington said, "because it stayed open all night and became a rendezvous for all the big stars and musicians on Broadway after they got through working."

It was there that Ellington first began to make the band his instrument as a jazz composer, using it to paint the tonal colors he heard in his head. The richness of his palette set the Washingtonians apart from other bands of the day, and by 1927, when the rechristened "Duke Ellington Orchestra" began a long-running stand at Harlem's Cotton Club, the colors had coalesced into what the world would know as the Ellington sound. His lifelong method was to hire brilliant individual musicians—some of the first were the drummer Sonny Greer, the saxophonists Harry Carney and Johnny Hodges, and the trumpeters Joe Nanton and Cootie Williams—and to blend them into an ensemble as individualistic as the soloists were on their own.

It helped that the pianist was a brilliant musician himself, broadly intelligent and endlessly probing. Initially Ellington had been

The postal service put Duke Ellington on its 22-cent stamp but properly portrayed him looking like a million dollars. His dress and demeanor were as elegant as his harmonies and orchestral arrangements.

inspired by the great Harlem stride pianists Luckey Roberts, James P. Johnson and Willie (The Lion) Smith. But now he moved beyond their athleticism to a smoother style that was unmistakably his own. "Let Duke strike a chord and you knew it was Duke and no one else," the critic Ralph Gleason once wrote. The new style was more elegant than that of the Harlem giants, befitting Ellington's persona. In photographs and films he invariably looks handsome and dapper, born to dukedom. The only other young prince-about-town who exerted the same kind of charisma was his near-twin George Gershwin.

Ellington never forgot that his identity was closely bound with the collective identity of his musicians, and he held his band together for five decades until he died in 1974—an astonishing feat of stamina, leadership and charm. Some of his musicians spent their whole careers with him; Harry Carney, hired in 1926 at the age of 16, was still playing at the end. In lean times Duke often used his own royalties to keep the men working, repeatedly taking them on concert trips and recording dates all over the world. If the big band was an American invention, Ellington's orchestra brought it to its artistic pinnacle, especially after the arrival in 1938 of the arranger, composer and pianist Billy Strayhorn.

A conservatory-trained kid from Pittsburgh, Strayhorn was just 23 when a friend recommended him to Ellington, who was in town on a concert tour. Duke was so taken by his composing talent that he urged him to write something for the band, meanwhile scribbling some directions for Strayhorn on how to reach his New York apartment. The notes were obviously subway-specific; Strayhorn turned up not long afterward with "Take the A Train," which soon became the band's signature song and has been a swing classic ever since.

Billy Strayhorn was everything Duke Ellington was not: small, shy, introspective, homosexual. But the two quickly fell into a composing relationship so symbiotic, the younger man habitually developing or completing Ellington's ideas, that nobody could tell—or knows to this day—who wrote what. "I've seen Strayhorn walk into Duke's dressing room," Ellington's sister Ruth recalled, "and Duke would say, 'Oh, Billy, I just want you to finish this thing for me.' Just like that. And Billy would sit and stare into his eyes, and Duke would stare back, and then Billy would say 'O.K.' They wouldn't even exchange a word. They'd just look into each other's eyes, and Billy would go out and write what Duke wanted."

The irony of a bond so mystical and trusting was not lost on Ellington's son. "[Duke] didn't like anybody who could read his mind," Mercer Ellington said. "That's what gave him his strength over people. Strayhorn was the only one. He let Strayhorn in the door. That door was *locked* for everybody else, and I do mean everybody—his family, women—and for me, too, before the old man was dying and I was the only one sitting there." Strayhorn's role as Ellington's alter ego, muse and amanuensis—and as the sole composer of "Lush Life," "Chelsea Bridge" and many other numbers associated with the band—ended only when he died in 1967, almost 30 years after the older man had let him in the door. He seems to have been a man without vanity, never resenting his often anonymous role, grateful for a safe environment and a regular outlet for his compositions and arrangements. His death shook Ellington with intimations of his own mortality. As Strayhorn's friend Lena Horne said, "Duke was young forever—listen to his music. He never aged a day, till Billy died."

Unlike America's other great songwriters—servants of a 32-bar story—Ellington was an impressionist, a master of lights and shadows, forever pushing himself into extended forms. Some of his most ambitious works were suites that aspired to portray the Negro experience in America, starting in 1931 with *Creole Rhapsody* and ending in 1970 with *New Orleans Suite*, a musical portrait of the jazz legends of that city, and famously including the 45-minute *Black, Brown and Beige*, composed for his Carnegie Hall debut in 1943, which Ellington said was "about the history of my race." One of his purest melodies, the hymnlike "Come Sunday," survives from that suite as a jazz standard, a reminder that religious feeling inspired much of Ellington's work, especially the three Sacred Concerts of 1965, 1968 and 1973. "His music's most basic concern is uplift of the human spirit," says Wynton Marsalis, the trumpeter and artistic director of Jazz at Lincoln Center.

But what we remember Ellington by are his popular songs, and we remember them because they aren't like anyone else's. They are the melodies of a jazz instrumentalist. (His only counterpart among the great songwriters is Hoagy Carmichael, a disciple of the cornetist Bix Beiderbecke.) Although the piano was Duke Ellington's forte, the piano is a percussion instrument, its sound quick to decay. I don't think the undulating line of a melody like "Sophisticated Lady" or "Prelude to a Kiss" would occur as naturally to a pianist as it would to someone who hears those descending notes being caressed by a saxophone or a trumpet or a clarinet. His melodic intervals often startle me. The 9-tone leap at the beginning of "I Got It Bad and That Ain't Good" ("Never TREATS me sweet and gentle . . . ") isn't a songwriter's interval or a singer's interval; it's a jazzman's interval.

Ellington's rhythms also sound instrumental to me, especially in their no-nonsense momentum. I'm struck by how many Ellington songs are in full motion before they even reach the first bar. Many popular songs have a few preliminary "pickup" notes leading to the opening bar and its downbeat. But usually there are only a few of those pickup notes, and their tempo is almost conversational:

It's ve-ry / CLEAR, our love is here to stay   [3 pickup notes]

I left my / HEART in San Francisco   [3 pickup notes]

It was / JUST one of those things   [2 pickup notes]

All very easygoing and chatty. Not so with Ellington; he uses a whole bunch of pickup notes, and they are anything but relaxed:

Missed the Sa-tur-day / DANCE   [5 pickup notes]

In a sen-ti-men-tal / MOOD   [6 pickup notes]

Do noth-ing till you hear from / ME   [7 pickup notes]

In a mel-low / TONE   [4 pickup notes]

Those pickup notes don't lead gently to the start of the song. They *are* the start of the song: "Missed the Saturday dance." WHAP! It's as if Duke couldn't wait to get things percolating. Maybe that's why he was America's best jazz composer. As one of his songs states the case, "It don't mean a thing if it ain't got that swing."

Hoagy Carmichael
(and Mitchell Parish)

Play me a Hoagy Carmichael song and I hear the banging of a screen door and the whine of an outboard motor on a lake—familiar sounds of summer in a small-town America that is long gone but still longed for. Often the imagery starts with the title. It may be the name of a place ("Memphis in June," "New Orleans," "Georgia," "Can't Get Indiana Off My Mind"), or a sentimental setting ("Riverboat Shuffle," "Old Rockin' Chair's Got Me"), or a bird ("Skylark," "Mister Bluebird"), or a flower ("Blue Orchids"), or an attribute of nature ("Star Dust," "Ole Buttermilk Sky"), or a bucolic moment ("One Morning in May," "Watermelon Weather," "In the Cool, Cool, Cool of the Evening"), or an allusion to the easy life ("Lazybones," "Lazy River"). Whatever it is, it invites us into an agreeable world. There's no winter in these songs—they're not called "Memphis in March" or "One Morning in February."

> Up a lazy river by the old mill run,
> That lazy, lazy river in the noonday sun,
> Linger in the shade of a kind old tree,
> Throw away your troubles, dream a dream with me . . .

Unlike Cole Porter, who left Indiana and never looked back, Hoagy Carmichael was a Hoosier in his bones. His melodies were as lazy as the lazy rivers he loved to write about, and the images in his songs were strictly rural: skylarks and star dust, old rockin' chairs and ole buttermilk skies. No other songwriter evokes so much nostalgia for a long-gone, simpler America.

That's one of Carmichael's own lyrics (an early song, written with Sidney Arodin), and it's a pure product of the rural America he grew up in—a classic of escapism. If the noonday sun is too hot you can linger in the shade of not just a tree, but a kind old tree. Among the great songwriters Carmichael was the great exception—not a city boy who wrote scores for Broadway and Hollywood, but a country boy who wrote individual ballads that became huge hits on their own: "Star Dust," "The Nearness of You," "I Get Along Without You Very Well," "Skylark."

Hoagy's people don't get indoors much. At the nearest—as in

this lyric by Paul Francis Webster—they sit on the porch, watchin' the neighbors go by and keeping an eye out for the moon:

Memphis in June, a shady veranda,
Under a Sunday blue sky . . .
Memphis in June, and cousin Amanda's
Bakin' a rhubarb pie.
Memphis in June, with sweet oleander
Blowing perfume in the air.
Up jumps the moon to make it that much grander . . .

I don't know what oleander smells like, but it sounds as if it smells as sweet as wisteria and honeysuckle. I also don't know what a buttermilk sky looks like, but it sounds pleasant. "What's the good word tonight? Are you gonna be mellow tonight?" the singer asks the buttermilk sky, beseeching it to "keep a-brushing those clouds from sight" when he pops the question to his girl.

Much is expected of the moon and the stars in Carmichael's songs. "I'm gonna get a moonburn when I'm out with you tonight," says the lyric of "Moonburn," explaining that when "the glowing stars above me . . . flash the words that you love me, it [the moon] will warm my heart." The moon also means home to a departed Hoosier. "I long for that moon country, that 'possum and 'coon country, that sycamore heaven back South," says "Moon Country," making no mention of animals that are up and about during the day, and in "Can't Get Indiana Off My Mind" the force that "calls me back home, anywhere I chance to roam" is "the moonlight on the Wabash that I left behind." Magical words: moonlight, Wabash, sycamore, 'possum, oleander, rhubarb, veranda, buttermilk, old mill, watermelon. They reach us not only through the eye, ear and nose but through two even more powerful transmitters: memory and yearning for the simplicities of yesterday.

Carmichael's melodies tug on the same nostalgia. They are wanderers, itinerant as a hobo, in no hurry to arrive. There's no big-city tension in them. Partly that's because they have almost no repeated notes. The melody of "Lazy River" is as lazy as the river, full of curves and bends that don't exactly repeat, just as different stretches of a river look alike without being alike. "Can't Get Indiana Off My Mind" is another meandering tune, rural in feeling. It wouldn't work if the lyric said "Can't get New York City off my mind."

By contrast, the tunes of urban songwriters take much of their insistence from repeated notes. George Gershwin's "They Can't Take That Away from Me" and "A Foggy Day" are the love songs of a cosmopolitan suitor, taking their emotion from their repetitive

Nobody remembers Jerry Franks, but everybody remembers Hoagy Carmichael's "Star Dust"; the song has been translated into 40 languages. The fact that the sheet music had a ukulele arrangement—little square boxes over every piano chord denoting the harmony for a stringed instrument— was important information in the self-entertaining 1930s. If nobody in the family could play the piano, somebody could probably play the uke.

clusters and melodic jumps; no curving rivers come to mind. When "A Foggy Day" declares "I viewed the morning with alarm, the British Museum had lost its charm"—one of Ira Gershwin's most engaging couplets—the words have a ruefulness because of the reiterated notes, like many Cole Porter ballads ("Just One of Those Things"). Porter was also from Indiana, but he was no gazer at the moonlight on the Wabash or fancier of Cousin Amanda's rhubarb pies. His river was the Seine, his pie was caviar, and his rhythms were those of New York society dance bands, punching us with short bursts of melody ("It's All Right With Me"). Vincent Youmans was a prince of the repeated note ("I Know That You Know"), Irving Berlin took vitality from it ("There's No Business Like Show Business"), and Richard Rodgers was no stranger to its romantic uses ("Where or When"). Harold Arlen's "Come Rain or Come Shine" begins with the same note repeated 13 times, and Jule Styne's "Just in Time" is built on the alternation of two notes that are only a half-tone apart. What makes them work is that the chords change interestingly beneath the uninteresting melody.

That's seldom true of Hoagy Carmichael. His melodies usually dictate one set of chords, the most obvious example being "Star Dust." Its opening phrase ("Sometimes I wonder why I spend each lonely night") descends and climbs back up mainly on the notes of the F-major chord (the song is in the key of C) and therefore demands an F-major chord underneath it, just as each subsequent phrase demands a specific chord: F-minor ("dreaming of a song"), C-major ("the melody"), E-minor ("haunts my reve-"), A-major ("rie"), etc. Carmichael's tunes don't often welcome improvisation because they sound like jazz improvisations themselves. Where a Gershwin song sounds constructed ("The Man I Love"), or a Rodgers song ("My Funny Valentine"), or a Berlin song ("How Deep Is the Ocean"), Hoagy's melodies sound intuitive and spontaneous, like the riff of a jazz instrumentalist. They could be played as instrumental solos without any harmony.

How those fluid lines got into his ear is no mystery. Born in Bloomington, Indiana, Hoagy was taught to play the piano by his mother, who accompanied silent films in a local movie house, and he also studied with a black ragtime pianist named Reggie Duval. His first important influence was the young cornetist from nearby Iowa, Bix Beiderbecke, whom he got to know in the early 1920s when Carmichael was attending college and pursuing a law degree at the University of Indiana. On the side he made money by playing the piano at fraternity parties and in local watering holes. Another big influence was Louis Armstrong, whose trumpet he first heard in 1924. He also listened to the jazz that was coming up the river from New Orleans to Chicago, and he hired himself out as a singer and pianist to the great jazzmen like "King" Oliver, the Dorsey brothers and Jack Teagarden, who were creating a new American sound, aided by the fast-growing infant called radio. In 1926 he sold his first song, "Riverboat Shuffle," which was widely played by local bands, including Beiderbecke and his Wolverines. When it was followed by a second hit, "Washboard Blues," he gave up the law for music.

Thus when we hear a Hoagy Carmichael song we hear music that brings back an idealized moment in the American past, the end of an era when the nation was still pastoral, and its perfect icon is "Star Dust," the most recorded popular song; at last count, there were 1,300 versions in 40 languages. Composed in 1927 as an up-tempo piano solo, it languished until it was set to words in 1929 by Mitchell Parish and recorded in 1930 by the bandleader Isham Jones. A fine songwriter himself ("It Had to Be You," "I'll See You in My Dreams," "The One I Love Belongs to Somebody Else"), Jones slowed "Star Dust" down and caught its soul. Its success neverthe-

Many American songwriters have achieved postal immortality. One recent set of stamps honored Hoagy Carmichael, Dorothy Fields, Harold Arlen and Johnny Mercer.

less defied the canons of public acceptance. As Alec Wilder notes in his classic book *American Popular Song*, "Star Dust" is "very far out for a pop song of any era, and absolutely phenomenal for 1929."

Parish's lyric, though skillful, doesn't say very much. The only information it conveys is that the song is about "star dust." Proceeding from that poet's image, the lyricist throws in a carload of "poetic" words: night, dreaming, reverie, love, kiss, garden wall, nightingale, fairy tale, paradise, roses, heart, memory. But the words don't add up to a story. The convoluted melody, on the other hand, moves with inexorable logic; otherwise it wouldn't lodge itself so snugly in the brain—part of America's collective memory for seven decades. Nobody seems to have any trouble figuring out where the song is going next.

"Star Dust" was no lucky one-shot for Mitchell Parish. Over a long career he provided lyrics for more than 600 melodies, including "Sweet Lorraine," "Stars Fell on Alabama," "Stairway to the Stars" and "Moonlight Serenade." Many of his lyrics gave commercial life to melodies that already existed: Duke Ellington's "Sophisticated Lady"; "Deep Purple," an instrumental by Peter DeRose; "The Lamp Is Low," originally Maurice Ravel's "Pavane for a Dead Princess"; and "Volare," an Italian ballad called "Nel Blu, Dipinto di Blu." Instrumentals were kind to Parish; big band treatments of "Star Dust" in the swing era by Benny Goodman, Tommy Dorsey and Artie Shaw swept it to world popularity, and Glenn Miller swung his own "Moonlight Serenade" to fame.

Like Irving Berlin, Mitchell Parish grew up on New York's Lower East Side, brought there as a child by immigrant parents from Lithuania. Like Hoagy Carmichael, he studied law, supporting himself as a court clerk at criminal trials in downtown Manhattan. Commenting on the paradox of so many astral bodies in his songs, he once said, "Growing up on the Lower East Side, we didn't see stars. I don't want to psychoanalyze myself, but I sometimes think that those song lyrics about the moon and the stars represented an escape. They expressed a longing for what I couldn't see."

Only in a few cases did Hoagy Carmichael work with a lyricist who bothered to create a narrative. Most of his songs just express the mood of the people singing them. Georgia is on their mind, or they can't get Indiana *off* their mind, or they know of a lazy river. Nobody actually visits any of those places. Hoagy's people are receivers; they receive dust from the stars, burn from the moon, fairy tales from the nightingale and help from the buttermilk sky.

Two lyricists, however, brought humor and humanity to his songs. Frank Loesser, who would later write the brilliant *Guys and*

Dolls, caught the eternal lovers' quandary of "Two Sleepy People" who are "too much in love to say goodnight," and in "Small Fry" he gently ribbed the tendency of elders to chide uppity youth ("My! My! Put down that cigarette; you ain't a grown-up, high and mighty yet"). But it was Johnny Mercer who wrote the lyrics for Hoagy Carmichael's best song ("Skylark"), his most characteristic song ("Lazybones") and his most exuberant song ("In the Cool, Cool, Cool of the Evening").

"Skylark" is Carmichael at the top of his mature form. Its tortuous main theme, both graceful and confident, is matched by lyrics that have all the right down-home images ("meadow," "mist," "valley," "spring," "blossom," "lane"), and its complex bridge, making two changes of key in eight bars, is a model of freshness and surprise. Mercer's accompanying words are just right:

> *And in your lonely flight*
> *Haven't you heard the music of the night?*
> *Wonderful music, faint as a will-o'-the-wisp,*
> *Crazy as a loon,*
> *Sad as a gypsy serenading the moon.*

"Lazybones" has a melody and a gait so easygoing that they almost compel us to lie down—pure essence of Carmichael—and Mercer's mildly chastising lyric ("Never get your day's work done, sleepin' in the noonday sun") loses its rebuke altogether in the droll release, which speculates that when the lazybones goes fishing he probably keeps wishing that the fish won't grab at his line.

"In the Cool, Cool, Cool of the Evening," the last collaboration of the two country boys, which won the Academy Award, is a flat-out ode to the anticipated pleasure of a small-town picnic. Its form is short and direct: a verse that lists different folks' preferred food ("Sue/ wants a barbecue/ Sam/ wants to boil a ham . . . "), followed by a chorus expressing the singer's assurance that he wouldn't think of missing it ("Tell 'em I'll be there"). The music and the lyrics are equally amiable, a summing up of the enjoyment that both Carmichael and Mercer took in their work and in the simple blessings of a simpler America.

Hoagy Carmichael's son, Hoagy Bix Carmichael, middle-named for Bix Beiderbecke, once told me: "My father wrote about what he knew best—that which had made the earliest and most indelible impression, and it was definitely not the streets of New York or the palm trees in Los Angeles. Cole Porter wrote about where he wanted to go; Dad wrote about where he had been, and he never tried to shake that."

Hoagy Carmichael put his long, quizzical face and hayseed voice to
prolific use in a late career as a performer—first, in 1944, as a honky-
tonk piano player in To Have and Have Not, with Humphrey Bogart
and Lauren Bacall. Here, as Hoagy sings his "How Little We Know," all
eyes are on Bacall and not on the piano player, though her smoldering
look is for him. His other memorable song in that film was the antic
"Hong Kong Blues" ("the story of a very unfortunate Memphis man").
After that Carmichael was much sought as a character actor, and in
eight subsequent films he recycled his old songs—"Lazy River" in The
Best Years of Our Lives—and introduced some new ones, such as
"Memphis in June," in Johnny Angel, in which he played a singing cab-
bie. He also appeared with Kirk Douglas in Young Man With a Horn,
a movie based on the life of his first and strongest influence, the cornetist
Bix Beiderbecke.

Late Rodgers & Hart

The period between 1935 and 1942 was the astonishingly golden age of Rodgers & Hart. In those eight years they wrote ten musicals that were a steady outpouring of songs so melodically rich and lyrically tender that they have been a staple for jazz musicians and singers ever since. The shows were *Jumbo, On Your Toes, Babes in Arms, I'd Rather Be Right, I Married an Angel, The Boys From Syracuse, Too Many Girls, Higher and Higher, Pal Joey* and *By Jupiter,* and some of the songs were "My Romance," "The Most Beautiful Girl in the World," "Little Girl Blue," "There's a Small Hotel," "Glad to Be Unhappy," "My Funny Valentine," "The Lady Is a Tramp," "I Wish I Were in Love Again," "Where or When," "Have You Met Miss Jones?", "I Married an Angel," "Spring Is Here," "Falling in Love With Love," "This Can't Be Love," "I Didn't Know What Time It Was," "It Never Entered My Mind," "I Could Write a Book," "Bewitched, Bothered and Bewildered" and "Wait Till You See Her."

Rodgers was then in his thirties, and his songs have the confidence of an athlete at the peak of his form. The melodies are strong and graceful ("I Could Write a Book," "Have You Met Miss Jones?"), often taking us by surprise with their contour ("My Romance"), or disarming us with their zest ("This Can't Be Love"). Beyond that, they are always interesting; we think, "Where did he find *that* one?" They also are grounded in the harmonies of a master craftsman. Good pianists and arrangers are seldom tempted to improve the bass line of a Rodgers song; it can't be done. The descending bass of "My Funny Valentine" is the foundation that holds up the whole song; the contrapuntal bass line of "I Didn't Know What Time It Was" invites an instrumentalist or a singer to improvise on the melody, secure in the elegant safety net below. And the waltzes! No other American songwriter came close to writing such waltzes: "Falling in Love With Love," "Over and Over Again," "Wait Till You See Her," "The Most Beautiful Girl in the World." Their lilt is contagious:

Songwriters are constantly asked: "Which comes first: the words or the music?" With most partnerships the answer is "both." This 1940 picture of Lorenz Hart and Richard Rodgers writing a song for "Pal Joey" pins down the process. Hart scribbles some lyrics against the nearest wall while Rodgers writes some notes at the piano, their nicotine fix—cigar and cigarette —momentarily put aside.

Rodgers and Hart's "The Boys From Syracuse" (1938), based on Shakespeare's "A Comedy of Errors," was choreographed—it says here—by George Balanchine. Two years earlier, for "On Your Toes," Rodgers composed the extended "Slaughter on Tenth Avenue" to accompany Balanchine's shootout involving a dancer (Ray Bolger) fatally in love with a stripper (Tamara Geva)—the first time ballet had been used as a dramatic component of a Broadway musical.

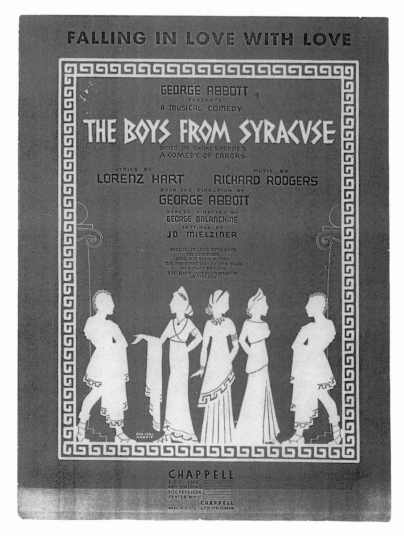

Falling in love with love is falling for make believe,
Falling in love with love is playing the fool . . .

So is their upward sweep in the final eight bars. Rodgers built his waltzes to their perfect emotional conclusion:

When my slippers are next to the ones that belong
To the one and only beautiful girl in the world.

Even if you don't know the words, you know it's a song about the most beautiful girl in the world. Musically, it couldn't be more romantic.

But Rodgers could also match his collaborator's pain. Lorenz Hart was a lyricist who never forgot that love goes wrong as often as it goes right, and some of Rodgers' most touching melodies are set to Hart's bittersweet reminders of that fact: "Little Girl Blue," "Glad

To Be Unhappy," "Spring Is Here," "Nobody's Heart Belongs to Me." By temperament Hart was the opposite of his contemporary Ira Gershwin. Gershwin, a married man of amiable disposition, liked to celebrate love at the moment of its hoped-for arrival ("Someone to Watch Over Me," "The Man I Love") or its actual arrival ("How Long Has This Been Going On?", "Our Love Is Here to Stay"). Hart, an unhappy man—dwarfish, homosexual, alcoholic—didn't shy away from being a poet of loss. The late Rodgers & Hart songs that linger in our emotional memory tend to be the losers' laments:

> Sit there and count the raindrops
> Falling on you,
> It's time you knew,
> All you can count on is the raindrops
> That fall on little girl blue.

> Once I laughed when
> I heard you saying
> That I'd be playing
> Solitaire,
> Uneasy in my easy chair,
> It never entered my mind.

> Spring is here,
> Why doesn't the breeze delight me?
> Stars appear,
> Why doesn't the night invite me?
> Maybe it's because nobody loves me.
> Spring is here,
> I hear.

> I fell in love with love,
> With love everlasting.
> But love fell out with me.

Among their many felicities of language, their internal rhymes and repetitions, these lyrics are deeply musical, perfectly tuned to the melodic line. The words about counting the raindrops that fall on Little Girl Blue fall on Rodgers' falling raindrops:

In "Spring Is Here" the phrase "maybe it's because nobody loves me" is a cry of pain set to ten consecutive rising notes, followed by an abrupt drop to the wistful "spring is here," followed by the final drop—almost a whisper—to the ironic "I hear." I think of these late Rodgers & Hart ballads as women's songs. No other American songwriters have given women cabaret artists such a sensitive literature.

But Hart was no sentimental softie. His view of human nature was cynical, and it turned up often in his situation songs, which satirized squalid behavior in such types as the rich ("Too Good for the Average Man"), the chic ("The Lady Is a Tramp") and the embattled married ("I Wish I Were in Love Again"):

> *When love congeals*
> *It soon reveals*
> *The faint aroma of performing seals,*
> *The double-crossing of a pair of heels . . .*

It's the Jonathan Swift school of lyric writing, and it reached its apogee in Rodgers & Hart's next-to-last show, *Pal Joey*, which was based on John O'Hara's acerbic *New Yorker* stories about a two-bit gigolo and an older woman. "It was a weird experience," Rodgers wrote about its genesis, "to be putting on a musical show in which none of the characters (with the exception of the ingenue) had even a bowing acquaintance with decency. It seemed time to us, however, that musical comedy get out of its cradle and start standing on its own feet, looking at the facts of life."

With Gene Kelly in his first leading role, as the hustling Joey, the show opened on Broadway in 1941, eliciting the revulsion of Brooks Atkinson, the *New York Times'* theater critic, for its "odious story." His review ended: "Although *Pal Joey* is expertly done, can you draw sweet water from a foul well?" If Atkinson could have listened only to the music he would have gone home bathed in one of Rodgers' most bountiful scores. But the words were gritty ("Bewitched, Bothered and Bewildered," "In Our Little Den of Iniquity," "Take Him"), and half of the first-night audience, as Rodgers recalled, "sat there in stony, stunned silence."

Like Atkinson, a man of old-school civility, the stunned 50 percent weren't ready for musical comedy to get real. Eleven years later, in 1952, *Pal Joey* had a smash revival of 542 performances and nobody found it even mildly distasteful, not even Atkinson. America had won the war and lost its innocence. So had the musical theater.

Rodgers himself had been one of the pioneers of the new reality. When he was offered the show that would become the groundbreak-

In "Pal Joey" (1940) Rodgers and Hart dared to write a musical whose hero was a heel—a heresy that was greeted with outrage by audiences and critics. When the show was revived a decade letter it was no longer outrageous.

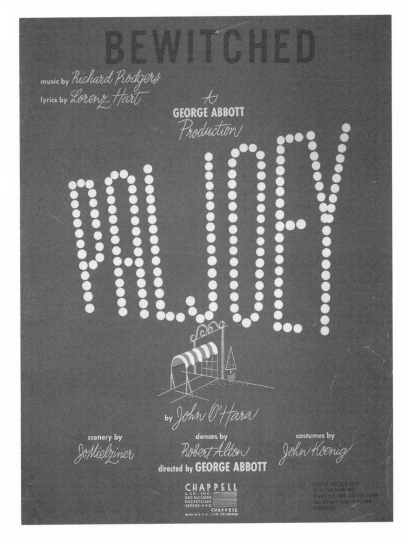

ing *Oklahoma!*, Hart had neither the strength nor the appetite for the project, and Rodgers took Oscar Hammerstein as his lyricist. So ended a partnership that produced more than a thousand songs of rare beauty and grace. Hart would live to see the opening of *Oklahoma!* in the spring of 1943, and with it the birth of the new age of musical theater, which brought his own era to an end. Six months later, weakened by drink and failing health, Lorenz Hart died at the age of forty-eight.

Harry Warren
(and Al Dubin and Mack Gordon)

Harry Warren was the great American hit machine. To this day, dozens of his melodies are as familiar as an old college roommate to anyone who listened to the radio from the early 1930s to the late 1950s. One of his ballads, "There Will Never Be Another You," is a classic; several others are near-classics ("The More I See You," "At Last," "This Heart of Mine," "I Only Have Eyes for You"), and the rest are merely good: "You'll Never Know," "September in the Rain," "Lullaby of Broadway," "Chattanooga Choo-Choo," "Jeepers Creepers," "On the Atchison, Topeka and the Santa Fe," "I Know Why (And So Do You)," "I've Got a Gal in Kalamazoo," "You Must Have Been a Beautiful Baby," "I Wish I Knew," "Boulevard of Broken Dreams," "My Heart Tells Me" . . . the list of hits seems to have no end. Three of his songs won an Academy Award and eight others were nominees. Forty-two made the top ten list on *Your Hit Parade*, the radio show that was the nation's index of commercial song popularity.

The familiarity of Harry Warren's songs is matched by the anonymity of the man. Perhaps because he stayed in Hollywood and didn't go East to write Broadway shows, like Jule Styne and Frank Loesser, or perform his songs, like Hoagy Carmichael and Johnny Mercer, he is the invisible man, his career a prime example of the oblivion that cloaked so many writers who cranked out good songs for bad movies. The irony was not lost on Warren; his one joke, often repeated, was that even his best friends hadn't heard of him.

Born Salvatore Guaragna, in 1893, the last of 13 children of immigrant parents from Calabria, he grew up in Brooklyn, where

Starting in 1933 with "Forty-Second Street," the composer-lyricist team of Harry Warren and Al Dubin became the hottest songwriters in Hollywood, turning out rapid-fire hits— "I Only Have Eyes for You," "I'll String Along With You," "Lulu's Back in Town," "Lullaby of Broadway"—for Warner Brothers musicals. Later, at 20th Century-Fox, with the lyricist Mack Gordon, Warren's output was no less amazing. For 60 years he wrote beautiful melodies that people loved and remembered. The only thing they couldn't remember was his name.

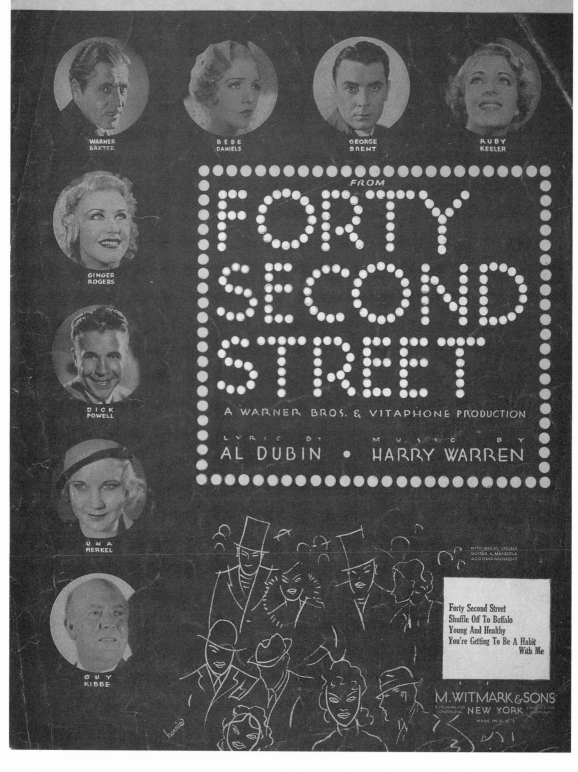

The movie musical was a dying species in 1932 when "Forty-Second Street" revitalized the form and made it one of Hollywood's most popular genres. It also raised to cinematic sainthood the choreographer Busby Berkeley, whose voyeuristic camera proved that chorus girls' legs could be seen from previously unimagined angles and heights.

he taught himself to play the piano in a neighborhood saloon called Blind Mike's, piecing out a living by working with small bands at local parties and bar mitzvahs. He wrote his first hit, "Rose of the Rio Grande," in 1922, and wrote his last song for the movie *Manhattan Melody* in 1981. Even his hero, Puccini, didn't have a 60-year output.

After a decade of composing Tin Pan Alley songs that didn't catch on, Warren found his popular touch in 1931 with "I Found a Million-Dollar Baby (in a Five and Ten Cent Store)." But the break that changed his life came in 1932, when Warner Brothers paired him with a gifted lyricist, Al Dubin, to write the score for *Forty-Second Street*. A landmark movie of the show-must-go-on genre, conferring instant stardom on Dick Powell and Ruby Keeler, with pyrotechnical dance routines by Busby Berkeley and amiable songs like "Forty-Second Street," "Shuffle Off to Buffalo" and "You're Getting to Be a Habit With Me," it raised the Hollywood musical to a new level and launched its long reign as an entertainment form. Adapted into a hit Broadway musical half a century later, it kept theatergoers humming Harry Warren's music for two seasons and still not bothering to learn his name.

Forty-Second Street set off a six-year gusher of Warner musicals with Warren-Dubin scores, including *Gold Diggers of 1933* ("We're in the Money," "Shadow Waltz"), *Moulin Rouge* ("Boulevard of Broken Dreams"), *Twenty Million Sweethearts* ("I'll String Along With You"), *Dames* ("I Only Have Eyes for You"), *Gold Diggers of 1935* ("Lullaby of Broadway"), *Broadway Gondolier* ("Lulu's Back in Town"), *Shipmates Forever* ("Don't Give Up the Ship"), *Gold Diggers of 1937* ("With Plenty of Money and You") and *Mr. Dodd Takes the Air* ("Remember Me?"). Some others—their titles alone a museum exhibit of the Warner years—were *Roman Scandals*, *Footlight Parade*, *Stars Over Broadway*, *Living on Velvet*, *Cain and Mabel*, *Melody for Two*, *Stolen Melody*, *The Singing Marine*, *San Quentin* and *Garden of the Moon*.

That this kind of studio dreck produced hundreds of America's beloved standards is a miracle often overlooked in the history of American popular song. We prefer to think the great songs came from the great musicals, like *The Wizard of Oz*. But Hollywood was a factory town, and steady employment had to be found for the stars on the studios' payroll to amortize their salaries. That fiscal fact gave steady work to songwriters, and none was kept busier than Harry Warren. In 1940 he moved to 20th Century-Fox and was teamed with another able lyricist, Mack Gordon. There his output was no less astonishing than it had been at Warner's. The movies were just as terrible, but the songs got even better.

Consider the year 1942, in which Warren & Gordon scores for three forgettable movies contained five memorable songs: *Iceland*: "There Will Never Be Another You"; *Springtime in the Rockies*: "I Had the Craziest Dream," and *Orchestra Wives*: "At Last," "Serenade in Blue" and "I Had a Gal in Kalamazoo." Consider 1943: "No Love, No Nothin'," from *The Gang's All Here*; "My Heart Tells Me," from *Sweet Rosie O'Grady*, and "You'll Never Know," from *Hello Frisco, Hello*. Looking up those movies in my guide to films on TV, I see that almost all of them get only two stars (**), and the casts tend to feature the same Fox employees: Alice Faye, Don Ameche, Betty Grable, John Payne, Cesar Romero, Sonja Henie and Carmen Miranda. That Miranda needed songs of Latin flavor was no problem for Harry Warren. His title song for *Down Argentina Way* was one of his Oscar nominees, and his hit song for *That Night in Rio* was the enjoyable "I, Yi, Yi, Yi, Yi (I Like You Very Much)."

The four Fox years, whose products included "The More I See You" and "I Wish I Knew" for *Diamond Horseshoe*, were followed by seven years at MGM, where, in 1945, Warren wrote "On the Atchison, Topeka and the Santa Fe" for *The Harvey Girls* and by seven more years at Paramount, where he would compose his last huge hit, the title song of the lachrymose movie *An Affair to Remember*. That continental melody, suggestive of sidewalk cafes on the Via Veneto—the Italian gene finally dominant—still tugs at our emotions on late-night television as it washes over the tormented lovers Cary Grant and Deborah Kerr.

The marvel of Warren's gift, I think, is that you only have to hear a Harry Warren song once to own it for the rest of your life. It doesn't even have to be one of his better songs. I still remember being taken as a boy in 1935 to *Shipmates Forever*, a navy movie whose Warren & Dubin score featured the patriotic rouser "Don't Give Up the Ship." I haven't heard the song since that day, but I have no trouble recalling every note. Think of any Warren song— "I Only Have Eyes for You," "I Had the Craziest Dream," "No Love, No Nothin'," "You Must Have Been a Beautiful Baby"—and the melody is instantly there, all 32 bars, none of the notes wanting to be changed.

A further marvel is that the songs are so varied. In this respect Warren reminds me of Richard Rodgers. Like Rodgers, he had a bottomless reservoir of melodies to dip into. "Jeepers Creepers" is full of bounce and merriment; "Serenade in Blue" is sinuous and chromatic; "Boulevard of Broken Dreams" is south-of-the-border sultry; "Forty-Second Street" is a minor-scale wanderer; "This Heart

It's safe to guess that these three films were not works of art. Harry Warren's fate as a Hollywood contract composer was to write superior songs—"The More I See You" is one of his best—for 77 such unexalted movie musicals.

that refresh us with a change of key in the second 8 bars, and "At Last" is one of the great beauties. Puccini would have been proud of his disciple.

But the crown jewel, "There Will Never Be Another You," doesn't remind me of Puccini or anyone else. It's wholly original. Mack Gordon's lyric is a succession of declarative sentences, which Warren matches with long and elegant musical sentences of his own:

> *There will be many other nights like this,*
> *And I'll be standing here with someone new,*
> *There will be other songs to sing,*
> *Another fall, another spring,*
> *But there will never be another you . . .*

That's the first 16 bars. Then the theme is repeated, and the song concludes with a 4-bar phrase that knocks me out every time I hear it. As a whole, it's a melody so serious and deeply felt that it would seem to lend itself only to a slow and serious rendition. Yet the song is also an icon to jazz musicians, who accelerate its tempo and revel in its fluid lines. It belongs to the elite company of romantic ballads that generations of jazzmen have embraced for their melodic energy and harmonic interest, like "How High the Moon."

One might think that when 20th Century-Fox received "There Will Never Be Another You" for its movie *Iceland*, the studio would have featured it as something special. But Harry Warren songs weren't the point of *Iceland*; Sonja Henie was the point of *Iceland*, just as Betty Grable was the point of *Diamond Horseshoe* and Harry James' orchestra and Carmen Miranda were the point of *Springtime in the Rockies*. Probably the only Harry Warren song that got presented with proper respect was "On the Atchison, Topeka and the Santa Fe." Sung by Judy Garland, it's the best-remembered moment in *The Harvey Girls*. But does anyone remember any of Warren's other songs being sung on the screen?

A similar peonage was the fate of Harold Arlen during his long residence in Hollywood. Typically, two of his gems, "Blues in the Night" and "This Time the Dream's on Me," were written for the dreadful *Blues in the Night*, and for the clinker *Casbah*, starring Tony Martin and Yvonne DeCarlo, he wrote no fewer than four superb songs: "Hooray for Love," "For Every Man There's a Woman," "It Was Written in the Stars" and "What's Good About Goodbye?" His lyricist for that movie was Leo Robin, another fine craftsman who labored honorably in the employ of the studio moguls. Those accidental Medicis never knew what gold they had struck. (Arthur Freed at MGM was the big exception.) They treated the songwriters

The older Harry Warren at home in Hollywood with his three Oscars. The Academy Award-winning songs were "Lullaby of Broadway," "On the Atchison, Topeka and the Santa Fe" and "You'll Never Know." Eight others were nominated for Oscars.

like caterers, to be paid when they delivered their product and sent back to the swimming pool, never to be told how—or even whether—their songs would be used.

Arlen at least got a few good movies to write songs for: *The Wizard of Oz, Cabin in the Sky, A Star Is Born*. He also kept his dignity by composing occasional Broadway musicals. Irving Berlin and Cole Porter stayed in New York and periodically answered Hollywood's call, thereby retaining at least a faint voice in decisions involving their work. But Harry Warren was the ultimate studio hireling. By my count he wrote songs for 77 movies, averaging five songs per movie, most of them above the norm in beauty and durability, and the best of all those films was the first one, *Forty-Second Street*.

E. Y. Harburg and "The Wizard of Oz"

The lyricist E. Y. Harburg was an incurable socialist and an incurable dreamer. That combination enabled him to write two of America's most powerful songs: "Brother, Can You Spare a Dime?", the ultimate hymn of the Depression, and "Over the Rainbow," the ultimate hymn of escape to a happier place.

Born Irwin Hochsberg on New York's Lower East Side, he never forgot the poverty of his upbringing or the toil of his immigrant parents in a garment industry sweatshop; social inequality is a recurring nag in his work. Only Irving Berlin, another urchin of that Jewish ghetto, was born as poor, and he didn't put politics into his songs. The other great songwriters were mostly children of bourgeois comfort. Richard Rodgers' father was a doctor; Jerome Kern, Vincent Youmans, Lorenz Hart, Burton Lane and Alan Jay Lerner were the sons of well-off businessmen; Harold Arlen's father was a respected cantor; Dorothy Fields' father was the popular comedian Lew Fields, and Oscar Hammerstein II came from a famous family of theatrical impresarios. They were also well educated. Johnny Green was a banker's son who went to Harvard; Cole Porter was a playboy who went to Yale; Rodgers, Hart, Hammerstein, Howard Dietz and Arthur Schwartz all went to Columbia, and Schwartz also had a law degree. So did Hoagy Carmichael.

That America's demotic song literature sprang from such middle-class soil might seem to be a paradox. But in fact the songwriters were writing for audiences very much like themselves: men and women who loved the theater and music and language and literature. Irwin Hochsberg raised himself into that bourgeoisie by going to City College, where he and Ira Gershwin wrote light verse for the campus newspaper. After graduation he opened an electrical sup-

That E. Y. (Yip) Harburg was photographed holding a bunch of flowers seems only proper. No other lyricist had such naive faith in life's simple blessings and possibilities. He believed in the ability—and the right—of every man, woman and child to fly over the rainbow and find love in Glocca Morra.

plies business that briefly made him rich. But the 1929 crash unmade him again. "All I had left was my pencil," he said, and he decided to use it to pursue his first love: writing lyrics. He also rechristened himself. An elfin man, not unlike the leprechaun of his later musical *Finian's Rainbow*, long called Yipper, from *yipsl*, the Yiddish word for squirrel, he took Yip as his middle name to go with Edgar and Harburg and was known as E. Y. (Yip) Harburg from that time on.

In 1932 Harburg and the composer Jay Gorney wrote the score for *Americana*, a musical about "the forgotten man" and his betrayal by greedy capitalism. They caught the bitter despair of the Depression in a number sung by a man standing in a breadline. Gorney's minor-key melody, a melody of unusual dignity, made a plaintive setting for Harburg's words:

> *Once I built a railroad,*
> *Made it run,*
> *Made it race against time.*
> *Once I built a railroad,*
> *Now it's done.*
> *Brother, can you spare a dime?*

The song so lacerated the national conscience that radio stations tried to ban it; they said it was "sympathetic to the unemployed." But there was no stopping the song's momentum, especially after it was recorded by Bing Crosby. "Brother, Can You Spare a Dime?" became the anthem of the Depression and a goad to Roosevelt's New Deal. It also entered the American language as an idiom, widely borrowed by advertisers, editorial writers and cartoonists.

Seven years later Harburg would create the even more potent metaphor of journeying over the rainbow. Meanwhile he had become a poetic and often impish lyricist—he was fond of truncations like "delish"— for musicals and movies, writing such standards as "It's Only a Paper Moon" with Harold Arlen and "What Is There to Say?" and "April in Paris" with Vernon Duke. In 1937 he and Arlen wrote a particularly amiable song, "In the Shade of the New Apple Tree," for the antiwar musical *Hooray for What!*, which caught the fancy of Arthur Freed at MGM. Freed, a former songwriter himself ("Singin' in the Rain"), was trying to get himself launched as a movie producer. He persuaded Louis B. Mayer that he had found the ideal screen property, L. Frank Baum's *The Wizard of Oz*, and the ideal songwriters to catch its fairy-tale spirit.

That hunch turned out to be brilliant. No lyricist was more suited than Harburg to imagine a kingdom over the rainbow where

At a studio piano on the MGM lot, E. Y. Harburg and Harold Arlen work on the score of "The Wizard of Oz." Harburg's words for songs like "If I Only Had a Brain" were more than just lyrics. They were miniature scenes, the dramatic glue that held the movie together. The two kibitzers are columnist Sidney Skolsky and a studio official.

happy little bluebirds fly and troubles melt like lemon drops. Harburg's achievement in *The Wizard of Oz* was to write memorable lyrics to Arlen's equally memorable music ("We're Off to See the Wizard," "The Merry Old Land of Oz," "If I Only Had a Brain," "Ding-Dong, the Witch Is Dead!") that served not only as songs but as entire scenes, stitching the narrative together and making *The Wizard of Oz* the first truly integrated movie musical.

As for "Over the Rainbow," the song is so encrusted with legend—it was cut three times from *The Wizard of Oz* and restored just before the premiere, going on to win the Academy Award—and is so entwined with the career of Judy Garland, who introduced it as Dorothy when she was 15 and sang it for the rest of her life as the symbol of her own yearning for a less complicated world, that it exists as a separate force, Judy's song having also become *our* song, *our* symbol of yearning for a less complicated world.

Stripped of those accretions, "Over the Rainbow" is a marvel of both grandeur and simplicity. Arlen's audacious leap of an octave ("Some-where") sends the melody soaring over the rainbow on the first two notes. But after that it could hardly be purer: the main theme is all major intervals, with none of Arlen's usual half-tone blue notes, and the release is as guileless as a nursery rhyme in its iterations. Harburg matched the notes with the oldest kind of nurs-

"Over the Rainbow" jumps an octave on its first two notes. What could be more suggestive of the journey that Dorothy (Judy Garland) was daring to imagine and hope for? The melody came to Harold Arlen while his wife Anya was driving him along Sunset Boulevard. He told her to pull over so he could write it down.

ery images: "a land that I heard of, once in a lullaby," "the dreams that you dared to dream really do come true."

The "lemon-drop kid," as Arlen called him, really believed that the dreams that you dared to dream really do come true, and his subsequent work continued to be an amalgam of naive hope and leftist prodding. It's all there in a single couplet sung by Ethel Waters in "Happiness Is a Thing Called Joe," written with Arlen in 1943 for the all-black movie *Cabin in the Sky*:

> *Sometimes the cabin's gloomy and the table bare,*
> *Then he'll kiss me an' it's Christmas everywhere.*

Cole Porter wouldn't have written that lyric. Bare tables don't occur to songwriters born with a silver spoon.

Harburg's Broadway shows always made me a little uncomfortable. I'm wary of messages in art, and I never knew when the political Yip would elbow aside the poetical Yip. Both were strongly present in the two richly integrated musicals—*Bloomer Girl* (1944) and *Finian's Rainbow* (1947)—that climaxed his career. *Bloomer Girl*, which had a sunny score by Harold Arlen ("Right As the Rain," "Evelina"), was set in the Civil War period and inspired by the reform campaigns of the suffragette Amelia Bloomer, providing the liberal lyricist with such inviting themes as early feminism and civil rights, and Arlen wrote one of his most exuberant melodies for Harburg's lyric, "The Eagle and Me," sung by a runaway slave, affirming the need of all God's creatures to be free.

But even the gentle Arlen wearied of Harburg's insinuation of "propaganda" into his lyrics. He declined to work with him on *Finian's Rainbow*, whose eventual composer, Burton Lane, also demurred, hesitating for three months while trying to decide whether Harburg would drive him crazy. Harburg did; afterward, Lane didn't speak to him for two years. Their show, however, was a triumph. Lane composed one of the most melodic of all Broadway scores ("How Are Things in Glocca Morra?", "Look to the Rainbow," "Old Devil Moon," "If This Isn't Love"), and Harburg's lyrics were properly whimsical, befitting an Irish fable about a get-rich-quick schemer who steals a crock of gold from a leprechaun. He was at his playful best in "When I'm Not Near the Girl I Love, I Love the Girl I'm Near." But inevitably the fable of stolen gold rested on— and kept insisting on—the evils of materialism, satirized by Harburg in songs such as "When the Idle Poor Become the Idle Rich." The old socialist never stopped being true to what he believed, even when he was blacklisted by Hollywood for his political views in the McCarthyist 1950s. That was another distinction that set him apart from his fellow songwriters.

OVER THE RAINBOW

THE WIZARD OF OZ

with

JUDY GARLAND
FRANK MORGAN · RAY BOLGER
BERT LAHR · JACK HALEY
BILLIE BURKE

Photographed in TECHNICOLOR

Directed by Victor Fleming

A Metro-Goldwyn-Mayer PICTURE

Produced by Mervyn LeRoy

Lyrics by
E. Y. HARBURG

Music by
HAROLD ARLEN

SONGS:

OVER THE RAINBOW
IF I ONLY HAD A BRAIN
DING-DONG! THE WITCH IS DEAD
THE MERRY OLD LAND OF OZ
WE'RE OFF TO SEE THE WIZARD

Leo Feist inc.

1629 BROADWAY · NEW YORK

JUDY GARLAND
as Dorothy

FRANK MORGAN
as The Wizard

RAY BOLGER
as The Scarecrow

BERT LAHR
as The Cowardly Lion

JACK HALEY
as The Tin Woodman

The Songs of World War II

It's almost impossible today to imagine the emotional power that was generated by the songs of World War II. A nation that had put seven million men into uniform and sent them all over the world suddenly needed songs to express the pain of separation, and many good ones were written. Half a century later those songs still touch a nerve in any man who once heard them overseas on Armed Forces Radio or in any wife or girlfriend who listened to them on the family radio back home.

Some of them were patriotic rousers, written to celebrate heroic military feats when the war was still going badly: "Coming in on a Wing and a Prayer," "Praise the Lord and Pass the Ammunition." Some were songs of parting: "I Left My Heart at the Stage Door Canteen," "Goodbye, Mama, I'm Off to Yokohama." Some were admonitions to the girl left behind: "Don't Sit Under the Apple Tree (With Anyone Else But Me)." Some were assurances of chaste behavior by that left-behind girl:

In the stunned aftermath of Pearl Harbor, Hollywood's studios threw themselves into the war effort with patriotic extravaganzas that used every star on the lot. The first entry in this catch-all genre was Paramount's "Star Spangled Rhythm," whose expedient score by Harold Arlen and Johnny Mercer included three home-front morale builders: "Old Glory," "On the Swing Shift" and "I'm Doing It for Defense."

No love, no nothin'
Until my baby comes home,
No sir! No nothin'
As long as baby must roam.
I promised him I'd wait for him
Till even Hades froze,
I'm lonesome, heaven knows,
But what I said still goes.
No love, no nothin'
And that's a promise I'll keep,
No fun with no one,
I'm getting plenty of sleep . . .

Beneath its ostensible good cheer that song by Harry Warren and Leo Robin contains three of the dynamite words of World War II balladry—"home," "lonesome" and "promise"—as well as the potent word "sleep," which turns up repeatedly in these ballads of sexual deprivation, along with "dream" ("I'm getting tired so I can sleep, I want to sleep so I can dream . . . "). Sleep was the most common of the monastic activities that the home-front girls claimed they were practicing "for the duration." Some other occupations were cards and reading and listening to the radio. Duke Ellington's 1942 "Don't Get Around Much Anymore," lyric by Bob Russell, begins with this verse:

> *When I'm not playing solitaire*
> *I take a book down from the shelf,*
> *And what with programs on the air*
> *I keep pretty much to myself.*
> [chorus]
> *Missed the Saturday dance,*
> *Heard they crowded the floor,*
> *Couldn't bear it without you,*
> *Don't get around much anymore . . .*

Never was so much reading done by American women. "When the phone starts ringing, I just let it ring," begins the verse of "Saturday Night Is the Loneliest Night of the Week," Jule Styne and Sammy Cahn's calendar of celibate days passing slowly—a condition that wouldn't end "until I hear you at the door, until you're in my arms once more." Similar abstinences are declared at the outset of the two blockbuster "walk" songs, also composed by Jule Styne, with lyrics by, respectively, Frank Loesser and Sammy Cahn:

> *All my friends keep knocking at the door,*
> *They've asked me out a hundred times or more,*
> *But all I say is "Leave me in the gloom,"*
> *And here I stay within my lonely room, 'cause*
> [chorus] *I don't want to walk without you, baby . . .*

> *They call, no date*
> *I promised you I'd wait,*
> *I want them all to know*
> *I'm strictly single-o.*
> [chorus] *I'll walk alone . . .*

I don't remember whether my fellow GIs and I, listening to those songs in our tents in North Africa and Italy, actually believed

With Arthur Schwartz the lyricist Frank Loesser (right) wrote the only funny song about wartime deprivation, "They're Either Too Young or Too Old," in which an older woman bemoans the shortage of virile males. Loesser also wrote one of the war's most sentimental ballads, "I Don't Want to Walk Without You," and one of its military rousers, "Praise the Lord and Pass the Ammunition."

that our wives and girlfriends were spending the war alone in their room and turning away their friends at the door. But we probably *wanted* to believe it. Helen Forrest certainly sounded as if she didn't want to walk without me; Dinah Shore certainly sounded as if she wanted to walk alone. Songwriters have always made their money on idealized love, and the wartime lyricists knew better than to get real. They preserved morale among the troops by preserving the fantasy that the relationships they left behind were still intact. As Frank Loesser once explained the wartime songwriter's task, "You give them hope without facts, glory without blood."

But the most emotional songs were the cries of yearning for the day when the endless war would finally end. "You'd be so nice to come home to," wrote Cole Porter, setting the words to one of his patented minor-key melodies. "We'll meet again, don't know where, don't know when," sang the British thrush Vera Lynn, her plaintive voice a pledge to all Yanks stationed in England, "but I know we'll meet again some sunny day. Keep smiling through, just like you always do, till the blue skies drive the dark clouds far away." Many

Today it's easy to forget how long the war—especially the war in the Pacific—went badly. Songs like "Praise the Lord and Pass the Ammunition" and "Coming in on a Wing and a Prayer" had only one purpose: to lift the spirits of a worried nation and to celebrate any glimmer of hope.

Praise The Lord And Pass The Ammunition!!

Words and Music by FRANK LOESSER

FAMOUS MUSIC CORP., • 1619 BROADWAY, New York City, N. Y.

of those poignant songs were by British songwriters, pluckily looking to the future. "When the lights go on again all over the world," one of them began, leaving no doubt that the lights would indeed go on. "There'll be bluebirds over the white cliffs of Dover, tomorrow, just you wait and see," said another, its melody as pure as honey, its words promising an ever-after of love and laughter. But the ultimate tomorrow song was American-born: "I'll Be Seeing You." Written in 1938 by Sammy Fain and Irving Kahal and resuscitated during the war, it became the talisman for all separated lovers longing to see each other again "in all the old familiar places."

For me the most insistent song was "Sentimental Journey." It was played day and night at the camp outside Naples where I waited unsentimentally in the fall of 1945 for a troopship to bring me home. "Home" was the destination of the journey the singer was "gonna take." Whenever I hear it I'm back in Naples, wondering whether that ship would ever arrive. Such associations still give the songs of World War II a powerful pull.

But those songs are also remembered, I think, because they were beautiful. "I'll Walk Alone," "We'll Meet Again," "I'll Be Seeing You"—all of them were melodies with simple lines, making plain musical statements about plain emotions.

> *You'll never know just how much I miss you,*
> *You'll never know just how much I care . . .*

So began one of the most popular wartime songs. Harry Warren knew just what to do with Mack Gordon's old-fashioned declaration of love, climbing up and down the scale in triads as elementary as the thoughts being expressed. Nobody who heard the song ever forgot it.

Johnny Mercer

Johnny Mercer is America's vernacular poet. A native of Savannah, he had a sure ear for idiom, slang and regional imagery. He was hip without being cute—"Goody-Goody," "Bob White (Whatcha Gonna Swing Tonight?)"—and he was endlessly versatile. Over a 45-year career, starting in 1930, he wrote lyrics for most of America's best songwriters, in each case matching and enhancing what was distinctive about them. Here's a partial list:

Harold Arlen ("Blues in the Night," "One for My Baby," "Accentuate the Positive"), Rube Bloom ("Day In, Day Out," "Fools Rush In"), Hoagy Carmichael ("Lazybones," "Skylark," "In the Cool, Cool, Cool of the Evening"), Gene De Paul ("Namely You"), Walter Donaldson ("Mister Meadowlark"), Duke Ellington and Billy Strayhorn ("Satin Doll"), Gordon Jenkins ("P.S. I Love You"), Jerome Kern ("I'm Old-Fashioned," "Dearly Beloved"), Henry Mancini ("Moon River"), Victor Schertzinger ("I Remember You," "Tangerine," "Arthur Murray Taught Me Dancing in a Hurry"), Jimmy Van Heusen ("I Thought About You"), Harry Warren ("Jeepers Creepers," "You Must Have Been a Beautiful Baby," "On the Atchison, Topeka and the Santa Fe"), and Richard Whiting ("Hooray for Hollywood," "Too Marvelous for Words").

Add to those classics the many songs for which Mercer wrote his own music ("Dream," "G.I. Jive," "I'm an Old Cowhand," "Something's Gotta Give"). Also add all the foreign hits for which he wrote English words ("Autumn Leaves," "Summer Wind," "When the World Was Young"). Also add all the movie themes that he fitted with lyrics and thereby brought into the repertory of American song: "Days of Wine and Roses," "Charade," "Laura." By itself David Raksin's brooding *Laura* theme would only survive as an obbligato to Clifton Webb's skulduggery on the screen. Instead a girl named Laura is somewhere in the memory of anyone who ever heard the song:

No lyricist wrote as many different kinds of lyrics as Johnny Mercer or wrote with so many composers. Whoever he worked with—Harold Arlen, Hoagy Carmichael, Jerome Kern, Jimmy Van Heusen, Harry Warren— wrote a little better when his melodies were hitched to Mercer's down-home idioms and images.

157

And you see Laura
On a train that is passing through.
Those eyes, how familiar they seem . . .

Train images and rural images recur in Mercer's lyrics. Just the euphonious name of the Atchison, Topeka and the Santa Fe Railroad inspired the rousing song that Judy Garland rousingly sang in *The Harvey Girls*, which won Mercer the first of of his three Academy Awards. (The others were for "In the Cool, Cool, Cool of the Evening" and "Moon River.") Untypically, the song was about a day-time train, its newly debarked passengers wanting "lifts to Brown's Hotel," because they had been "travelin' for quite a spell, all the way from Philadelphi-ay, on the Atchison, Topeka and the Santa Fe."

Usually Mercer's trains run through the American night, generating loneliness and longing. Laura, glimpsed on a train that is passing through, is surely a night rider, and "I Thought About You" takes place entirely in a Pullman sleeper. Mercer's deceptively simple lyric, set to Jimmy Van Heusen's gentle melody, begins, "I took a trip on the train" and proceeds to mention various sights, seen from the window, that remind the singer of the girl or boy who has been left behind. The plain nouns with their small-town images—train, track, town, lane, parked cars, stars, moon, stream—carry all the pain of parting. They also remind us of what it was once like to travel in America.

But although Mercer's roots were in the South, he was nobody's rube. Humor ran through his work, and it knocked off many a pre-tender, often with a sly nudge, as in the last line of the song about the South American siren Tangerine ("Oh, she's got them all on the run, but her heart belongs to just one, her heart belongs to Tangerine"), or in the song that begins "Hooray for Hollywood! Where you're terrific if you're even good." The marvel of his lifelong achievement—650 published songs—was that he could solve every problem and adapt to every composer. I can't imagine anyone else putting coherent words to "Satin Doll." What the jazzmen Ellington and Strayhorn wrote was a series of short musical jabs that give a lyricist almost nothing to work with: five syllables, three syllables, five syllables, three syllables. What Mercer wrote was the ultimate jazz lyric:

Cigarette holder
Which wigs me,
Over her shoulder
She digs me,
Out cattin'
That satin doll.

Baby, shall we go
Out skippin'
Careful, amigo,
You're flippin'
Speaks Latin,
That satin doll . . .

Yet the same man wrote the ultimate regional lyric, "Moon River," in slow waltz time—sung by Audrey Hepburn in the movie *Breakfast at Tiffany's*—for the composer Henry Mancini, Ellington's metabolic opposite.

. . . Two drifters
Off to see the world,
There's such a lot of world to see.
We're after the same rainbow's end,
Waitin' round the bend,
My huckleberry friend,
Moon River
And me.

I don't know what a huckleberry friend is, but I think I'd like to have one, and I'm glad Mercer added it to the American language.

Mercer's words and phrases always "sang" easily because he was a great jazz singer himself; he first caught on with Paul Whiteman's band in 1930. One of the earliest of the relaxed crooners, along with Bing Crosby, he charmed radio and television audiences—and record buyers—with his Southern drawl and engaging personality; between 1938 and 1952 he had 29 hit singles. In 1942 he also co-founded Capitol Records and made it a hospitable label for good singers and musicians. Meanwhile he also wrote all those lyrics.

Harold Arlen was the composer with whom Mercer consistently did his best writing, just as it was with Mercer that Arlen did his best composing. They were from opposite ends of the cultural landscape— one Northeastern Jewish, the other Southern Episcopalian—but the sound they created together was distinctively American. In Johnny Mercer, Arlen got a lyricist whose colloquial ear and swinging rhythm were tuned to who he was. During their Hollywood collaboration in the early 1940s, Mercer found the perfect solution for whatever Arlen threw at him: the poignant "This Time the Dream's on Me," the stately "My Shining Hour," the meandering "That Old Black Magic," the easygoing "Let's Take the Long Way Home," the august "Out of This World," the bluesy "One for My Baby," the spiritual-like "Accentuate the Positive," the hip "Hit the Road to Dreamland."

It was no accident that Mercer and Arlen achieved together the two high points in their separate careers: one of the best American songs, "Blues in the Night," and one of the best Broadway scores, *St. Louis Woman*. Remembered mainly for its hit ballad, "Come Rain or Come Shine," and for two droll Pearl Bailey numbers, "A Woman's Prerogative" and "Legalize My Name," the musical was a tapestry of lullabies, cakewalks and blues ("I Had Myself a True Love," "Any Place I Hang My Hat Is Home"). Such was the surfeit of riches that the superb "I Wonder What Became of Me" was cut from the show, but it survives in the repertory of cabaret singers, a classic example of Arlen's elegant harmonic structure and Mercer's poetry of sights and sounds:

Lights are bright,
Pianos making music all the night,
And they pour champagne
Just like it was rain,
It's a sight to see,
But I wonder what became of me . . .

The talents that flowered so abundantly in *St. Louis Woman* can be traced back to the wail that was "Blues in the Night." In 1941 Arlen and Mercer were hired to write the score for a movie about an American jazz band and to include one hit song of a blues nature. "I went home and just thought about it for two days," Arlen told me. "After all, anybody can write a blues song. The hard thing is to write one that doesn't sound like every other blues song. Finally I decided to cast it in the traditional form of the early American blues: three sections of 12 bars each, not in the conventional 32-bar Tin Pan Alley shape."

He met his challenge by writing three of his most haunting melodies, then repeating the first 12 bars and adding a 4-bar coda. Mercer did the rest with nighttime rain sounds, train sounds, winds, breezes, crying trees, hiding moons, grieving mockingbirds, Southern place names and lonesome whistles, hums and "whooees." Is there a more evocative American song?

[A]
My mama done tol' me
When I was in knee pants,
My mama done tol' me, son,
A woman'll sweet talk
And give ya the big eye,
But when the sweet talkin's done

A woman's a two-face,
A worrisome thing
Who'll leave ya t'sing
The blues in the night.

Musically, that theme is not only catchy; it gets locked into the brain by the blues convention of repetition. First it's repeated twice exactly. Then it's repeated twice metrically, but with different notes ("A woman'll sweet talk, And give ya the big eye"). Then the same meter recurs once more, again with different melodic notes ("A woman's a two-face"). Then the section is satisfyingly concluded by descending to the low tonic note ("night"). Lyrically, "sweet talk" and "two-face" are gaudy idioms, and "worrisome" may be the best thing in the whole song.

[B]
Now the rain's a fallin',
Hear the train a-callin'
Whoo-ee,
(My mama done tol' me),
Hear that lonesome whistle
Blowin' 'cross the trestle,
Whoo-ee,
(My mama done tol' me),
A whooee-duh-whooee,
Ol' clickety-clack's
A-echoin' back
The blues in the night.

Musically, the song breaks out of the tight blues format and begins to swoop and soar in sorrowful cadences. Lyrically, nobody ever wrote 12 better bars. Listen to all those heartbreaking sounds.

[C]
The evenin' breeze'll start
The trees to cryin'
And the moon'll hide its light
When you get the blues in the night.
Take my word, the mocking bird'll
Sing the saddest kind of song,
He knows things are wrong,
And he's right. [whistle]

Musically, that's Arlen at his bluest—all those seventh chords straining and resolving into each other. Lyrically, I especially like the

Humor was a strong current in Mercer's lyrics. It was also part of his personality as one of the best popular singers of his generation. The writer of "Pardon My Southern Accent" didn't mind putting his easy-going drawl to use. It helped to give him 29 hit singles and make him a household favorite on radio and television.

mockingbird who is right for knowing things are wrong. Unlike all those dumb birds in Hoagy Carmichael songs, this one is advancing the plot.

[A]
From Natchez to Mobile,
From Memphis to St. Jo,
Wherever the four winds blow,
I've been in some big towns
An' heard me some big talk,
But there is one thing I know,
A woman's a two-face,
A worrisome thing
Who'll leave ya t'sing
The blues in the night. [hum]

Musically, that's a classic blues recapitulation. Lyrically, the first three lines are pure American poetry, so representative of all the pleasure Mercer has given me that I'll leave the final words to him:

[Coda]
My mama was right,
There's blues in the night.

Laura

Featured by FREDDY MARTIN and his Orchestra

Lyric by JOHNNY MERCER
Music by DAVID RAKSIN

Theme melody from the
20th CENTURY-FOX PICTURE
"LAURA" featuring GENE TIERNEY

ROBBINS MUSIC CORPORATIO

Made in Hollywood: "As Time Goes By" and "Laura"

Probably no popular American song carries such strong associations for so many people as "As Time Goes By." Those emotions have nothing to do with real life: the memory of a college prom or a broken romance. The song takes its resonance solely from its use in *Casablanca*—a movie made more than 50 years ago. In that triangular romance of World War II the song isn't merely played and sung by the pianist Dooley Wilson. It keeps returning as a leitmotif, so suggestively serving the purposes of flashback and narrative, of love remembered and love renounced, that it has become a character in the film, as memorable as Humphrey Bogart, Ingrid Bergman, Claude Rains, Peter Lorre and the other usual suspects.

Herman Hupfeld had no such visions of eternal life for "As Time Goes By" when he wrote it for a 1931 Broadway musical called *Everybody's Welcome*. He was a type familiar to us from the literature of small-town America: the gifted boy who lives with his mother all his life and dies on the same street where he was born. The town was Montclair, New Jersey, and Hupfeld was a piecework provider of specialty songs for Broadway musicals that had a hole to fill. I remember several from my own boyhood: "Sing Something Simple," "When Yuba Plays the Rhumba on the Tuba," "Let's Put Out the Lights and Go to Sleep." In the case of "As Time Goes By," Hupfeld gave the show its hit. It was sung by Frances Williams, who also made a record of it, as did Rudy Vallee, conferring on the song a brief moment of fame.

So fetching was Miss Williams' record that a Cornell student named Murray Burnett fell in love with it—or, it would seem, with

David Raksin's haunting background theme for the mysteriously missing Laura (Gene Tierney) became a huge commercial hit when Johnny Mercer later set it to an evocative lyric.

Miss Williams—and played it more often than his roommates thought necessary. But all that repetition would linger. In 1938 Burnett took a trip to Europe that left him stunned by the Nazi harassment of Vienna's Jews and their sudden vulnerability. On the way home he happened to visit a bar in France that had an exotic clientele and a black man playing the piano. Back in New York, he wrote his impressions into a play set in French North Africa called *Everybody Goes to Rick's*, which Warner Brothers would buy to make into *Casablanca*. The script specifies that when Ilsa first comes into Rick's bar she asks the black piano player to play "As Time Goes By."

In that golden age of Hollywood production all the studios had eminent staff composers—Franz Waxman, Erich Korngold, Alfred Newman, Hugo Friedhofer, Bronislaw Kaper, Dimitri Tiomkin— who were kings of the background score, their lush themes grandly

From the Warner Bros. picture "CASABLANCA"

AS TIME GOES BY

Words and Music by HERMAN HUPFELD A.S.C.A.P.

WARNER BROS. PICTURES, INC. PRESENTS

Humphrey BOGART *Ingrid* BERGMAN *Paul* HENREID

IN

"CASABLANCA"

A HAL B. WALLIS PRODUCTION
A WARNER BROS.-FIRST NATIONAL PICTURE

manipulative of the emotions of moviegoers watching grand passions on the screen. None was more esteemed than Max Steiner, whom Jack Warner signed for *Casablanca*. Steiner had scored more than 300 movies, including *Gone With the Wind*, for which he wrote well over three hours of music. His most recent score, for Bette Davis' renunciatory *Now, Voyager*, had won the Academy Award, its theme becoming a song called "It Can't Be Wrong."

That was a common birthing sequence for Hollywood songs, and the studio composers were proud of their ability to create themes that could be converted into pop ballads. One of the most famous of those hits, "Laura," almost didn't get born. Otto Preminger, the film's notoriously autocratic director, told the composer David Raksin that he wanted to use Duke Ellington's "Sophisticated Lady" for the theme that establishes the character of Laura (Gene Tierney) while detective Dana Andrews combs her apartment for clues to her apparent death. Preminger said he thought of Laura as somewhat wanton and promiscuous. Raksin disagreed—and not just because Hollywood composers don't like to have other people's songs foisted onto their score. He told Preminger that "Sophisticated Lady" was totally wrong for *Laura*: "It has nothing to do with your movie." Preminger, unaccustomed to mutinous behavior, said, "This is Friday. Come in Monday with something you like better. Otherwise we use 'Sophisticated Lady.'"

"All weekend I struggled with the idea," Raksin recalled many years later. "Ordinarily, music flies out of me in all directions, but this time I was tied up in knots, in trouble emotionally and out of touch with myself." He had just received an unwelcome letter from his wife and had put it in his pocket to avoid dealing with it. By Sunday night, he said, "I knew my big chance was fading fast: I didn't really believe in any of the themes I had written. As a boy, when the music wouldn't flow, I would prop a book or a poem on the piano and improvise. The idea was to divert my mind from the conscious awareness of music-making. I hadn't done that for a long time, but I took the letter out of my pocket, put it up on the piano and began to play.

"Suddenly the meaning of the words on the page became clear to me. She was saying: Hail, farewell, better luck next life—and get lost! Knowing that, I felt the last of my strength go, and then, without willing it, I was playing the first phrase of what you now know as 'Laura.' I knew it was the real thing, and I stumbled through it again and again in a sweat of catharsis and self-indulgence." Johnny Mercer would later add the lyric that made it a commercial song. (Raksin's theme for *The Bad and the Beautiful* is another Hollywood gem.)

In *Casablanca* Max Steiner was offered no such escape. He didn't much like "As Time Goes By" and didn't want it in his movie, but Jack Warner did, and it was also an element in the script. Stuck with the song, Steiner accepted his fate with remarkable charity, painting the song in many colors and weaving it through a score that also included "The Marseillaise," "Watch on the Rhine" and scraps of American standards like "It Had to Be You" and "Avalon," which symbolized Rick's cafe as an American haven in a world falling apart. "As Time Goes By" duly became a hit when the movie was released in 1942, achieving its second moment of fame—and, anyone might have thought, its last.

But nothing connected with *Casablanca* was orthodox, starting with its makeshift creation. The mystery of its excellence—that a film so unified, so sensitively tuned to the patriotic needs and political nuances of the early war years, emerged from such a haphazard process—has been explored in many books and academic journals. Seven writers ultimately worked on the script, rewriting it from day to day during production, still undecided on how it would end. Ingrid Bergman kept asking director Michael Curtiz which man she was supposed to be in love with. He couldn't tell her. Bogart's last line, "Louis, I think this is the beginning of a beautiful friendship," wasn't written until after the shooting was over and the cast had flown. Bogart was called back to the studio to dub it.

The canonization of the movie was equally unpremeditated, the last lucky accident. Not long after Humphrey Bogart died in 1957, crossing over into culthood himself, an art cinema near Harvard Yard, the Brattle Theater, started holding Bogart festivals, which always ended with *Casablanca*. Harvard students began to attend the movie with ritual frequency, seeing it again and again, speaking the lines along with the actors, and rising to sing "The Marseillaise." From Harvard the worship of Bogart and his alter ego Rick fanned out to other campuses, gradually becoming an object of cultural homage (Woody Allen's *Play It Again, Sam*) and scholarly exegesis, each new college generation finding in the Bogartian themes of honor and resistance some allegory for its own needs in a world no less fluid and complex than Rick's. Since the mid-1970s *Casablanca* has been the most popular film shown on television; four of its lines have made it into *Bartlett's Familiar Quotations*.

But the glue holding it together is "As Time Goes By." For more than half a century Herman Hupfeld's song has reinforced the movie and the movie has reinforced the song—twin icons, joined at the hip. It isn't really a very good song; jazz musicians seldom play it except when someone asks for it. They don't like it much more than Max Steiner did. Melodically it's inert, lyrically it's platitudinous. But emotionally it's off the charts.

Kurt Weill
(and Ira Gershwin and Vernon Duke)

I didn't know anything about the composer Kurt Weill when I went to see the new hit musical *Lady in the Dark* in 1941. I knew about the lyricist, Ira Gershwin, finally back at work after several years of stunned inactivity following the death of his brother George. I knew about the librettist, Moss Hart, finally on his own after writing all those hilarious plays like *You Can't Take It With You* and *The Man Who Came to Dinner* with George S. Kaufman, and I knew about the star, Gertrude Lawrence. But I had never heard of Kurt Weill. I had also never heard of Victor Mature. Or Danny Kaye.

Mature was making his Broadway debut, fresh from Hollywood success as the hunter Tumak in *One Million B.C.*—a role that brought "hunk" into the American language. In *Lady in the Dark*, as a movie star wooing Gertrude Lawrence, he was described to her as "the most beautiful hunk of man you ever saw," and when he appeared, clad in pink circus tights and leopard-skin briefs, he didn't disappoint. Mature's more modest opinion of himself, over a long film career in which he played the Sioux warrior in *Chief Crazy Horse* and pulled down the temple of Solomon in Cecil B. De Mille's *Samson and Delilah*, would enable him to triumph over all the early tittering. Rejected for membership by the Los Angeles Country Club because it didn't take actors, he said: "Hell, I'm no actor, and I've got 28 pictures and a scrapbook of reviews to prove it."

Danny Kaye, also making his Broadway debut in *Lady in the Dark*, was a no less remarkable force of nature. Playing a circus ringmaster and other antic roles, he stopped the show near the end—the applause was long and incredulous, and Gertrude Lawrence was seriously displeased—with an Ira Gershwin number

Kurt Weill and his wife, the singer Lotte Lenya, came to America in the mid-1930s. An influential composer in Germany after World War I, Weill re-established himself as a major composer for the American musical theater, and Lenya starred in a long-running English-language version of their German hit, "Die Dreigroschenoper" ("The Three-Penny Opera").

171

called "Tschaikowsky," in which he sang the names of 49 Russian composers in 39 seconds:

> There's Malichevsky, Rubinstein, Arensky and Tschaikowsky,
> Sapelnikoff, Dimitrieff, Tscherepnin, Kryjanowksy,
> Godowsky, Arteiboucheff, Moniuszko, Akimenko,
> Solovieff, Prokofieff, Tiomkin, Korestchenko.
> There's Glinka, Winkler, Bortniansky, Rebikoff, Ilyinksy.
> There's Medtner, Balakireff, Zolotareff and Kvoschinsky,
> And Sokoloff and Kopyloff, Dukelsky and Klenowsky,
> And Shostakovich, Borodin, Gliere and Nowakofski.
> There's Liadoff and Karganoff, Markievitch, Pantschenko,
> And Dargomyzski, Stcherbatcheff, Scriabin, Vassilenko,
> Stravinsky, Rimsky-Korsakoff, Mussorgsky and Gretchaninoff,
> And Glazounoff and Caesar Cui, Kalinikoff, Rachmaninoff,
>   Stravinsky and Gretchaninoff,
>   Rumshinky and Rachmaninoff,
> I really have to stop, the subject has been dwelt upon enough!

Sharp-eyed observers of that Slavic soup will recognize two composers who left their imprint on American popular culture. Dimitri Tiomkin, one of many conservatory-trained Russians who found employment in Hollywood, composed more than 60 movie scores, most famously the Academy Award-winning theme for *High Noon* ("Do not forsake me, oh my darling"), Gary Cooper's only companion as he waits in stoic solitude for the three baddies to arrive on the midday train. Vladimir Dukelsky brought with him from Russia a melodic gift that caught the ear of his new American friend George Gershwin. Gershwin urged him to write theater songs and popular songs and to use the name Vernon Duke. That advice would result in some of our most urbane standards—"April in Paris," "I Can't Get Started," "Autumn in New York," "What Is There to Say?", "I Like the Likes of You"—and the Broadway score *Cabin in the Sky*, in which Ethel Waters sang the graceful title song and "Taking a Chance on Love."

As for Danny Kaye, he didn't stay a novice for long; Cole Porter grabbed him to be the star of his new musical, *Let's Face It*. That show revealed his boundless talents as an entertainer and propelled him into a movie career that lasted well into the 1970s. Watching him now on late-night TV, I wonder if we ever fully appreciated what a good singer and dancer he was—on a par with Fred Astaire and Gene Kelly and the most effortlessly nimble of the three; with his elongated legs he seems to be dancing on air. But he never forgot the number that made him famous, often singing "Tschaikowsky" for children on his many world tours for the United Nations Children's Emergency Fund. Once, in Barcelona, he announced that he was going to try for a new record and brought the song in at 36 seconds. Later, in Madrid, he was timed at 31.

Lady in the Dark, which ran for 467 performances, is almost alone among American musical theater classics in being an original, not derived from an existing book or play. The only other one I can think of is Meredith Willson's *The Music Man*. Historically, from *Show Boat* to *Oklahoma!*, from *Carousel* to *South Pacific* to *The King and I*, from *Kiss Me, Kate* to *West Side Story*, from *Guys and Dolls* to *My Fair Lady*, from *Cabaret* to *Gypsy* to *Fiddler on the Roof*, the great musicals have been based on stories that had already proved their appeal. *Lady in the Dark* is also the only great musical that has never had a major revival in this country. (There was one recent revival in England.) Perhaps, with its three elaborate dream sequences, the show is too technically complex. Or maybe its subject, psychoanalysis, is to blame; Dr. Freud's method, like the doctor himself, has steadily lost favor.

But in 1941 it was revolutionary. Shrinks were the new craze, the lifeblood of cocktail party conversation, and for Moss Hart to address that clinical experience seriously in a musical was audacious. (This was two years before *Oklahoma!* gave musicals tacit permission to move beyond romantic fluff.) Hart's libretto was about a glamorous and seemingly successful fashion-magazine editor named Liza Elliott (Gertrude Lawrence), who, as we learn when she starts seeing a psychoanalyst, is immobilized by doubts and fears going back to her childhood. Those sessions with her analyst, delving into her subconscious mind, come to life in three mini-operas that Kurt Weill and Ira Gershwin lodged within the larger show.

I still remember those brilliant dream sequences. I had never seen such an imaginative fusion of all the theatrical arts: revolving stages and sets, surrealistic lighting, glittering costumes, fairy-tale lyrics, mood-altering melodies and orchestrations. Weill's score was what made it all work. The straight ballads like "This Is New" were the solid fare of Broadway musical theater, but the dream numbers had a mysterious quality, perfect for Gershwin's fantasy words in which an adoring public dotes on Liza Elliott or she sings her own fantasies of being adored:

> *Huxley wants to dedicate his book to me*
> *And Stravinsky his latest sonata,*
> *Seven thousand students say they look to me*

THIS IS NEW
Sam H. Harris presents
Gertrude Lawrence in
Lady in the Dark
by
Moss Hart
music by
Kurt Weill
lyrics by
Ira Gershwin
PRICE
60¢
Production by
HASSARD SHORT
Musical Direction by
MAURICE ABRAVANEL
ONE LIFE TO LIVE
MY SHIP
THIS IS NEW
THE PRINCESS OF PURE DELIGHT
GIRL OF THE MOMENT
JENNY
TSCHAIKOWSKY
CHAPPELL
& CO · INC ·
RKO BUILDING
ROCKEFELLER
CENTER · N · Y · C
CHAPPELL
& CO · LTD · LONDON
MADE IN U · S · A

To be at the Yale-Harvard regatta.
Epstein says I simply have to pose for him,
No refusing these artistic ultimata,
Dupont wants me wearing the new hose for him,
Oh how thrilling to be the world's inamorata!

Liza's cure hinges on recalling the words to a tune from her childhood, which she hums for the psychiatrist and which Weill weaves through the score in disturbing, unresolved harmonies. When she finally remembers the song, "My Ship," Weill replaces the haunting harmonies with major chords, and Liza emerges from her depression to sing the sunny, child-like lyrics. "My Ship" is one of Weill's purest melodies, a durable American standard.

That Kurt Weill could reinvent himself as a popular American songwriter in the second half of his life was a feat of cultural adaptation. Born to Jewish parents in Dessau in 1900 and schooled in classical composition and conducting, he became one of Germany's most influential modern composers in the 1920s. Together with the ironic left-wing poet Bertolt Brecht, he composed the socially activist operas—especially *Mahagonny* and *Die Dreigroschenoper*—that made his reputation and that of his wife, the sandpaper-voiced singer and actress Lotte Lenya. Three decades later *Die Dreigroschenoper* (*The Three-Penny Opera*) and its sardonic song "Mack the Knife," adapted by Marc Blitzstein, would run for seven years in an off-Broadway theater, with Lenya as its star. "Mack the Knife" would also give Louis Armstrong his most improbable hit.

Weill's music from that early European period can't be mistaken for anyone else's. With its deliberately tinny jazz rhythms and astringent harmonies, it reflected the cynical mood of post-World War I Germany—an era that the later American musical *Cabaret* would catch in all its nihilism and foreboding. In 1933 Weill fled Germany with Lenya and made his way to the United States. Starting over, he composed an antiwar musical called *Johnny Johnson*, with Paul Green, for the leftist Group Theatre. Then he put social protest behind him and teamed with the playwright Maxwell Anderson on a romantic musical about early New York, *Knickerbocker Holiday*, which gave him his first American hit, "September Song." Memorably sung by Walter Huston as the aging Peter Stuyvesant, it seemed to be a simple 32-bar ballad. But there was no escaping the Weill tinge of desolation. It came in the very first bar:

Refrain (*with expression*)

But it's a long, long while From May to De - cem - ber,—

The C-minor chord that falls on "long, long while" is as bleak as the days that dwindle down to a precious few for an old man in love with a young girl.

Weill was eager to collaborate with the best American writers and to develop an American voice as a musical theater composer. Working with Ira Gershwin on *Lady in the Dark* hastened that process, and he went on to compose excellent songs with various homegrown lyricists, especially the popular standard "Speak Low," with Ogden Nash, for *One Touch of Venus*. Some others were "Here I'll Stay" and "Green-up Time," with Alan Jay Lerner, for *Love Life*, and "Stay Well," "Lost in the Stars" and "The Little Gray House," with Maxwell Anderson, for *Lost in the Stars* (1949), a musical play based on Alan Paton's best-selling novel about a black minister's son in Johannesburg who accidentally kills a white man. It was to be Weill's last Broadway score, its rueful melodies well matched with Paton's somber story of failed racial dreams in South Africa.

But for me all the old and new Kurt Weills came together most emotionally in *Street Scene* (1947), an opera full of soaring solos, duets and vocal ensembles, derived from Elmer Rice's Pulitzer Prize winning play about Manhattan tenement life, which is now in the repertory of the New York City Opera. At the time of Weill's sudden early death at the age of fifty, in 1950, he was starting on a musical based on the most American of novels, *Huckleberry Finn*.

Ira Gershwin worked with Weill on two other ambitious shows: a Broadway musical play about Benvenuto Cellini, *The Firebrand of Florence*, and a Hollywood film, *Where Do We Go From Here?*, in which music and lyrics told the story in extended opera-like episodes, one of them lasting 12 minutes, the longest such sequence in Hollywood history. Both were box-office disasters. Two other movie scores were kinder to his songs. "Long Ago and Far Away," written with Jerome Kern for *Cover Girl*, became the biggest single hit he ever had in one year, with sheet music sales of 600,000, and "The Man That Got Away," written with Harold

Ira Gershwin was Kurt Weill's lyricist for an ambitious movie musical as well as for Broadway's "Lady in the Dark." Here he works on his last score, the film "A Star Is Born," starring Judy Garland and a song (music by Harold Arlen) about a man that got away.

Arlen for *A Star Is Born*, gave Judy Garland one of the biggest hits *she* ever had.

Ira didn't appreciate the movie reviewers who improved his English and referred to "the man who got away." The only men who get away, he said, are criminals. He understood that just as fishermen weep for the one that got away, so would a jilted woman. The lyricist responsible for bringing the fresh air of American idiom into American popular song in the 1920s knew that kind of thing in his bones.

Rodgers & Hammerstein

In March of 1943 I began tracking the out-of-town fortunes of a new Theatre Guild musical called *Away We Go!* Some of the Broadway kibitzers who attended the tryouts in New Haven and Boston urged the Guild to close the show. They said it was too staid and too square—too different from what audiences expected and wanted a musical to be. It didn't even have a chorus line. No legs, no chance.

But it was Richard Rodgers' first collaboration with his new lyricist, Oscar Hammerstein II, and anything Rodgers wrote I wanted to hear. I went around to the St. James Theater and bought two tickets for the matinee that would follow the show's opening night on Broadway—there was no line at the box office—and I asked my mother if she would like to go along. We wouldn't be having another outing soon; I had a date with the army a few days later. I warned her that we might be in for a dud.

During its Boston run the show made some alterations, changed its name to *Oklahoma!* and opened to reviews so ecstatic that it stayed at the St. James for almost six years. We saw the second of those 2,212 performances. This time there was a line at the box office.

I've never forgotten the overwhelming freshness of that matinee. Until then I hadn't heard a note of the Rodgers & Hammerstein score, which, overnight, would be played and sung everywhere, part of the acoustical backdrop of the war years. One after another, the sparkling songs—"People Will Say We're in Love," "The Surrey With the Fringe on Top," "Many a New Day," "Out of My Dreams," "Kansas City," "I Cain't Say No," "Oklahoma!"—cascaded over me, starting with "Oh, What a Beautiful Mornin'," sung with utmost simplicity by Alfred Drake as the cowboy Curley,

Richard Rodgers and his new lyricist Oscar Hammerstein II began their groundbreaking collaboration with "Oklahoma!" in 1943. Hammerstein would write the lyrics first, at his farm in Pennsylvania, and Rodgers would then set them to music, reversing the order he had used with Lorenz Hart. The result was a more spacious musical voice.

standing alone on the stage. Were these people really letting just one actor kick off a musical?

From that revolutionary beginning *Oklahoma!* continued to break the old musical comedy conventions. The book faithfully adhered to Lynn Riggs' play about cowboys and homesteading farmers, *Green Grow the Lilacs*; the songs delved into character and advanced the plot ("Pore Jud Is Dead," "Lonely Room"), and the ambivalence of the heroine Laurey was resolved in a dream ballet choreographed by Agnes De Mille. The fact that De Mille had been recruited from the Olympian slopes of classical dance was hailed as a daring departure, though Rodgers himself had broken that barrier seven years earlier, in *On Your Toes*, by composing "Slaughter on Tenth Avenue" for a cops-and-robbers ballet choreographed by George Balanchine. But it was *Oklahoma!* that made ballet acceptable—and commercially popular—on Broadway, pioneering for choreographers like Jerome Robbins (*West Side Story*), Michael Kidd (*Guys and Dolls*) and Bob Fosse (*The Pajama Game*) a golden era of dance in the musical theater.

Oklahoma! became the musical theater's second redefining event. Like *Show Boat*, it set a higher standard for the form, opening the door for all the mature and intelligent musicals that were to follow, from *Bloomer Girl* and *Finian's Rainbow* to *Gypsy*, *Fiorello!* and *My Fair Lady*. Hammerstein, however, didn't rest easy in his triumph. A modest man, well aware that the gods of Broadway are capricious, he took an end-of-the-year ad in *Variety* that said:

Holiday Greetings

OSCAR HAMMERSTEIN, II

author of

Sunny River
(Six Weeks at the St. James Theatre, New York)

Very Warm For May
(Seven Weeks at the Alvin Theatre, New York)

Three Sisters
(Six Weeks at the Drury Lane, London)

Ball At The Savoy
(Five Weeks at the Drury Lane, London)

Free For All
(Three Weeks at the Manhattan Theatre, New York)

✦ ✦ ✦ ✦ ✦ ✦

I'VE DONE IT BEFORE AND I CAN DO IT AGAIN

He needn't have worried. *Oklahoma!* was only the first step in a journey of tremendous growth for Rodgers and Hammerstein. The new emperors of Broadway didn't sit contented on the throne. In their next four shows—*Carousel* (1945), *Allegro* (1947), *South Pacific* (1949) and *The King and I* (1951)—they continued to expand the possibilities of the musical. Except in the case of *Allegro*, an original Hammerstein libretto, they worked from material so seemingly unsuitable that the choice always took old theater hands by surprise. *Carousel*, derived from Ferenc Molnar's gloomy play *Liliom*, had a hero who gets killed in the first act. *South Pacific* was pieced out of James Michener's disconnected tales of World War II in the Pacific, and *The King and I* was made from Margaret Landon's book, *Anna and the King of Siam*, whose hero, an Asian monarch unattainable by the heroine, dies at the end.

In telling those stories Rodgers and Hammerstein further dared to confront "forbidden" interracial themes and to use methods that were innovative for their time: the eight-minute "Soliloquy" in *Carousel*; the casting of the Metropolitan Opera basso Ezio Pinza as the French planter Emile de Becque in *South Pacific*; the allegorical "Uncle Tom's Cabin" ballet in *The King and I*. The result was that they deepened the original book or play—they didn't just decorate it with songs—and created a vibrant new work of art. *The King and I* is far more moving than *Anna and the King of Siam* because the addition of music and lyrics and dance turned up the emotional voltage. "Shall We Dance?" is the most electrifying moment in all Rodgers & Hammerstein musicals: a Siamese king and an English governess dance the mutual attraction that they can't declare even to each other. It's a love scene without the usual assertions of love.

Richard Rodgers found a new voice when he began working with Hammerstein. Their output would also include the Broadway shows *Me and Juliet* (1953), *Pipe Dream* (1955), *Flower Drum Song* (1958) and *The Sound of Music* (1959), the movie *State Fair* (1945), and the TV musical *Cinderella* (1957). His melodies often turned stately ("Some Enchanted Evening," "We Kiss in a Shadow"), or grandiose ("Bali Ha'i," "If I Loved You"), or pretentious ("You'll Never Walk Alone," "Climb Every Mountain"). Partly this was because he was now setting tunes to Hammerstein's lyrics, reversing the order he used with Lorenz Hart. Pre-written lyrics can do that to a composer, suggesting melodies different from the ones he might have created on his own; nothing that Rodgers wrote with Hammerstein reminds me of anything he wrote with Hart. A lyricist's words, however, can also inspire. Hammerstein's lilting lyric for "It Might As Well Be Spring," from *State Fair*, led Rodgers by the hand to one of his most delicate melodies.

But another reason for the serious new voice was that Rodgers was now composing musical plays, not musical comedies. It was as if he had been waiting all his life for someone to give him real characters to write for, and he threw himself into telling their stories, tapping a deeper vein than he had found with Hart. (Perhaps the only figure who was more than cardboard in all the Rodgers & Hart musicals was the heel Joey in *Pal Joey*.) Now the ambitious melodies came flooding out: the "Soliloquy" written for the circus barker Billy Bigelow in *Carousel* as he faces the prospect of fatherhood; "I'm in Love With a Wonderful Guy," written for the navy nurse Nellie Forbush in *South Pacific* who was "as corny as Kansas in August," and "This Nearly Was Mine," written for the French planter who thought he had lost her; "Hello, Young Lovers," written for Anna in *The King and I*, who once had a love of her own, and many more. Rodgers obviously loved writing music for those people.

Explaining how Rodgers differed in that respect from other songwriters, Oscar Hammerstein said: "All composers have a reservoir of melodies which come to them at different times and which they write down in a sketchbook. When they start work on a new musical, they play over these melodies for their collaborator, and it is decided which ones can be used. Dick Rodgers, however, does not work in this way. He writes music only for a specific purpose. Ideas for tunes seldom come to him while he is walking down the street or riding in taxicabs, and he doesn't rush to his piano very often to write a tune just for the sake of writing a tune. I don't think either Dick or I would be very successful as popular songwriters—writers of songs detached from plays. We can write words and music best when they are required by a situation or a characterization in a story."

I don't like Rodgers & Hammerstein songs as much as I like Rodgers & Hart songs. The music is a little too middle-aged, the lyrics a little too Hallmark; I miss the wit and the youthful buoyancy of the earlier partnership. But it's a no less remarkable body of work. Hammerstein had no yen to be Hart—he also was as corny as Kansas in August, and that was his strength. He wrote out of who he was and what he believed; his lyrics have absolute integrity. Rodgers' new melodies were no less sincerely felt. The waltzes continued to soar like nobody else's ("Out of My Dreams," the *Carousel* waltzes, "My Favorite Things"), and here and there, amid all the heavy lifting, an old-fashioned zinger in 2/4 time ("There Is Nothing Like a Dame") served notice that the young man who lit up Broadway in *The Garrick Gaieties* was still alive and well.

Rodgers and Hammerstein's only movie score was for "State Fair," in 1945. Besides "It Might As Well Be Spring," wistfully sung by Jeanne Crain from an upstairs window, it included the ballad "That's for Me" and one of Rodgers' soaring waltzes, "A Grand Night for Singing."

That kid came back for an encore in the first show Rodgers composed after Hammerstein died: *No Strings*, in 1962, for which he wrote his own lyrics. I went to the out-of-town tryout, eager to hear my first Rodgers & Rodgers songs, and when "The Sweetest Sounds" jumped out of the unpretentious score I almost jumped out of my seat. Where did that stunning melody come from? It was still another Richard Rodgers, younger than springtime.

Today his music is played more than that of any other American songwriter. Turn on any car radio, stroll through any mall or airport, listen to any jazz singer or pianist—you'll soon hear a Rodgers song.

Have Yourself A Merry Little Christmas

Words and Music by HUGH MARTIN and RALPH BLANE

M-G-M's
Meet Me in St. Louis
STARRING
JUDY GARLAND
WITH
MARGARET O'BRIEN

MARY ASTOR • LUCILLE BREMER • TOM DRAKE • MARJORIE MAIN

Photographed in TECHNICOLOR   A METRO-GOLDWYN-MAYER PICTURE

Directed by VINCENTE MINNELLI   Produced by ARTHUR FREED

Leo Feist inc.

Singers of the Song

Hugh Martin and Ralph Blane, who first made their name on Broadway with the genial musical *Best Foot Forward* ("Buckle Down, Winsocki!", "Every Time"), wrote three superior songs in 1944 for the movie *Meet Me in St. Louis*. "The Trolley Song," "The Boy Next Door" and "Have Yourself a Merry Little Christmas" were principal players in the film, contributing to its turn-of-the-century charm. But we remember them because they were memorably sung by Judy Garland, the last two with her trademark wistfulness. "Have Yourself a Merry Little Christmas," a major-scale melody of fierce purity, is, in the context of the story, enormously sad.

Without singers there would be no song, and Judy Garland was one of the great deliverers of what the great craftsmen wrote, starting at the age of 15 with the movie *Broadway Melody of 1938*, in which she sang "You Made Me Love You (I Didn't Want to Do It)" to a photograph of Clark Gable, and ending in 1954 with "The Man That Got Away" in *A Star Is Born*. When I watch her old movies today—Judy and Fred Astaire, for instance, singing and hoofing to Irving Berlin's "A Couple of Swells" in *Easter Parade*—I marvel not only at the voice and the diction and the phrasing, but at Garland the total professional. She moves and dances as well as she sings. Above all, she works very hard; nobody is more endearingly committed to putting over whatever material she has been given.

When great singers introduce a song they often take such authoritative possession of it that it can never really belong to anyone else. Just as Judy Garland owns "Over the Rainbow" (*The Wizard of Oz*), Ethel Merman owns "There's No Business Like Show Business" (*Annie Get Your Gun*), Gertrude Lawrence owns "Hello, Young Lovers" (*The King and I*), Julie Andrews owns "I Could Have Danced All Night" (*My Fair Lady*), Vivian Blaine owns "Adelaide's Lament" (*Guys and Dolls*), Joel Grey owns "Wilkommen" (*Cabaret*) and Barbra Streisand owns "People" (*Funny Girl*). I'm

Hugh Martin and Ralph Blane's Christmas song still comes calling every December, part of the seasonal landscape of our lives. But it was Judy Garland who established it as an icon, just as she had with "Over the Rainbow." Judy was one of the great ladies who could fix a song in America's collective memory. Some others were Ella, Ethel and Barbra.

stuck with the stamp of the singer's personality on the song as I first encountered it. When I hear "One for My Baby (and One More for the Road)" I picture Fred Astaire closing the bar ("It's quarter to three") in the movie *The Sky's the Limit*, kicking away not only his blues but all the martini glasses on the shelves. But I'm aware that Frank Sinatra sings it just as well, if not better. It's a saloon song, and Frank is the ultimate saloon singer.

Most people of a certain age first heard the hit songs of their era on the radio or on a record. I didn't happen to be a radio listener or a record buyer; the big band sound that intoxicated my generation left me sober. I learned the songs mostly by seeing the musicals and movies they were written for. When my friends reminisce about old hits, I'm struck by what different routes we took to the same literature. "That's a Jo Stafford song," they say, or "Peggy Lee did that with Benny Goodman," or "Remember the Helen Forrest record?" Their memories are a roll call of great bandleaders (Tommy Dorsey, Glenn Miller, Harry James, Artie Shaw, Kay Kyser, Woody Herman) and great arrangers (Fletcher Henderson, Paul Weston, Nelson Riddle) and great vocalists: Bing Crosby, Billie Holiday, Nat King Cole, Maxine Sullivan, Dinah Shore, Dick Haymes, Connie Boswell, Helen O'Connell, Helen Ward, Margaret Whiting, the Mills Brothers, the Andrews Sisters, the Ink Spots, Anita O'Day, Fran Warren, Bob Eberly, Patti Page, Billy Eckstine, Sylvia Syms, Louis Armstrong, Vic Damone, Steve Lawrence, Bobby Darin, Johnny Mathis, Julius La Rosa, Ray Charles, Johnny Mercer, Dean Martin, Perry Como . . . Each of them brought something distinctive to the songs they sang, and that's what is still remembered.

My own interest wasn't in the jazz singers, but in the cabaret singers—Lee Wiley, Mabel Mercer, Bobby Short—who took as their repertory the overlooked show tunes and the art songs of composers like Alec Wilder ("While We're Young") and Bart Howard ("Fly Me to the Moon") and handled the lyric with immaculate care. I thought of jazz and popular song as dwelling in different rooms. Then, in 1956, with "The Cole Porter Song Book" (two LPs, 32 songs), Ella Fitzgerald broke down the walls. Until then she had been mainly identified with swing tunes, bebop numbers and scat novelties. The Porter album, a stunning revelation of her intelligence and breadth, was followed by the "Song Books" of George and Ira Gershwin (five LPs, 53 songs), Irving Berlin, Harold Arlen, Rodgers & Hart, Jerome Kern, Johnny Mercer and Duke Ellington. When she was finished, in 1964, the giant songwriters had their definitive reference shelf. "I never knew how good our songs were," Ira Gershwin said, "until I heard Ella Fitzgerald sing them."

What she brought to that literature was not only the flexibility of an African-American jazz singer, but an understanding of what the songs were saying, both musically and lyrically. Her voice wasn't merely her instrument; her voice was *herself*, and she used it with the joy that was part of her character, making even the sad numbers seem to be not the end of the world. Often her choice of tempo and style came as a surprise to those of us who thought we knew the songs well. But the choice always seemed exactly right.

There's no counting the number of vocalists who took from that body of work a new sense of possibility. The years since Ella's "Song Books" have been blessed with singers who were touched by her influence, especially Sarah Vaughan (her only peer), Mel Tormé, Carmen McRae, Barbra Streisand, and those two wise elders Rosemary Clooney and Tony Bennett, singing better than ever, their delivery pared to a simplicity that has endeared them—and the great standards—to a new generation. With no vocal or bodily mannerisms to get in the way, they are pure servants of the song.

But one figure towers over the whole long cavalcade. Frank Sinatra made his first record in 1939—with Harry James, at the age of 24—and in the 1990s he was still at it. During those six decades Sinatra sang a prodigious number of ballads—not only the theater and movie songs of the Gershwins, Arlen, Porter, Kern, Rodgers & Hart, Berlin, Arthur Schwartz, Jule Styne and Jimmy Van Heusen, but the great one-shots: "In the Wee Small Hours of the Morning," "You Make Me Feel So Young," "Angel Eyes," "Witchcraft," "Young at Heart." Wherever the songs were born, he made them all seem like old friends. With the generosity of his embrace he broadened the literature of American popular song and defined the term "standard." Somewhere on the radio, from early morning to late at night, his voice continues to be the codifying presence and connecting thread. Mel Tormé said that Sinatra epitomized the "three C's" that are required for being a great popular singer: consistency, concentration and credibility.

I never get tired of hearing Sinatra sing whatever he chooses to sing. His intention is always serious, his voice always true, his rhythm always hip, his enunciation always clear, his phrasing always faithful to the words as they would be conversationally spoken. He had a writer's ear for language and a troubadour's sense of romantic love; he never forgot that his job was to tell a story. Of all America's popular singers, Sinatra was the one who most truly seemed to believe the words he was singing. No wonder the multitudes of bobby-soxed girls swooned over him at the Paramount Theater in 1942. Some part of us is swooning over him still.

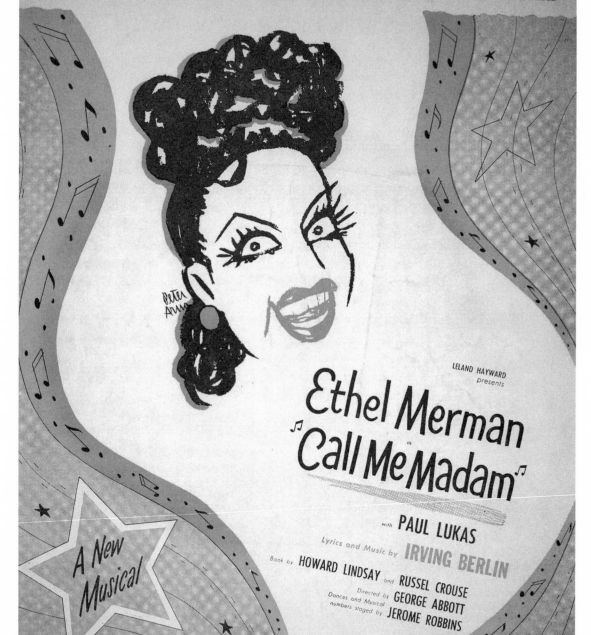

Irving Berlin:
The Theater Songs

Irving Berlin's movie music consisted of more than the three classic scores he wrote for Fred Astaire and Ginger Rogers. Hollywood also called on him for, among other films, *Holiday Inn*, whose songs included "White Christmas," the biggest hit of his career. But Berlin was essentially a man of the theater. Starting in 1908, when he contributed some songs to a revue called *The Boys and Betty*, and ending in 1962 with *Mr. President*, his words and music were heard on Broadway for more than five decades. He also took personal possession of both World War I and World War II with *Yip, Yip, Yaphank* (1918) and *This Is the Army* (1942), forever capturing the plight of the newly inducted soldier—his sudden loss of civil liberties—in "Oh, How I Hate to Get Up in the Morning" and "This Is the Army, Mr. Jones."

The songs Berlin wrote for the theater took their nature from what was needed at that moment in the show; he was a chameleon, changing colors from one number to the next. Of the many gems in his 1933 revue *As Thousands Cheer*, "Easter Parade" was radiant, "How's Chances" was torchy, "Heat Wave" was hot, and "Suppertime" was a dirge. Sung by Ethel Waters as a woman mourning the husband who has been lynched and won't be coming home for dinner, "Suppertime" might have been written by Harold Arlen—it has his sadness of line. Berlin had never written anything like it before and never would again.

For *Call Me Madam*, in 1950, an Ethel Merman musical suggested by the career of Perle Mesta, President Truman's feisty ambassador to Luxembourg, he wrote "The Hostess With the Mostes' on the Ball." Of all the brassy numbers written for Merman over the years, none more perfectly served her voice and personality;

Ethel Merman first conquered Broadway in 1930, singing the Gershwins' "I Got Rhythm" in "Girl Crazy." Cole Porter subsequently wrote five shows for her, and then Irving Berlin took over the Merman franchise. With "Call Me Madam" and "Annie Get Your Gun" he gave her two scores that made rich use of her glass-shattering voice and sure comic sense.

from the first clarion note the audience knew she was the hostess with the mostes'. The score also included the feathery "It's a Lovely Day Today," the beautiful Russian-flavored ballad "The Best Thing for You Would Be Me," and the famous double song, "You're Just in Love," in which, first, a young man sings an easygoing melody about his mysterious new symptoms:

> *I hear music and there's no one there,*
> *I smell blossoms and the trees are bare,*
> *All day long I seem to walk on air,*
> *I wonder why? I wonder why?. . .*

Then the woman responds with a counter melody, telling the kid that his problem isn't serious:

> *You don't need analyzing,*
> *It is not so surprising*
> *That you feel very strange but nice.*
> *Your heart goes pitter-patter,*
> *I know just what's the matter*
> *Because I've been there once or twice . . .*

Then the two sing their choruses simultaneously, coming out even after 16 bars and again after 32 bars. The musically untrained Berlin could do anything he set out to do, apparently without exertion; his instincts were infallible. Again, the marvel of the *Call Me Madam* score is its variety. No two songs are anywhere near alike.

But the supreme display of Berlin's genius was *Annie Get Your Gun*, in 1946. Its producers, Richard Rodgers and Oscar Hammerstein, had commissioned Jerome Kern and Dorothy Fields to write the score. When Kern suddenly died, they asked Irving Berlin to take over the assignment. Berlin demurred. He was wary of trying to replace Kern, his lifelong idol, and he also didn't know whether he would be able to write what he called hillbilly music. But as a trial balloon he agreed to check into a hotel in Atlantic City for a weekend and see what he could come up with. He returned on Monday with five songs: "Doin' What Comes Natur'lly," "They Say It's Wonderful," "The Girl That I Marry," "You Can't Get a Man With a Gun" and "There's No Business Like Show Business." Most people wouldn't mind having written those songs in a lifetime. Or just "There's No Business Like Show Business."

Two months later the job was done—15 numbers, each one giving total satisfaction at the moment of delivery. The funny songs were truly funny: "Doin' What Comes Natur'lly," "You Can't Get a Man With a Gun," "I'm an Indian Too," "Anything You Can Do I

One of the best Broadway scores, "Annie Get Your Gun," was written by Irving Berlin, who took the assignment reluctantly after Jerome Kern died. A weekend in Atlantic City proved that he was the right man for the job.

Can Do Better," "I'm a Bad, Bad Man" and "Moonshine Lullaby." The romantic songs were truly romantic—"They Say It's Wonderful," "The Girl That I Marry," "I Got Lost in His Arms," "My Defenses Are Down" and "I'll Share It All With You"—and the others—"I've Got the Sun in the Morning," "Who Do You Love, I Hope?" and "Colonel Buffalo Bill"—had that old-time Broadway effervescence, the sound that makes show business like no business.

Other great Broadway scores have been more complex (*Guys and Dolls*), or more elegant (*My Fair Lady*), or more unified (*Kiss Me, Kate*), or more lyrical (*Carousel*). But no score was ever better at what it set out to be—more flat-out successful—than *Annie Get Your Gun*. And no weekend in Atlantic City was ever better spent.

Jule Styne
(and Sammy Cahn)

I first noticed Jule (pronounced Joo-lee) Styne early in World War II, when he wrote the music for three of the war's sentimental block-busters: "I Don't Want to Walk Without You," "I'll Walk Alone" and "Saturday Night Is the Loneliest Night of the Week." The first had lyrics by Frank Loesser. The other two were by Sammy Cahn, and, as it turned out, they were just the first trickle in the Styne-Cahn oil well. Suddenly their movie songs were everywhere—gigantic hits—and they kept coming: "I've Heard That Song Before," "It's Been a Long, Long Time," "Five Minutes More," "Let It Snow! Let It Snow! Let It Snow!," "I Fall in Love Too Easily," "Time After Time," "It's the Same Old Dream," "There Goes That Song Again," "Guess I'll Hang My Tears Out to Dry," "Three Coins in the Fountain," "The Things We Did Last Summer," "It's Magic." They were all supreme-ly catchy, Styne's melodies easy to hum, Cahn's lyrics easy to identify with. "Sammy loved that big-band sound," Styne said of his lyricist, "so every song had that big-band sound." Fifteen were Number 1 on the charts.

The composer Jule Styne wrote powerful melodies that propelled three pop divas to their highest peaks. One, Barbra Streisand (below, with Styne), became a star with "Funny Girl." The other two were Carol Channing, in "Gentle-men Prefer Blondes," and Ethel Merman, in "Gypsy." Earlier Styne had composed many huge movie hits with the lyricist Sammy Cahn.

Nor were all of them as simple as they seemed. "Guess I'll Hang My Tears Out to Dry" is full of surprises. Its opening melodic curve ("When I want rain, I get sunny weather") is unlike that of any other popular song; it also has a 9-note drop in the 6th bar ("pull MY-SELF together"), and the bridge changes key twice. "I Fall in Love Too Easily" charms us with its unusual opening phrase and then tells its entire story in only 16 bars—a gem of com-pression. "Time After Time" is a superior example of the A-B-A-B form, soaring upward into B in the 9th bar ("So lucky to be . . . ") and building to an emotional climax at the end. It's such a strong song that it serves notice of the strong composer who was about to break out of the Hollywood cocoon.

The eight-year-old Julius Stein was a piano prodigy. Here, suitably garbed for the higher realms of classical music, he makes his debut with the Chicago Symphony.

Born in England to Jewish immigrant parents from the Ukraine who owned a butter-and-egg store, Julius Stein was smitten by the theatrical virus at the age of three, when the family attended a vaudeville performance by Harry Lauder, the beloved Scottish entertainer. At one point young Julius startled the audience by running onto the stage and singing a song. Afterward, Lauder advised his parents to buy the boy a piano. That was beyond their income, but his mother did manage to rent a piano and arrange for her son to take lessons.

When Julius was eight, the family came to the United States, settling in Chicago. There he studied at the Chicago College of Music and became a child pianist with the Chicago Symphony and other symphony orchestras. But adolescence sang a different tune to him, and he began playing at high-school dances and in burlesque houses and nightclubs. His parents were not pleased, especially when the kid started writing songs. Styne (as he reconfigured his name) once remarked that his dad would have disliked his success as a songwriter. "My father said he never paid for me to be a composer; he paid for me to be a pianist. He would tell people,

'You ought to have heard him play when he was eight years old.'"

Landing a job at 20th Century-Fox in the late 1930s, Styne became a studio arranger and a vocal coach for Fox stars, including Shirley Temple, and then moved to horsy Republic Pictures, where he wrote songs for Gene Autry and Roy Rogers. "I did just about anything they asked me to do," he recalled, adding that he would gladly have played the piano for Trigger. Teaming with Sammy Cahn in 1942 sprang him from such Augean toil. Assigned to a succession of movies like *Follow the Boys*, *It Happened in Brooklyn*, *Anchors Away*, *Romance on the High Seas*, *Stork Club* and *Tars and Spars*, the team turned on the spigot of mega-hits.

Still, I never thought of Jule Styne as more than a 32-bar tunesmith with a rich melodic gift—a gift, I assumed, that was just big enough for Hollywood's modest needs. Then he moved to New York and rapidly developed into a major composer of Broadway musicals, starting in 1947 with the long-running *High Button Shoes*, for which he and Sammy Cahn wrote such high-energy theater numbers as "Can't You Just See Yourself?", "I Still Get Get Jealous (When They Look at You)" and "Papa, Won't You Dance With Me?" In 1949 the even longer-running *Gentlemen Prefer Blondes* paired Styne with the adroit lyricist Leo Robin, whose "Little Girl From Little Rock" and "Diamonds Are a Girl's Best Friend" helped to make an instant star of Carol Channing. In addition to those show-stoppers, Styne's ballads ("Bye, Bye, Baby," "Just a Kiss Apart," "You Say You Care") were more gentle and lyrical than his earlier Hollywood fare. "You write as well as who you write with," Styne once said, and Robin stretched him to a new level of sophistication. His next lyricists, Betty Comden and Adolph Green, evoked some of his most touching melodies in the musicals *Peter Pan* ("Never Never Land") and *Bells Are Ringing* ("The Party's Over," "Just in Time," "Long Before I Knew You"). Finally, in 1959, with *Gypsy*, Stephen Sondheim put him over the top.

If you write as well as who you write with, Styne wrote stunningly well with Sondheim. *Gypsy* was based on the memoirs of the upscale stripper Gypsy Rose Lee and her ferociously pushy mother Rose, played by Ethel Merman, and it's one of the all-time great Broadway scores, unendingly fresh and various. Ranging from the the tender ("Small World") to the angry ("Some People"), from the childlike ("Let Me Entertain You") to the declamatory ("Everything's Coming Up Roses"), from the ardent ("You'll Never Get Away From Me") to the jaunty ("Together Wherever We Go"), Sondheim's flawless lyrics were matched by Styne in every nuance of fierce ambition and failed theatrical dreams. How Merman must have loved sinking her vocal chords into "Everything's Coming Up Roses":

Diamonds are a Girl's Best Friend

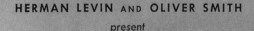

HERMAN LEVIN AND OLIVER SMITH
present

GENTLEMEN PREFER BLONDES

A New Musical Comedy

Music by
JULE STYNE

Lyrics by
LEO ROBIN

Book by
JOSEPH FIELDS
and
ANITA LOOS

BYE BYE BABY

JUST A KISS APART

YOU SAY YOU CARE

SUNSHINE

DIAMONDS ARE A GIRL'S
BEST FRIEND

A LITTLE GIRL FROM LITTLE ROCK

IT'S DELIGHTFUL DOWN
IN CHILE

Dances and Musical Scenes by AGNES De MILLE

Settings by OLIVER SMITH · *Costumes by* MILES WHITE

Entire Production Staged by JOHN C. WILSON

 J. J. ROBBINS & SONS, INC.
221 WEST 47th STREET, NEW YORK 19

Even that number was just a warm-up for the climactic "Rose's Turn," which gave Merman the most powerful moment of her Broadway career. The song confirmed Styne in the small company of theater composers who can elevate stars of the highest wattage or launch new ones overnight. He had done it with Carol Channing and would do it again with Barbra Streisand in *Funny Girl* (lyrics by Bob Merrill). Styne pushed Streisand to the highest altitudes with four dynamic songs: "I'm the Greatest Star," "Don't Rain on My Parade," "The Music That Makes Me Dance," and "People." Compare the complex 46-bar "People" with Styne's early movie songs like "It's Been a Long, Long Time." The 32-bar tunesmith of Hollywood had come a long way. Ultimately he would write almost 20 Broadway shows, including *Do Re Mi* ("Make Someone Happy"), *Say, Darling, Subways Are for Sleeping* and *Hallelujah, Baby!*

Styne's journey from Hollywood to Broadway, like the similar journey of Frank Loesser, is a textbook illustration of the difference between the popular song and the theater song—and of the differences in temperament and ambition that go into their creation. Harry Warren and Jimmy Van Heusen were content to stay in California and write 32-bar songs for the studios to use without further consultation. They lived well and were well rewarded. Other great melodists—Richard Rodgers, Irving Berlin, Frederick Loewe— regarded themselves as theater composers and stayed close to New York. Their pleasure was to write scores that contained many kinds of songs, tailored to specific situations and characters. They were deeply involved in how their songs served the show, often writing new numbers during the tryout to fix scenes that weren't working.

Jule Styne learned his trade in Hollywood but wasn't content to write movie songs forever. Some inner flame took him to Broadway, and he succeeded there because his instincts were theatrical. "Jule was a dramatist," Betty Comden told me. "To him the show was always the most important thing. He was always asking what's right for this scene and what's right for this character? He was very intuitive about it. It's not something that everybody has."

Frank Loesser

Frank Loesser (pronounced Lesser) was the other Hollywood songwriter who exhilarated me when he came to Broadway after World War II. His arrival was doubly impressive because he had doubled his skills and was now also a composer.

I had been aware of Loesser since the 1930s as a deft and witty lyricist for Hollywood songs: "Small Fry" and "Two Sleepy People" (Hoagy Carmichael), "They're Either Too Young or Too Old" (Arthur Schwartz), "Let's Get Lost" (Jimmy McHugh). I also knew that during the war he had begun to compose his own music, writing such hits as the patriotic "Praise the Lord and Pass the Ammunition" and the tender "Spring Will Be a Little Late This Year." But I wasn't prepared for the broad and inventive score of his first Broadway musical, *Where's Charley?*, in 1948. And I certainly wasn't prepared for *Guys and Dolls* two years later. It struck me then—and still does—as the best of all Broadway scores.

Born in New York in 1910, Loesser was a musically gifted addition to a Jewish family steeped in classical music; his older brother Arthur Loesser was a concert pianist. But Frank's ambitions were not Arthurian; he refused to study music formally and instead began trying to write popular songs. He was also in love with language, and after dropping out of City College he supported himself with such odd jobs as editing a small suburban newspaper and writing radio scripts and vaudeville sketches. At one point he sang for little more than his supper in a Manhattan club called the Back Drop Inn.

In 1931 his aptitude for language landed him a contract as a lyricist in Hollywood. There he spent a decade writing the words for songs in more than 60 movies, including "See What the Boys in the Backroom Will Have," huskily sung by Marlene Dietrich in *Destry Rides Again*, and "(I've Got Spurs That) Jingle, Jangle, Jingle." The distinctive Loesser humor, which would bloom so extravagantly in

Frank Loesser on a park bench in Manhattan. The day looks hot, but Loesser wouldn't want to be anywhere else. During his long employment as a Hollywood lyricist he never stopped dreaming of Broadway, and when he finally got there he took full possession. Nobody ever wrote a better musical than "Guys and Dolls."

Composer Irving Actman and lyricist Frank Loesser were a young songwriting team for Universal Pictures in the mid-1930s. Here they audition an unidentified aspiring actress. At least her hair was right for the period.

Guys and Dolls, couldn't help surfacing in songs like "I Get the Neck of the Chicken," music by Jimmy McHugh, and "Then I Wrote the Minuet in G," music by Ludwig von Beethoven, from *Hawaiian Nights.* Even more useful to the studios was Loesser's knack for the expedient solution, especially when the screenplay took a turn for the Polynesian. The grass-skirts genre gave him one of his biggest early hits, "Moon of Manakoora," sung by Dorothy Lamour in *The Hurricane.* Some others were "The White Blossoms of Tah-ni," from *Aloma of the South Seas;* "Moon Over Burma," from *Moon Over Burma,* and "Pagan Lullaby," from *Beyond the Blue Horizon,* later to be recycled for another movie as "Malay Lullaby," probably sung against the same swaying palms.

But essentially it was ten years of servitude. Typical of the indentured status of the Hollywood songwriter in those Depression days was Loesser's collaboration with the young composer Irving Actman, for Universal Pictures, from 1936 to 1938. Some of their movies were *Postal Inspector, Flying Hostess* and *Swing That Cheer,* and some of the songs they wrote were "Bang, the Bell Rang," "Let's Have Bluebirds," "Hot Towel" and "Chasing You Around." Universal paid them $200 a week and retained ownership of the copyrights and most of the proceeds, plus the right to "adapt, arrange, change, transpose, add to or subtract from" their songs. The contract also obliged Loesser and Actman to comport themselves "with due regard to public conventions and morals" and to refrain from "any act that will tend to degrade them in society or bring them into public hatred, contempt, scorn or ridicule."

Loesser wrote whatever was demanded; it was the Depression, and he was glad to have work. But his heart was never in California, or Manakoora, or any other tropical paradise. The only moon he cared about was the moon over Manhattan. A chain-smoking workaholic, notoriously impatient, he was immune to the languors of Movieland. "He always wanted to get to Broadway," his widow Jo Sullivan said. "In Los Angeles he would go outside and look at the sun and say, 'O.K., I'll give you ten minutes.'"

World War II was his escape—and his conservatory. As an army private for three years, assigned to an entertainment unit, he began writing entire shows—both lyrics and music—that were performed for soldiers around the world. He also turned out such military morale builders as "What Do You Do in the Infantry?", "First-Class Private Mary Brown" and the extended "Ballad of Rodger Young." All that on-the-job training paid off after the war when he finally got to Broadway with *Where's Charley?* Harold Arlen had been signed to compose the music, with Loesser doing the lyrics. When Arlen withdrew because of another obligation, Loesser nominated himself for the job, and the producers Cy Feuer and Ernest Martin, who knew his army work, decided to take a chance, though it was their first show and they had a lot to lose. They didn't regret it—their next project was *Guys and Dolls*.

The song in *Where's Charley?* that notified me that I was in the presence of a playful spirit was "Make a Miracle," in which Ray Bolger describes to his dilatory girl—the show is set in Edwardian times—some technological marvels of tomorrow. "Someday," he sings, "there'll be horseless carriages that fly . . . But who knows when that age of miracles will come to be? So meanwhile, darling, make a miracle and marry me." Contrapuntally, the girl sings "Horseless carriages, I can't believe it!", and so the song proceeds, the girl exclaiming over each future miracle and missing the proposal of marriage. In its antiphonal form the song foreshadowed the brilliant "Fugue for Tinhorns" that opens *Guys and Dolls*, just as "The New Ashmolean Marching Society and Students' Conservatory Band" anticipated with its barbershop-quartet flavor "The Oldest Established Permanent Floating Crap Game in New York." But Loesser was also a romantic, and in *Where's Charley?* his sentimental

Loesser's first Broadway hit, "Where's Charley?", also had a Hirschfeld drawing on its sheet music. The signature is at the end of Ray Bolger's scarf. Bolger sang the show's sentimental hit, "Once in Love With Amy."

side found its outlet in the beautiful "My Darling, My Darling" and in the sweet and simple "Once in Love With Amy," sung by Ray Bolger. Bolger's soft-shoe dance on a sanded floor always stopped the show.

Seeing *Guys and Dolls* on its opening night in 1950 was my nirvana as a musical comedy fan. Each of the 15 songs, starting with the hilarious racetrack fugue, was such a perfect blend of music and lyrics that I couldn't imagine how the next one would be as good, but it always was, whatever form it took, and the forms varied widely, from the pure "More I Cannot Wish You" to the comic "Sue Me" and "Take Back Your Mink," from the perky "A Bushel and a Peck" to the pulsing "Luck Be a Lady," from the heartfelt "I'll Know" and "If I Were a Bell" to the streetwise "Guys and Dolls" and "My Time of Day" and the revivalist "Sit Down You're Rockin' the Boat." (The show's musical director, incidentally, was Irving Actman, Loesser's fellow slave back at Universal Pictures.)

Although the melodies in *Guys and Dolls* were warm and pleasant, the lyrics were doing the real work, seamlessly woven in and out of Abe Burrows' droll libretto based on the Broadway fables of Damon Runyon. Loesser's songs went beyond advancing the plot; they also developed character. "Adelaide's Lament," in which a no-longer-young showgirl diagnoses her nasal allergies as psychosomatic, the result of being chronically deserted just short of the altar by Nathan Detroit, is both funny and poignant, and Nathan's response, "Sue Me," is the autobiography of every gambling man who doesn't want to be tied down.

Loesser's ear was infallible, his language pure Broadway in its humor and intonations. A less savvy lyricist might have blown the title song with inexact rhymes for "doll." Loesser took care to find words that rhyme with how "doll" is properly pronounced in New York:

> When you meet a gent
> Paying all kinds of rent
> For a flat that could flatten the Taj Mahal,
> Call it sad, call it funny,
> But it's better than even money
> That the guy's only doing it for some doll . . .
> When you meet a mug
> Lately out of the jug
> And he smells from Vitalis and Barbasol . . .

In the third chorus the girl is strung with platinum fol-de-rol.

Loesser would stretch himself still further in 1956 with *The Most Happy Fella*, a near-opera based on Sidney Howard's play,

MAKE A MIRACLE

LYRICS AND MUSIC BY *Frank Loesser*

CY **FEUER** and ERNIE **MARTIN** in association with GWEN **RICKARD**

PRESENT

RAY BOLGER

IN A NEW MUSICAL COMEDY

Songs from the Score

MY DARLING, MY DARLING
ONCE IN LOVE WITH AMY
LOVELIER THAN EVER
AT THE RED ROSE COTILLION
PERNAMBUCO
WHERE'S CHARLEY?
THE YEARS BEFORE US

where's charley?

BASED ON
BRANDON THOMAS'
"CHARLEY'S AUNT"

BOOK BY
GEORGE ABBOTT

LYRICS AND MUSIC BY
FRANK LOESSER

CHORAL DIRECTOR **GERRY DOLIN**

ORCHESTRATION BY **TED ROYAL**

SETTINGS AND COSTUMES BY **DAVID FFOLKES**

DANCES BY **GEORGE BALANCHINE**

PRODUCTION DIRECTED BY **GEORGE ABBOTT**

SUSAN PUBLICATIONS, INC.

EDWIN H. MORRIS AND COMPANY, INC.
Sole Selling Agents

1619 BROADWAY • NEW YORK 19, N. Y.

When Frank Loesser hit the jackpot on Broadway with "Guys and Dolls" he didn't forget the young composer with whom he had written songs like "Hot Towel" for all those B movies at Universal; the man conducting the orchestra was Irving Actman. Director George S. Kaufman was best known as the co-author with Moss Hart of "The Man Who Came to Dinner" and other Broadway comedies.

They Knew What They Wanted, about an aging California vineyard owner who orders a young mail-order bride. Loesser, now a triple talent, wrote the words, the music and the libretto. The show was too long, with 42 musical numbers, but it was a treat for the ear, a parade of beautiful melodies, including operatic duets and Verdi-like ensembles, as well as such pop winners as "Big D" and "Standing on the Corner (Watching All the Girls Go By)." Loesser made no apologies for the surfeit of music. "I like a great frequency of songs," he said. "I may give the impression that this show has operatic tendencies. If people feel that way, fine. Actually all it has is a great frequency of songs." Those songs still have many devotees; today *The Most Happy Fella* is regularly revived by small opera and musical theater companies in many parts of the country.

Luck was not a lady for Loesser in his next musical, *Greenwillow* (1961), a short-lived fantasy based on B. J. Chute's novel; the only hit song was "Never Will I Marry." But he rebounded a year later with the amiable satire *How to Succeed in Business Without Really Trying* ("I Believe in You," "A Secretary Is Not a Toy"), which won the Pulitzer Prize. He also wrote the score for the movie *Hans Christian Andersen* ("Anywhere I Wander," "No Two People"), starring Danny Kaye, as well as such pop classics as "Baby, It's Cold Outside" and "A Slow Boat to China."

But *Guys and Dolls* is his monument, and no American songwriter has a better one. Frank Loesser had an original turn of mind and turn of phrase, and the characters who give voice to that turn of mind, like the allergic Adelaide, stay with us for the rest of our lives:

> *You can spray her all day with the Vitamin A*
> *and the Bromo-fizz,*
> *But the medicine never gets anywhere near*
> *where the trouble is,*
> *If she's getting a kind of a name for herself*
> *and the name ain't his,*
> *A person can develop a cold.*

Betty Comden
and Adolph Green

No entertainers have conveyed more enjoyment over more decades than the lyricists Betty Comden and Adolph Green. Photographs from the early 1940s show them radiating youthful energy and pleasure as members of a satirical comedy act called "The Revuers" at the Village Vanguard—an act that included the also-still-unknown Judy Holliday. Photographs from the 1990s show them radiating the same youthful energy and pleasure in two-person performances drawn from their life work, which ranges from the musical *On the Town* (they wrote the book and the lyrics and acted in the original production) to the movie *Singin' in the Rain* (they wrote the story and the screenplay) to the musical *Bells Are Ringing* (they wrote the book and the lyrics). And that's the merest tip of the oldest established permanent floating collaboration in the American theater. The two aging juveniles are heaped with Kennedy Center honors, Academy Award nominations, Screen Writers' Guild Awards and Tony Awards.

On the Town was the show that got it all started—a skyrocket exploding over sober wartime Broadway in 1944. Comden and Green took the idea for their musical from a ballet, *Fancy Free*, that two young friends of theirs, the composer Leonard Bernstein and the choreographer Jerome Robbins, had created for Ballet Theatre. The story was about three sailors on 24-hour shore leave, exploring New York and looking for romance. Bernstein was signed to write the music and Robbins to stage the dances. Thus four brilliant careers were born on one night. The prodigy known as Lenny would go on to make the whole world of music his domain. Robbins kept one foot in the theater as a choreographer and a director, putting his hugely innovative stamp on more than a dozen musicals, including

Adolph Green and Betty Comden in "On the Town" (top), for which they also wrote the book and lyrics, and (below) in a show built around songs from their subsequent long career as lyricists, especially for Jule Styne ("Just in Time," "The Party's Over"). As screenwriters for MGM they wrote the hilarious "Singin' in the Rain."

The King and I, The Pajama Game, Bells Are Ringing, West Side Story, Gypsy, A Funny Thing Happened on the Way to the Forum and *Fiddler on the Roof.*

Humor was one of Robbins' strengths—his Mack Sennett chase in and out of a row of bathhouses in *High Button Shoes* was as funny as dance can get—and in Comden and Green he had the ideal co-conspirators. Reviewing *On the Town* in *The New Yorker*, the critic Wolcott Gibbs said that the show, besides being "young, bright and lovingly executed," had an "air of careless improvisation, as if the actors were making things up for their private amusement as they went along. That is one of the most valuable and mysterious things that can happen on a stage. The tendency of the average

musical is to vary and elaborate whatever effects are being successful at the moment; this one obviously doesn't give a damn for *Oklahoma!* or anybody else." With that observation Gibbs put his finger
on the insouciance that has always made Comden and Green's work
seem brighter than almost everybody else's.

Not that they couldn't be serious. Three of the songs in *On the
Town* were ballads of unusual feeling: "Lucky to Be Me," "Lonely
Town" and, especially, "Some Other Time," the plaintive next-to-last
number in which the sightseeing sailors and their newfound girls
have to say goodbye:

> *Where has the time all gone to?*
> *Haven't done half the things we want to.*
> *Oh, well. We'll catch up some other time . . .*

The song is still around, its wartime words of separated love never
out of date.

But the best-known legacy from the score is its opening number, "New York, New York," now part of the city's mythology; every
tourist venturing into the subway knows that the Bronx is up and
the Battery's down. Three comic situation songs were no less exuberant: "Carried Away," "Come Up to My Place" and "I Can Cook,
Too." At every turn the youthful Leonard Bernstein responded to
Comden and Green's essential joy. He would never again write a
score so young and fresh.

Comden and Green worked with Leonard Bernstein on one
more musical, *Wonderful Town*, again eliciting three ballads of great
purity—"Ohio," "It's Love" and "A Quiet Girl"; the more angular
Bernstein of *West Side Story* and *Candide* was still waiting in the
wings. After that, Comden and Green teamed with the ever melodi-
ous Jule Styne, writing no fewer than nine shows with him over the
next three decades (*Two on the Aisle, Peter Pan, Bells Are Ringing,
Say, Darling, Subways Are for Sleeping, Do Re Mi, Fade Out-Fade In,
Hallelujah, Baby!* and *Lorelei*), as well as two with Cy Coleman
(*On the Twentieth Century* and *The Will Rogers Follies*).

It's an astounding output of lyrics, all doing useful work in the
service of the plot, like the hilarious "Captain Hook's Waltz" in *Peter
Pan*, wherein Hook gloats in his fame as the slimiest pirate of all.
Perhaps because Comden & Green's songs were so plot-related, only
three ever became hits on their own: "Make Someone Happy," from
Do Re Mi, and "Just in Time" and "The Party's Over," from *Bells Are
Ringing*. "The Party's Over" is a particular gem. Set to Jule Styne's
bittersweet melody, the lyric, a distant echo of *On the Town's* "Some
Other Time," carries all the finality of the clock running out.

JUST IN TIME
THE THEATRE GUILD
presents
JUDY HOLLIDAY
in
Bells are Ringing
A NEW MUSICAL
BOOK AND LYRICS BY
BETTY COMDEN and ADOLPH GREEN
MUSIC BY
JULE STYNE
ENTIRE PRODUCTION DIRECTED BY
JEROME ROBBINS
DANCES AND MUSICAL NUMBERS STAGED BY
BOB FOSSE and JEROME ROBBINS
Barbelle
CONTENTS
LONG BEFORE I KNEW YOU
BELLS ARE RINGING
HELLO, HELLO, THERE
THE PARTY'S OVER
JUST IN TIME
MU-CHA-CHA
PRICE
50c
STRATFORD MUSIC CORPORATION
CHAPPELL & CO., INC. AND G. SCHIRMER, INC.,
SOLE SELLING AGENTS
RKO BLDG. ROCKEFELLER CENTER, NEW YORK

Judy Holliday, who began her career with Comden and Green in a nightclub act called the Revuers, was reunited with them as the star of their musical, "Bells Are Ringing." Another figure from Comden and Green's past was the choreographer Jerome Robbins. After "On the Town" he choreographed many of Broadway's pioneering musicals.

But the most fondly remembered of the team's achievements took place far from the city where the Bronx is up and the Battery's down—at MGM in Hollywood. *Singin' in the Rain* (1952), which Comden and Green conceived and wrote, is generally agreed to be the most enjoyable movie musical ever made and can also be found on various lists of the ten all-time best American films. Starring Gene Kelly, Debbie Reynolds and Donald O'Connor, with period songs from the 1920s, it lampooned Hollywood's dawning era of "talkies" and the accompanying discovery that the silent movie stars didn't always sound as good as they looked.

Along with two subsequent films that Comden & Green also wrote—*The Band Wagon* and *It's Always Fair Weather*, both of which were nominated for an Academy Award—*Singin' in the Rain* raised the Hollywood musical to a standard of serious intention that would become the norm for such literate films as *A Star Is Born, Funny Face, My Fair Lady* and *Gigi*. Until then the genre hadn't been troubled by high aspirations. The Warner Brothers musicals of the 1930s and 20th Century-Fox musicals of the 1940s were content to keep the customers mollified with material that didn't tax the I.Q.

It's safe to guess that Betty Comden and Adolph Green grew up on those movies, grateful, as I was, for their simple pleasures—all those Harry Warren melodies and Sonja Henie skating routines and Carmen Miranda fruited hats. But when Comden and Green went to Hollywood as writers they brought with them more than their obvious affection for the form. They brought intelligence and humor. They couldn't help wanting to crank the Hollywood musical up a notch, and beneath the song-and-dance glitter of their three best films—*Singin' in the Rain, The Band Wagon* and *It's Always Fair Weather*—they took some hard looks at human nature and at the demons of vanity and disillusion. Their work never lost the satiric edge—the impatience with pretension—that they started out with as a nightclub act.

But they also didn't lose the ingredient that had always kept them young—the impression that they were having a wonderful time.

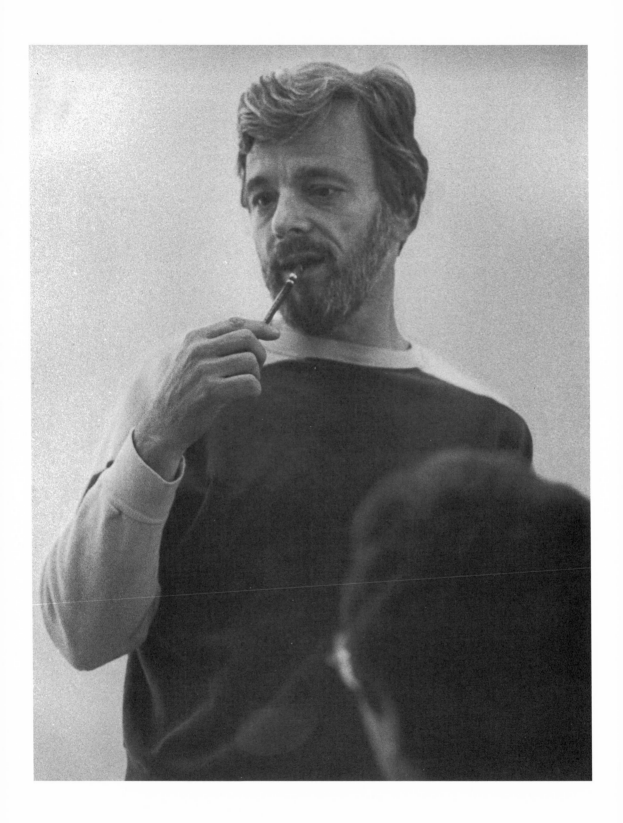

Stephen Sondheim
(and Leonard Bernstein)

In their long and eminent careers both Stephen Sondheim and Leonard Bernstein became so much more than songwriters that they belong in this book only at its margins.

Bernstein stopped composing for Broadway after his fourth show, *West Side Story*, in 1957, returning only for a final musical, *1600 Pennsylvania Avenue*, with Alan Jay Lerner, in 1976. That visit to the White House was a flop. But otherwise the Bernstein decades were a whirlwind of glamour and glory. Lenny was the perpetual motion machine of classical music: composer, concert pianist, recording artist, writer, teacher, lecturer, conductor of the finest orchestras around the world. Finally slowed by failing health, he died in 1990 at the age of seventy-two.

Sondheim, a classically trained composer, achieved his first Broadway successes as a lyricist, with *West Side Story* and *Gypsy*. In 1962 he began his dual career, writing the music as well as the words for *A Funny Thing Happened on the Way to the Forum*, a Roman farce loosely derived from Plautus, starring the manic Zero Mostel. Sondheim's sunny and melodic score had as its opening number one of the most enjoyable of songs, "Comedy Tonight." In the forthcoming revels, Mostel tells the audience, the cast will stop at no device, however threadbare, to generate laughs:

> *Nothing with kings, nothing with crowns,*
> *Bring on the lovers, liars and clowns . . .*
> *Old situations, new complications,*
> *Nothing portentous or polite.*
> *Tragedy tomorrow, comedy tonight! . . .*
> *Nothing that's grim, nothing that's Greek,*
> *She plays Medea later this week . . .*

One of the giants of the American musical theater, Stephen Sondheim first made his name as the lyricist of "West Side Story" and "Gypsy." Later, as the composer and lyricist of "Company," "Follies," "Pacific Overtures," "Sweeney Todd" and other innovative musicals, he boldly took the musical theater into new territory.

"Comedy Tonight" belongs on the same mountaintop as Irving Berlin's "There's No Business Like Show Business" and Dietz & Schwartz's "That's Entertainment." No musical was ever more pleasurably launched.

But that was Sondheim's last homage to musical theater tradition. After that he systematically reshaped the form with shows that broke every notion of what kind of stories a musical could tell. Mostly cynical in outlook, brittle in their lyrics and unorthodox in their extended musical forms, they first laid claim to Broadway in 1970 with *Company*, an interlocking portrait of five unhappily married couples. *Follies*, a year later, took place at a reunion of ex-Follies stars and showgirls looking back over lives more bleak than their smiling stage personalities suggested.

Next came *A Little Night Music*, Sondheim's most lyrical and unified score, composed entirely in three-quarter time and containing his only popular standard, "Send in the Clowns." Based on Ingmar Bergman's film *Smiles of a Summer Night*, about the Swedish leisure class at the turn of the century, it occupied itself with the romantic skirmishes of a lawyer and various wives, lovers, ex-mistresses, mothers, sons and guests at his country estate one night. A score consisting only of waltzes might seem a good bet to wear out its welcome. But these weren't ordinary waltzes—the heavily stressed oom-pah-pahs of a Johann Strauss. The beat, as in "Send in the Clowns," was stressed just enough to insinuate itself into the listener's metabolism, an easygoing lilt that became a running commentary on the long night's affairs of the heart.

Pushing into still more eclectic subject matter, *Pacific Overtures* (1976) dealt with the history of modern Japan, starting in the 19th century, as it was experienced by the Japanese people, using Japanese actors and stagecraft and Japanese-inflected music; *Sweeney Todd* was a grisly thriller about the infamous Fleet Street barber who cut the throats of his customers and baked them into meat pies; *Sunday in the Park With George* examined the life and art of the French pointillist painter Georges Seurat; *Into the Woods* explored the often dark world of fairy tales, and *Assassins* looked at some of history's political killers and the nature of murderous violence.

Nobody could accuse Sondheim of playing it safe or coddling his audiences with melodies to hum as they went out. Over the years the critics tended to respect the shows but not to like them very much. I'm one of those infidels at the Sondheim shrine; I find his music intellectual and cold. But no better lyricist ever worked on Broadway. Sondheim's lyrics dazzle me with their dexterity and precision, their internal rhymes and sonorities, their sardonic humor and psychological tension. If I don't think of him as a songwriter, I salute him as a musical dramatist of originality and courage, his canonical reputation secure.

The two heavyweights Stephen Sondheim and Leonard Bernstein worked together only once, in 1957, but on that occasion they created a popular masterpiece. *West Side Story* was a seamless welding of book (Arthur Laurents), lyrics (Sondheim), music (Bernstein) and dance (Jerome Robbins). Borrowing from Shakespeare's *Romeo and Juliet* the idea of two warring clans and their doomed young lovers, Laurents wrote a story of two New York street gangs—the "American" Jets and their enemies, the Puerto Rican Sharks. True to Shakespeare, the Jets' Tony falls in love with the Puerto Rican girl Maria, sister of one of the Sharks, and after a fatal knife fight the plot moves inevitably to a tragic conclusion.

This was stark stuff for a musical, straight out of the morning newspaper, and Bernstein's music and Sondheim's words and Robbins' dances were wholly of the moment: street-smart and dynamic. Bernstein's score had an undertow of rhythm, not unlike two earlier scores whose subterranean tempos caught the vitality of a self-contained community—Jerome Kern's *Show Boat* and George Gershwin's *Porgy and Bess*. With that fluidity *West Side Story* often felt more like an opera than a musical.

But its individual songs had the haymaker punch of Broadway show tunes, starting with two knockouts: the "Jet Song" ("When you're a Jet . . . ") and "Something's Coming," in which Tony describes the "something" that he can feel "around the corner or whistling down the river." Sondheim's lyric, full of imagery and wonder, holds its own with the momentum of the music—language moving at toboggan speed:

> *Could be.*
> *Who knows? . . .*
> *It's only just*
> *Out of reach,*
> *Down the block,*
> *On the beach,*
> *Under a tree.*
> *I got a feelin' there's a miracle due,*
> *Gonna come true,*
> *Comin' to me . . .*

Stephen Sondheim with
Leonard Bernstein, his
earlier collaborator on
"West Side Story," on
the occasion of "Sond-
heim: A Musical Tribute"
(1973), one of several
shows—another was
"Side by Side by Sond-
heim"—that looked back
over his extensive body
of work.

Farther along, three soaring ballads—"Maria," "Tonight" and
"One Hand, One Heart"—gave the show an emotional grandeur,
and two comic numbers lightened the general gravity. "America"
ironically compared the merits of the new country with the recol-
lected pleasures of Puerto Rico. The other, "Gee, Officer Krupke!",
found the Jets explaining to the cop on their block that they aren't
inherently bad, but just victims of adverse forces in society ("We're
misunderstood/ Deep down inside us there is good").

Throughout *West Side Story*, Sondheim's lyrics struck me as so
right that I was surprised to find him displeased with one of them
when I interviewed him for a magazine article soon after the show
opened to rave reviews. The song was "I Feel Pretty," in which Maria
blurts out the joy of being newly in love:

> *I feel pretty, oh, so pretty,*
> *That the city should give me its key.*
> *A committee*
> *Should be organized to honor me . . .*

The words state a simple emotion clearly, yet they're not dry; they have a girlish sparkle, a touch of humor and an element of surprise in the triple, mainly internal rhyme. But when Sondheim heard the song at the out-of-town tryout he felt that it was wrong for Maria. He didn't think she would use a three-syllable word or express herself in such a complex pattern, and he asked Laurents and Bernstein and Robbins to drop the number. They turned him down.

I still remember Sondheim's dismay because it symbolized for me the essence of his skill as a lyricist. His words for *West Side Story* and *Gypsy* grip us not only because they fit the narrative need of the moment; they are organic to the entire show and to the psyche of its characters. Thus, early in *Gypsy*, in the voracious song "Some People," when Rose announces that it's all right for some people to go on "living life in a living room," but not for *her*, we know that cold ambition is to be the goad for everything that follows, and whatever she sings thereafter reveals some facet of that ambition.

"Those are the lyrics that come easiest," Sondheim told me. "The ones that deal with bitter, driving, hostile people."

Jimmy Van Heusen
(and Johnny Burke and Sammy Cahn)

Jimmy Van Heusen's easygoing melodies always take me slightly by surprise with their unexpected curves. They are totally relaxed. To hear a Van Heusen tune—"It Could Happen to You," "Here's That Rainy Day," "Darn That Dream," "Imagination," "Sunday, Monday or Always," "Like Someone in Love," "But Beautiful"—is to understand why he was the house Mozart for America's two princes of relaxation, Bing Crosby and Frank Sinatra. Twenty-three Crosby movies had music by Van Heusen, including *The Road to Morocco* and five other *Road* films, and Sinatra recorded 77 of his songs, including "All the Way," "The Tender Trap," "The Second Time Around," "Call Me Irresponsible," "Come Fly With Me" and "Nancy With the Laughing Face," written for Sinatra's daughter. Van Heusen even moved to Palm Springs to be near the two crooners for whatever service they might need from him at any hour: 32 bars of music, 18 holes of golf, or an all-night round of the clubs.

"He was one of the world's greatest swingers," Sammy Cahn said when the composer died in 1990. "He was in charge of Sinatra from eight at night until five in the morning."

Van Heusen was born Chester Babcock, in 1913, in Syracuse, New York. He hated the name. By the age of 16 he was singing and playing the piano on a local radio station—a gig that Babcock *père* ended by sending him to Syracuse University to get him educated for the family construction business. But the son mainly educated himself by writing songs for varsity shows. His father, like Jule Styne's father and Cole Porter's grandfather and many other parental figures in Tin Pan Alley lore, frowned on what they perceived as frivolous work, though the sons often turned out to earn

Jimmy Van Heusen at his keyboard in Palm Springs, where with endless ease he wrote graceful melodies that perfectly suited the personality of his swinging friends Bing Crosby and Frank Sinatra. "Frank hung on every note Jimmy wrote," said the arranger Joe Derise. Originally his name wasn't Jimmy—or Van Heusen.

Van Heusen with Johnny Burke, his longtime lyricist for the Bing Crosby and Bob Hope "Road" movies of the early 1940s, like "The Road to Morocco." Burke's many meteorological lyrics ("Moonlight Becomes You," "Swinging on a Star," "Polka Dots and Moonbeams") strained credulity but not the singer.

far more money writing songs than they would have made in the family firm. Vincent Youmans' father sold a lot of hats, but not *that* many hats. Johnny Mercer paid off more than a million dollars of personal debts that his father, a respected Savannah banker, incurred in 1927 when land values abruptly dropped.

The boy from Syracuse solved the parental problem by eloping to New York and solved the Chester Babcock problem by getting rid of that person: he took the name Van Heusen from the shirt company because he thought it sounded classy. "Chester Babcock" would make only one more appearance—as the character played by Bob Hope in *The Road to Hong Kong*. In Manhattan the new husband paid the rent with musical odd jobs, finally composing his first hits in the late 1930s: "It's the Dreamer in Me," with Jimmy Dorsey, and "Heaven Can Wait (This is Paradise)," "All This and Heaven Too" and "Darn That Dream," with Eddie DeLange.

I first noticed Jimmy Van Heusen's ingratiating melodic gift in

Van Heusen at work with Bing Crosby and at play (croquet) with Frank Sinatra. Twenty-three of Bing's movies had songs by Van Heusen, and Frank recorded 77 of his songs, including most of the late hits like "All the Way" and "The Tender Trap" that revived his flagging career.

Like Harry Warren,
Jimmy Van Heusen
enjoyed the good life
of California and wasn't
particular about what
kind of movies his songs
were in. The melodies
that he wrote for Bing
Crosby were unfailingly
pleasant. Who cared if
the plots were fluff? And
who didn't like Dorothy
Lamour?

1942 in *The Road to Morocco*, when Bing Crosby sauntered into a patio and crooned "Moonlight Becomes You" to Dorothy Lamour, standing Juliet-like on a balcony:

Moonlight becomes you, it goes with your hair,
You certainly know the right things to wear . . .

Song and singer were perfectly matched: romantic drivel delivered with conviction and absolutely no strain; it was as if Crosby had been born to sing it. That was also my first exposure to Johnny Burke's feel-good lyrics. Van Heusen's principal collaborator from 1940 to 1953 was a bubbling well of metaphors:

Did you ever swing on a star,
Carry moonbeams home in a jar?

Hide your heart from sight,
Lock your dreams at night,
It could happen to you . . .

This road leads to Rainbowville,
Going my way?
Up ahead is Bluebird Hill,
Going my way?
Just pack a basket full of wishes . . .

I've never been able to remember a single lyric by Johnny Burke; the words leach out of my brain like moonbeams from a jar or wishes from a basket. I need words I can get a grip on. The only early Van Heusen song whose words I can recall from beginning to end, "I Thought About You," has a narrative lyric by Johnny Mercer that's grounded in the American landscape—familiar sights seen from a Pullman window.

The melodies Van Heusen wrote with Burke are so interesting that many of them survive on their own as jazz standards, much loved by musicians, like the wonderful "Here's That Rainy Day," or "Polka Dots and Moonbeams," whose words are too cute for any but the strongest stomach: "In my frightened arms, polka dots and moonbeams sparkled on a pug-nosed dream." Burke had been gazing skyward ("Pennies From Heaven," "Sing a Song of Sunbeams") and boning up on metaphors ("I've Got a Pocketful of Dreams," "My Heart Is Taking Lessons") long before he teamed with Van Heusen. Except for "Pennies From Heaven," a great standard and a pleasant lyric, I find Burke's stuff hard to swallow. I'm aware, however, that I'm a minority crank; the man has many admirers.

What gives Jimmy Van Heusen's melodies their signature

beauty is that his mind tended to work in eight-bar segments. Jerome Kern was his earlier counterpart—and, incidentally, his idol. The first eight bars of almost any Kern melody—"The Way You Look Tonight," "All the Things You Are," "Long Ago and Far Away"—move in a continuous line, not pausing to develop what has gone before. Other composers tend to write in shorter bursts that build on earlier material, especially Cole Porter: "I've got you under my skin." *Stop; repeat and amplify earlier idea*: "I've got you deep in the heart of me." *Stop; repeat and amplify*: "So deep in my heart . . . " Or George Gershwin: "Embrace me, my sweet embraceable you." *Stop; repeat the idea on a higher note*: "Embrace me, you irreplaceable you . . . "

Van Heusen, like Kern, usually keeps his initial idea flowing for eight bars:

> *Lately I find myself out gazing at stars, hearing guitars,*
>   *like someone in love.*

> *Call me irresponsible, call me unreliable, throw in*
>   *undependable, too.*

> *Love is lovelier the second time around,*
>   *just as wonderful with both feet on the ground.*

These are beautiful fluid lines, pleasing in their originality and lilt, their perfect confidence in where they are headed. Van Heusen then winds the song back down (if it's an A-B-A-B song) with an 8-bar counter-melody, maintaining its unruffled gait. "Call Me Irresponsible" continues:

> *Do my foolish alibis bore you?*
> *I'm not too clever, I just adore you.*

After that he repeats the first 8 bars and then wraps up the song— no extra bars or frills. He was content to stay within his melodic gift, especially during the Bing Crosby era, America's last age of innocence, seeming to not want to put Bing—or himself—to any exertion.

In 1954 Van Heusen's career got a second life when Frank Sinatra paired him with Sammy Cahn for a television version of *Our Town*, in which Sinatra played the stage manager and sang "Love and Marriage." So began a fertile collaboration with Cahn that would win three Academy Awards—for "All the Way," "High Hopes" and "Call Me Irresponsible"—and would play a major role in reviving Sinatra's beached career.

Songwriters who become the court favorite of a ruling singer

are no less fortunate than Bach or Beethoven in obtaining steady employment from a royal patron. But Sinatra was also shrewd enough to recognize in Van Heusen and Cahn the ideal providers of fare for his older voice and self. Tougher than Bing Crosby, an embodiment of the country's darker new emotions, he took off with the swinging songs from the new team—"The Tender Trap," "Come Fly With Me," "Come Dance With Me," "Only the Lonely," "The Second Time Around," "My Kind of Town," "September of My Years," "All the Way" and many more—and rode them to a new level of popularity and record sales.

Cahn gave Sinatra a solid language of the heart to work with. He wasn't into moonbeams or dreams; he wrote words that people would really say, expressing thoughts they would really think:

> *When somebody loves you*
> *It's no good unless she loves you*
> *All the way . . .*

Unlike Crosby, Sinatra was an up-front singer, his feelings available to his public. The seemingly genial Bing wore a veil telling the public not to come too close, and in all those love songs that Van Heusen and Burke wrote for him they were careful not to require Crosby to say "I love you." Love was declared by indirection:

IT COULD HAPPEN TO YOU

Words by JOHNNY BURKE   Music by JIMMY VAN HEUSEN

AND THE ANGELS SING

STARRING Dorothy LAMOUR * Fred MacMURRAY * Betty HUTTON

a Paramount Picture

SCORE

IT COULD HAPPEN TO YOU • HIS ROCKING HORSE RAN AWAY • MY HEART'S WRAPPED UP IN GINGHAM • KNOCKIN' ON YOUR OWN FRONT DOOR • THE FIRST HUNDRED YEARS • BLUEBIRDS IN MY BELFRY • WHEN STANISLAUS GOT MARRIED • HOW DOES YOUR GARDEN GROW

FAMOUS MUSIC CORPORATION · 1619 Broadway · New York City, N.Y.

It COULD happen to you.

IF I say I love you, it's not just because I love you, although moonlight becomes you so.

Lately I seem to walk AS THOUGH I had wings, bump into things, LIKE someone in love.

There was no "could" about Sinatra, no "if" or "as though" or "like." Van Heusen and Cahn's ballads enabled him to extend intimate invitations to the good life ("Come fly with me") or to share the late-night melancholy that only the lonely know.

"Frank hung on every note Jimmy wrote," I was told by the arranger and vocalist Joe Derise, who met Van Heusen in 1950 when he arranged and sang "Sunshine Cake" for Claude Thornhill's band in the movie *Riding High* and remained a close friend of the composer for the rest of his life. "Jimmy was a big man—six foot two, with a barrel chest," Derise said. "But when he sat down at the piano to play one of his songs you heard this warm, *tiny*, breathy voice come out of this huge man."

Sammy Cahn, like so many other songwriters, was born on New York's Lower East Side, the son of Jewish immigrant parents. Unlike the others, he took up the violin because his mother told him to ("in her mind the girl played the piano and the man played the violin"), becoming a teenage fiddler at weddings and other social occasions. Taking up lyric writing when his mother finally released him from his fiddling vows, he struck gold with his adaptation of the Yiddish song, "Bei Mir Bist du Schoen," which, improbably, gave the Andrews Sisters their first hit.

Looking back over Cahn's career, I can only guess that no other lyricist had so many huge commercial hits—not only all those early blockbusters with Jule Styne and all those late bloomers with Jimmy Van Heusen, but the many standards he tucked in along the way with other composers: "Please Be Kind" and "Until the Real Thing Comes Along" (Saul Chaplin); "I Should Care" and "Day By Day" (Axel Stordahl and Paul Weston); "Teach Me Tonight" (Gene DePaul). He made the job look so easy that he made himself easy to overlook and to underestimate. But to achieve such authentic simplicity is one of the hardest of artistic tasks.

Alan Jay Lerner and Frederick Loewe

The songwriting team generically known as Lerner & Loewe won't be remembered for pushing the musical theater into new terrain. If anything, they were a throwback to the earlier generic team of Gilbert & Sullivan. Of all American lyricists, Alan Jay Lerner was the nearest descendant of W. S. Gilbert; he could have written lyrics for Sir Arthur Sullivan. The composer Frederick Loewe was also a residual product of the 19th century; he could have written melodies for Gilbert. Born in Vienna in 1901, the son of an actor who starred in Franz Lehar's *The Merry Widow*, he was reared on the romantic strains of European operetta. When he began to collaborate with Lerner, in 1942, his work continued to sound Viennese. No jazz rhythms or blue flavors from the new musical America of Irving Berlin and George Gershwin crept into his melodies.

Nor did the team have any yen to tell modern stories. Lerner & Loewe's first Broadway hit, *Brigadoon*, was about a Scottish village that comes to life for one day every 100 years; their second, *Paint Your Wagon*, was about the California gold rush, and their three huge achievements—the musicals *My Fair Lady* and *Camelot* and the movie *Gigi*—were set in Edward VII's London, King Arthur's Cornwall and Colette's turn-of-the-century Paris.

But, hey, who's complaining? These guys gave us *My Fair Lady*. Never was a more elegant banquet for the eye, the ear and the mind served by the musical theater. Adapted from George Bernard Shaw's play *Pygmalion*, it opened in 1956, ran on Broadway for six and a half years, and has been playing in some part of the world ever since. There have been other musicals that I enjoyed more: *Oklahoma!, Guys and Dolls, Gypsy, St. Louis Woman, Annie Get Your Gun*; I felt connected to their American humor and idiom.

Composer Frederick Loewe and lyricist Alan Jay Lerner at a backstage piano. Five cups of coffee and one pack of cigarettes don't seem to have helped in their search for a melodic or lyrical fix. Writing songs as technically perfect as the numbers in "My Fair Lady" is the result of long and agonizing work.

And yet. . . whenever I roam the TV channels and run across the movie version of *My Fair Lady*, which is closely based on the Broadway show, I can't turn it off. One after another the plot-advancing, character-defining songs come along—"You Did It," "Show Me," "A Hymn to Him" ("Why Can't a Woman Be More Like a Man?")—and I get caught up again in their perfection.

Alan Jay Lerner was almost 20 years younger than "Fritz" Loewe. Born in New York in 1918 to the family that owned the Lerner shoe stores, a graduate of Harvard, he was still another songwriting son of the affluent, educated class. Like Oscar Hammerstein, he was also a librettist, writing the book for his musicals as well as the lyrics. Turning *Pygmalion* into a musical was a test of those twin skills that would have undone a writer less intellectually agile. Shaw's play had already defeated a long line of suitors eager to marry it to music and lyrics. When Lerner first wrestled with it, in 1952, Hammerstein asked him how he and Loewe were coming along. "Slowly," Lerner told him. Hammerstein said, "It can't be done. Dick [Rodgers] and I worked on it for over a year and gave it up."

Pondering this news, Lerner and Loewe also dropped the project for several years. Two obstacles had blocked them. One was that they felt bound by certain conventions from the great musicals of the previous decade, especially those of Rodgers and Hammerstein. There had to be an ensemble of local residents: *Oklahoma!* had its farmers and cattlemen, *Carousel* its New England villagers, *South Pacific* its seamen. There also had to be a subplot, preferably romantic: Liat and Lieutenant Cable in *South Pacific*, Tuptim and Lun Tha in *The King and I*. And at some point—so said Agnes De Mille and Jerome Robbins—there had to be a ballet: Laurey's dream in *Oklahoma!*, the Civil War ballet in *Bloomer Girl*, the "Uncle Tom's Cabin" allegory in *The King and I*, the cops-and-robbers chase in *High Button Shoes*.

The second problem was that George Bernard Shaw was a man of many words, and the best musicals use very few, paring their book to keep things moving with a minimum of gab. Words, however, were the whole point of *Pygmalion*. Shaw's comedy is about an imperious professor of phonetics, Henry Higgins, who bets that he can pass off the Cockney flower girl Eliza Doolittle as a duchess at an embassy ball by refining her manners, her accent and her use of the English language. For a musical hoping to enter that world there would be no escaping the Shavian torrent.

In 1954, however, Lerner and Loewe decided to try again. Cultural changes in the theater, they felt, had begun to loosen the old rules. But their big breakthrough was the realization that Shaw was not the problem but the solution. He had written one plot so compelling that they didn't need a subplot, and he had created characters so interesting—especially Henry Higgins—that they didn't need a supporting population of local folk, like the Scottish folk in *Brigadoon* or the Irish folk in *Finian's Rainbow*. Nor would they need a ballet to express in dance what might be tiresome in words. They looked the demon in the eye—language—and didn't blink. Lerner incorporated whole chunks of Shaw's dialogue in his book and wrote some of the most word-heavy songs in Broadway history.

Not all of them were verbose. Three were simple beauties, lyrically direct, musically tender: "Wouldn't It Be Loverly?", "On the Street Where You Live" and "I Could Have Danced All Night" (the most popular of all Lerner and Loewe songs). Two others, "With a Little Bit o' Luck" and "Get Me to the Church on Time," sung by Eliza Doolittle's Cockney father, were knockabout tunes in the English music-hall tradition. But the rest were mostly patter songs of the Gilbert & Sullivan school—intricate, witty and meticulous in their meter and rhyme.

Lerner was lucky in having two actors of impeccable diction—Julie Andrews and Rex Harrison—to deliver these rapid-fire philippics and philosophical discourses. As Eliza Doolittle, Andrews told off her tormentor Harrison in "Just You Wait, 'enry 'iggins!" and "Without You," and told off the fatuous swain Freddie in "Show Me." But Harrison got the great set pieces that give the show its intellectual center: "Why Can't the English?", "I'm an Ordinary Man" and "A Hymn to Him". Those numbers tell us the three things Shaw wanted us to know about Professor Higgins: that he passionately loved the English language and considered it England's ultimate class barrier, that he was a particularly smug male, and that he had a low opinion of women. Think how much dramatic exposition those three songs accomplish.

It was through Rex Harrison that Lerner discovered his Shavian voice. Trying to learn "Why Can't the English?", Harrison told Lerner that the song made him feel like a second-rate Noël Coward. Puzzled by the complaint, Lerner finally saw that the problem might lie in the rhyme scheme. He had initially written:

Why can't the English teach their children how to speak?
In Norway there are legions
Of literate Norwegians . . .

He rewrote it:

Why can't the English teach their children how to speak?
This verbal class distinction by now should be antique . . .

The change "made the lyric less 'lyricky' and more actable," Lerner recalled, "and made Rex comfortable. [After that,] the more I worked on his material, the more I began to enjoy it and the more at home I became. Somehow I had the feeling that in finding a style for Rex I was also finding a style for myself. To this day I find myself instinctively writing for Rex and constantly reminding myself that I am not. Nevertheless he was then and will always be my natural extension."

Changing that lyric, I think, was the moment when Alan Jay Lerner separated himself from other American lyricists and crossed over into Gilberthood. The couplet about the legions of literate Norwegians is not only pure Noël Coward; it's pure Lorenz Hart and Ira Gershwin and E. Y. Harburg and, especially, pure Cole Porter. The quick, facile rhyme provides instant gratification. Lerner was after a longer line—a declarative sentence—and a slower payoff:

I've grown accustomed to her face!
She almost makes the day begin.
I've grown accustomed to the tune
She whistles night and noon,
Her smiles, her frowns,
Her ups, her downs
Are second nature to me now,
Like breathing out and breathing in . . .

That's one of the great American theater songs, set to one of Loewe's most understated melodies. It makes a perfect ending for *My Fair Lady* and for Henry Higgins' hesitant journey into the *terra incognita* of the heart.

Lerner would continue to write for his alter ego when he wrote lyrics for Louis Jourdan and Maurice Chevalier in *Gigi*, in 1958, and for Richard Burton in *Camelot*, in 1960. Jourdan, singing the soliloquy "Gigi," about the girl whose blossoming he has finally noticed ("Have I been standing up too close, or back too far?"), could be Rex Harrison soliloquizing about Eliza Doolittle. Or, singing "She's Not Thinking of Me," he could be Harrison expatiating on the fickleness of the female. Chevalier got from Lerner two charming Gallic disquisitions on love, "Thank Heaven for Little Girls" and "I'm Glad I'm Not Young Any More," plus one of the most wise and compassionate of all situation songs, "I Remember It Well," in which he and Hermione Gingold recall—very differently—the details of their long-ago romance.

Camelot, the last Lerner and Loewe collaboration, based on T. H. White's Arthurian epic *The Once and Future King*, was *My Fair Lady* untamed—an avalanche of fastidious words and lush melodies, of opulent costumes and sets. On its much-trumpeted opening night in Toronto it ran four and a half hours. The corrective surgery hospitalized Lerner with an ulcer and director Moss Hart with a heart attack and left the show bleeding badly. But it recovered and ran for 873 performances, an honorable survivor, its score full of melodic gems—"If Ever I Would Leave You," "Camelot," "I Loved You Once in Silence," "How to Handle a Woman"—and loquacious lyrics: "I Wonder What the King Is Doing Tonight," "The Simple Joys of Maidenhood," "C'est Moi," "What Do the Simple Folk Do?", "The Lusty Month of May," "Then You May Take Me to the Fair." Lerner had out-Gilberted W. S. Gilbert, and his three stars—Richard Burton as King Arthur, Julie Andrews as Queen Guinevere, and Robert Goulet as Lancelot—out-Rexed Harrison.

The genius of Fritz Loewe's achievement with Lerner was to write melodies that always sounded pleasant and that perfectly served the densely worded lyrics. They are major-scale melodies, with almost no half-tones. They never did stop sounding Viennese in their hint of violins and their accelerations of tempo ("I Could Have Danced All Night"). Nor did Loewe ever forsake for the new world the pleasures of the continent that had reared him and that remained his favorite sandbox. Between shows with Lerner he played the chemin-de-fer tables at Cannes for months at a time, and in his sixties he largely gave up composing, seemingly without regret.

Lerner got the impatient American gene: he was a man who had to keep busy. One activity that kept him busy was being married eight times. He was also an MGM screenwriter, winning an Academy Award for his screenplay of the Gershwin pastiche, *An American in Paris*. Another of his films, *Royal Wedding*, best known for the scene in which Fred Astaire dances up and down the walls of a room and across its ceiling, had among its songs—by Lerner and Burton Lane—the fine standard "Too Late Now."

It was with Lane that Alan Jay Lerner would write his last Broadway hit, *On a Clear Day You Can See Forever*, in 1965. Four unsuccessful shows were to follow: *Coco* (Andre Previn), *1600 Pennsylvania Avenue* (Leonard Bernstein), *Carmelina* (Burton Lane) and *Dance a Little Closer* (Charles Strouse). But he remained a craftsman to the end, his work serious and intelligent. If none of it matched *My Fair Lady*, he had set the standard impossibly high.

John Kander and Fred Ebb
(and Jerry Bock and Sheldon Harnick)

John Kander, composer with the lyricist Fred Ebb of *Cabaret* and *Chicago* and other Broadway hits, remembers the exact moment when he realized that the golden age of American popular song was over. His story comes in two installments.

In 1966, he told me, he went to Boston for the out-of-town try-out of *Cabaret*. Unpacking his bags in his hotel room, he turned on the radio and got a station that was playing popular songs, which included some of his own from *Cabaret*. The moment wasn't all that unusual; individual songs had always been the bread and butter of disk jockeys. A year later, out of town with his next show, *The Happy Time*, Kander turned on the radio again. This time he didn't hear any of his own songs—or anybody else's show tunes or standards. All he could find was rock.

Rock, or rock 'n' roll—a term loosely embracing a cluster of new musical forms that emphasized the performer, or the performing group, or the performer-composer, rather than the song itself—had been in the air for a decade. But not until the mid-1960s did it dislodge standards and jazz as the dominant popular music form in America. With its insistent pulse, its repetitive lyrics and its amplified volume the new music turned on the young and turned off their elders, who had been reared on melody and narrative and a lower decibel count.

It was a split as wide as a chasm, severing the old American tradition of a musical heritage that was shared by all generations.

Lyricist Fred Ebb and composer John Kander working on the score of "Chicago." The creators of "Cabaret" are still active as a songwriting team, the last custodians of the tradition of the well-constructed musical play that began with "Show Boat."

I remember a summer evening when I happened to catch one of Mitch Miller's sing-alongs in a small Midwestern town. Almost every song was familiar to almost everyone in the audience—songs like "For Me and My Gal," "Let Me Call You Sweetheart," "If You Were the Only Girl in the World," "You Are My Sunshine," "By the Light of the Silvery Moon," "Till We Meet Again," "Take Me Out to the Ball Game," "When Irish Eyes Are Smiling" and "A Bicycle Built for Two"—though none of them had been written during our lifetime. They were all hand-me-downs; we had learned them from our parents or our grandparents, who had learned them from *their* parents. Or we had sung them around the campfire at summer camp. Or we had heard them in all those turn-of-the-century Betty Grable movies like *Sweet Rosie O'Grady*.

That continuity between the generations was snapped when rock became the secular religion of American youth and the propellant of its various social revolutions in the late sixties. Soon rock itself would splinter into many mongrel forms with mongrel names like folk-rock and funk and disco. But by any name the new arrivals became the country's new popular music literature. Today the iconic songs from the age of Woodstock are as bathed in nostalgia as the popular standards of earlier decades. Aging baby boomers, hearing on the radio an old Grateful Dead or Rolling Stones number, are no less carried back in time than their parents hearing an old Gershwin song.

But to become a new George or Ira Gershwin was no longer a possibility—the 32-bar standard was dead. Even giants like Hoagy Carmichael couldn't get their new songs published or played. Jazz was also unwanted; nightclubs closed, and dozens of great jazzmen simply disappeared or went to Europe to scrape together a living. The last outlet for the well-constructed narrative song was the Broadway musical theater, now almost suicidally expensive, and a few theater composers and lyricists managed to do solid work well into the 1970s.

Two of the best were Jerry Bock and Sheldon Harnick, whose *Fiorello!*, based on the life of New York's peppery Mayor LaGuardia, won the Pulitzer Prize in 1959. Its score was a skillful mixture of musical comedy elements, catching the rowdiness of big-city politics ("Gentleman Jimmy," "The Bum Won," "Politics and Poker"), the higher goals of the reform mayor ("The Name's LaGuardia"), and the yearnings of the women around the edge ("When Did I Fall in Love?", "The Very Next Man"). Bock's melodies had an urban energy as well as a softer side of great beauty ("Till Tomorrow"), and Harnick's lyrics matched their warmth and their humor, especially

Jerry Bock and Sheldon
Harnick at the recording
session for "The Apple
Tree" in 1966.

"Little Tin Box," one of the all-time hilarious show tunes, in which
a machine politician, queried about the source of his considerable
wealth, attributes it to the thrifty habits of a lifetime: putting coins
into a little tin box "that a little tin key unlocks."

Bock and Harnick revisited bygone New York in their next
show, *Tenderloin*, and followed it with *She Loves Me*, an intimate
musical based on the old Hollywood bonbon, *The Shop Around the
Corner*, a tale of two pen-pal lovebirds in Budapest unknowingly
working in the same candy shop. *Fiddler on the Roof*, in 1964, greatly
broadened their canvas. Based on Sholem Aleichem's story, *Tevye
and His Daughters*, it was a boisterous tapestry of life in a Jewish
village in Russia in the early 1900s. With its underlying theme of

poverty and persecution it broke every theory of what Broadway musical audiences would put up with. But obviously this fiddler struck many universal chords, not the least being Tevye's efforts to marry off those five daughters. The show ran for 3,242 performances—almost eight years. Once again, as in *Fiorello!*, Bock and Harnick's score perfectly served the plot. Harnick's lyrics were steeped in shtetl wisdom and humor ("Tradition," "If I Were a Rich Man," "Matchmaker, Matchmaker"), and Bock's melodies were Old World Jewish in their minor colors, especially "Sunrise, Sunset." But after two more musicals, *The Apple Tree* and *The Rothschilds*, the team broke up.

Another pair that separated too soon—the composer Charles Strouse and the lyricist Lee Adams—wrote another of my favorite musicals, *Bye Bye Birdie*, an affectionate spoof of the impact of a Presley-like rock star on the teenagers of a small American town. "Put on a Happy Face" was typical of the score's geniality; "The Telephone Hour" and "Kids" were typical of its humor—one lampooning the teenagers' addictive use of the phone, the other satirizing the self-righteousness of their parents—and "An English Teacher," "Talk to Me" and "Rosie" were gentle beauties. Strouse's rich melodic gift, which would adorn such later Strouse-Adams musicals as *All-American* and *Applause*, produced the guileless "Tomorrow," in 1974, when he teamed with the lyricist Martin Charnin for *Annie*.

Two other strong Broadway songwriters of the period were Jerry Herman and Cy Coleman. Herman, who wrote both music and lyrics, is best remembered for the long-running *Hello, Dolly* and *Mame* and their title songs—rousers of the kind that pit orchestras were born to play. But that reputation overlooks many fine songs of lower voltage in *Hello, Dolly* ("It Only Takes a Moment"), in *Mame* ("If He Walked Into My Life"), in *Mack and Mabel* ("I Won't Send Roses"), and in *La Cage Aux Folles* ("Look Over There"). Coleman did his best composing with two women. Carolyn Leigh was his lyricist for a handful of hits ("Witchcraft," "It Amazes Me") before the team succeeded on Broadway with the musicals *Wildcat* and *Little Me*. The other collaborator was Dorothy Fields, whose lyrics for *Sweet Charity* and *Seesaw* ("Big Spender," "If My Friends Could See Me Now") were a good fit for Coleman's jazz-flavored style.

But the true survivors on Broadway are John Kander and Fred Ebb. They have stayed together as a composer-lyricist team and are still doing with excellence what they began in 1964 with *Flora, the Red Menace* and continued with *Cabaret*, *The Happy Time*, *Zorba*, *70 Girls 70*, *Chicago*, *The Act*, *Woman of the Year*, *The Rink*, *Kiss of the*

Spider Woman and *Steel Pier*. Both *Cabaret* and *Chicago* have been strikingly reimagined and revived; a collage of 22 Kander & Ebb songs, *And the World Goes Round*, had a long off-Broadway run, and two musicals-in-progress—one adapted from Friedrich Dürrenmatt's play *The Visit*, the other from Thornton Wilder's play *The Skin of Our Teeth*—will continue their work in the new century.

John Kander also perpetuates one of this book's recurring themes: a boy from a supportive Jewish home picking out tunes on the family piano and growing up in a society that valued music. "I found the piano when I was about five," says Kander, who was born in 1927 in Kansas City; his father, who was in the poultry and egg business, loved to hear him play. "One day," Kander told me, "my Aunt Rheta put her hands over mine and we made a C-major chord. That was a great moment—when I found I could do that. Music was part of American life. We were always being taken to children's concerts and to all those little opera companies that came through Kansas City, and our schools had all those music appreciation programs. Today it's mostly gone."

Kander also had an old-fashioned craft apprenticeship. He wrote musicals in high school, became involved in musical theater at Oberlin College and then got his M.A. in music at Columbia. There one of his mentors, Douglas Moore, chairman of the music department and composer of *The Ballad of Baby Doe* and other American operas, told him, "If I had it to do all over again I'd write for Broadway." Kander says: "That was the kick in the ass I needed. Moore legitimized me. I took an assistantship in an opera workshop, I accompanied and coached singers, I conducted in summer stock, I arranged dance music. The result was that I eased into the business. All those jobs kept me from being frightened when my own time came to write musicals. It held less mystery for me."

In 1963 a music publisher paired Kander with Fred Ebb, and the first song they wrote, "My Coloring Book," was introduced by Sandy Stewart on Perry Como's television show. The show received thousands of letters responding to the song, and 40 different recordings were made. What the letter writers were responding to was a fresh approach to an overworked subject. Kander's quiet waltz had a strong narrative line and Ebb's forlorn lyric came at the age-old story from a new direction:

> *These are the eyes that watched him as he walked away.*
> *Color them gray.*
> *This is the heart that thought he would always be true.*
> *Color it blue . . .*

Fred Ebb was born in New York in 1932—his father was a salesman—and went to New York University and got an M.A. in English literature from Columbia. "I always loved the theater," he told me, "and after college I started writing lyrics. But I became profoundly depressed because I couldn't also write music. One night I had a blind date with a girl named Patsy Vamos, and I put my problem to her. She said that she knew Phil Springer, composer of 'Santa Baby' and 'Moonlight Gambler,' which was a big Frankie Laine hit, and that he needed a lyricist. I auditioned for him, and the first song we wrote got recorded by Carmen McRae. It was called 'Never Loved Him Anyhow.' ('Well anyhow, not much.') None of our other songs caught on—in our first year we made about $80—and after a while Phil left and took a job in the music business."

But it was a start, and Ebb still thinks of Patsy Vamos with gratitude and wonders where she is today. Next, with the composer Paul Klein, he struck it big with a country song called "That Do Make It Nice," featured by Eddie Arnold, and the team also wrote some popular children's songs, especially "The Horse in Striped Pajamas," which was in fact a zebra. "Paul was very good," Ebb says, "but he didn't have the commitment to starving that I had. He got married and said he had to earn a living and went into another field." Ebb meanwhile supported his art in the nether regions of the job market. He was a credit authorizer; he worked on a truck for Valcort Hosiery, whose slogan, he remembers, was "One Woman Tells Another," and he bronzed baby shoes for an ornamental iron company.

Rescue came with his introduction to John Kander, which resulted in *Flora, the Red Menace*. It was Liza Minnelli's first big role and the start of a long triple friendship. Minnelli would star in Kander & Ebb's *Chicago* on Broadway and in the movie of their *Cabaret*, for which she won an Academy Award, and would sing their title song on the soundtrack of the movie *New York, New York*. Today "New York, New York" is a cultural icon lodged in the brain of baseball fans; Frank Sinatra's recording is played over the public address system at Yankee Stadium after every Yankees home game—a songwriter's dream. Of all the odes written to the Big Apple, none can match the swagger of Ebb's career-counseling lyric: "If you can make it there you'll make it anywhere."

Flora was also the start of Kander and Ebb's long association with Harold Prince, the most innovative producer-director of the modern musical theater. Their next show together, *Cabaret*, was a strikingly confident score for two young songwriters on only their second effort. *Cabaret* was already a thrice-told tale: first a book by

Christopher Isherwood, *Berlin Stories*, about Berlin between the wars; then a play by John van Druten, *I Am a Camera*, and then a movie of the same title, based on the play. But Kander's music and Ebb's lyrics and Prince's staging gave the story a sordid new vitality, starting with the brilliant "Wilkommen," in which the cynical host of the Kit Kat Klub welcomes the audience in three languages. Kander's score evoked the tinny orchestrations of Kurt Weill's bitter German operas of the same period; Ebb's lyrics ("Two Ladies," "Money, Money," "What Would You Do?") reflected the hollow values of the time and place, and "Cabaret" has been an international standard ever since.

"*Cabaret* broke new ground," Kander says, "by moving away from the linear shape of the Rodgers & Hammerstein musicals. The show was very presentational—songs like 'Wilkommen' were presented directly to the audience—and one of our later shows, *Chicago*, was *all* presentation; we called it 'vaudeville.' But at the time nobody thinks, 'Now I'm breaking new ground.'" Ebb strongly concurs. "You *never* think that," he says. "You only think about serving the moment." My impression was of two modest men, uninflated by their Kennedy Center honors and other awards, going about their work as seriously as when they were starting out.

Revisiting that body of work on the CD of *And the World Goes Round*, I find Kander's music unfailingly melodic. It has great theatrical energy when energy is called for ("All That Jazz," "Cabaret," "The Kiss of the Spider Woman"). But more often his melodies— and Ebb's lyrics—are tender and emotional: "Colored Lights" and "Marry Me," from *The Rink*, "I Don't Remember You," from *The Happy Time*, "A Quiet Thing," from *Flora, The Red Menace*, "Sometimes a Day Goes By," from *Woman of the Year*. Ebb's lyrics also have a lot of humor.

"There's a river of music going on in my head all the time," Kander told me. "When a song is needed I dip into it and see if I can use it." His hero is Jerome Kern: "There's something about the melodic and harmonic invention; it has a warmth to it." Ebb's heroes are Lorenz Hart, Cole Porter and Frank Loesser. "Those are men I've revered all my life," he says. Of his own songs, his favorite is "But the World Goes Round," from *New York, New York*, which sums up his view of the big picture:

> Somebody loses and somebody wins,
> One day it's kicks, then it's kicks in the shins,
> But the planet spins
> And the world goes round and round.

Life goes on, and the point is to endure. "I'm proud of sticking to it," Ebb says of his career, grateful for the planet's many favorable spins since he was working on Valcort's hosiery truck and bronzing baby shoes.

Kander is grateful for the accident of timing that enabled him and Ebb to invade Broadway before high costs made producers fearful of taking a risk on new talent. "Along with Steve Sondheim and Jerry Herman and Harnick and Bock," he says, "we were the last generation of songwriters who were allowed to fail. Even before *Flora* opened, before anyone knew how it would go over, Hal Prince said to Fred and me, 'We'll meet on Sunday to talk about the next show.' Which turned out to be *Cabaret*. Today, younger writers don't get that break—the opportunity to learn their craft by failing. We all had it."

★   ★   ★

My journey ends with Kander and Ebb because they are the last custodians of the well-made musical play. I don't mean that musicals are dead; on the contrary, Broadway today has more long-running blockbusters than ever before—shows like *Les Misérables* and *The Phantom of the Opera* and Disney's *Beauty and the Beast* and *The Lion King* may well be around when another century turns. Their prophet and pioneer was the British composer Andrew Lloyd Webber, whose *Cats* ran for 18 years.

But those musicals are a whole new breed—high-tech spectacles that rely for their appeal on size and special effects, nearer to IMAX or the ice show than to the theater. Their audiences are also a new breed. Historically, people went to the musical theater for language as much as for music; shows like *The King and I* and *Guys and Dolls* and *My Fair Lady* captivated audiences with words and ideas. Today's audiences are children of the new age of electronic entertainment; they want visual dazzle and a lot of sound. They also don't require more than a general idea of what the songs are about, especially because so many of them are tourists from other countries. In this respect they are like operagoers. Audiences at *La Bohême* only need to know that Mimi is dying in a Paris garret to be moved by Puccini's music. If Andrew Lloyd Webber isn't Puccini—if the glutinous melodies don't linger in the memory or in the heart—nobody much cares. The score has done its expected job of wrapping the audience in a cocoon of amplified music, now the habitat of much of the population of the globe. A tourist from Kazakhstan would be puzzled by the revival of *Kiss Me, Kate* but would get along fine at *The Phantom of the Opera*.

This is the cultural shift that finally killed the musical theater of Rodgers & Hammerstein and Frank Loesser and Lerner & Loewe. Obviously costs were a contributing cause; producers became afraid to invest in any show that wasn't a guaranteed crowd pleaser. Rock was also a factor; it altered the way Americans listened to popular song, siring a generation that wanted its music electrified and didn't insist on songs that told a story or had rhymes that exactly rhymed. But those were just tremors in the larger revolution. What fundamentally changed was the audience. The love affair with language was over.

The great American songwriters wrote for men and women who cared about literary forms, the end product of a heritage that esteemed the written and the spoken word. Gilbert and Sullivan were inseparably joined, but it was the lyricist Gilbert who fixed the songs in our memory. George and Ira Gershwin were inseparably joined, but it was Ira who gave the melodies their meaning and their emotion: "a foggy day in London town," "they can't take that away from me." When I think of Jerome Kern, what I hear is Hammerstein's "old man river" and Dorothy Fields' "the way you look tonight." When I think of Richard Rodgers, I hear Hart's "my funny valentine" and Hammerstein's "oh, what a beautiful mornin'." When I think of Harold Arlen, I hear Harburg's "somewhere over the rainbow" and Mercer's "my mama done tol' me." When I think of the composer-lyricist Irving Berlin, I hear "there's no business like show business" and "I left my heart at the stage-door canteen." When I think of the composer-lyricist Cole Porter, I hear "every time we say goodbye" and "it was just one of those things." When I think of the composer-lyricist Frank Loesser, I hear "once in love with Amy."

But of course I wouldn't recall any of those phrases if they hadn't been set to music. They needed exactly the right melodies to bring them to life, just as the melodies needed exactly the right words. That's the marriage I never get tired of celebrating. The songs of the great American songwriters have never stopped reverberating through my days and nights, easy to remember and impossible to forget.

SONGS BY CATEGORY

Time

Soon
Time After Time
Time on My Hands
Just in Time
Bidin' My Time
I Didn't Know What Time It Was
As Time Goes By
It's Been a Long, Long Time
At Last
At Long Last Love
Always
How Long Has This Been
  Going On?
Once in a While
My Shining Hour
Round Midnight
From This Moment On
Some Other Time
Some Enchanted Evening
Some Day My Prince Will Come
Never in a Million Years
Day In, Day Out
Day By Day
Days of Wine and Roses
What a Difference a Day Made
Long Ago and Far Away
Yesterdays
If I Could Spend One Hour
  With You
Five Minutes More
Sunday, Monday or Always
Till Tomorrow
Too Late Now
The Party's Over

Weather

Soon It's Gonna Rain
Here's That Rainy Day
Isn't This a Lovely Day
  (to Be Caught in the Rain)?
Singin' in the Rain
Raindrops Keep Falling on
  My Head
Come Rain or Come Shine
Stormy Weather
A Foggy Day
Too Darn Hot
Heat Wave
Blue Skies
It's a Lovely Day Today
It's a Lovely Day Tomorrow
In the Cool, Cool, Cool of
  the Evening
Let It Snow! Let It Snow! Let
  It Snow!

Meteorology

Star Dust
Stars Fell on Alabama
I've Told Every Little Star
Ill Wind
They Call the Wind Maria
Ole Buttermilk Sky
My Blue Heaven
Pennies From Heaven
Paper Moon
Blue Moon
Moonglow
Moonlight Becomes You
Moonlight in Vermont
Polka Dots and Moonbeams
That Old Devil Moon
East of the Sun
  (and West of the Moon)
Over the Rainbow
Sunrise, Sunset
On a Clear Day You Can
  See Forever

The Seasons

June in January
Spring Will Be a Little Late
   This Year
It Might As Well Be Spring
Suddenly It's Spring
Spring Is Here
Spring Can Really Hang You Up
   the Most
April in Paris
I'll Remember April
Easter Parade
One Morning in May
June Is Bustin' Out All Over
Summertime
The Things We Did Last
   Summer
Autumn Leaves
Autumn in New York
September Song
September in the Rain
Winter Wonderland
White Christmas

You

You Must Have Been a Beautiful
   Baby
You Do Something to Me
You Are Too Beautiful
You Make Me Feel So Young
You Go to My Head
You Were Never Lovelier
You Keep Coming Back Like
   a Song
You Took Advantage of Me
You and the Night and
   the Music
You'd Be So Nice to Come
   Home To
Namely You
Embraceable You
All of You
I Remember You

I Thought About You
I'll String Along With You
It Had to Be You
How About You?
The Very Thought of You
The Nearness of You
Getting to Know You
All the Things You Are
The Way You Look Tonight
Any Old Place With You
Thou Swell
Of Thee I Sing
You're the Top

Idioms

Fools Rush In
I Should Care
I've Got the World on a String
I'm Putting All My Eggs in
   One Basket
Look for the Silver Lining
Between the Devil and the Deep
   Blue Sea
Come Rain or Come Shine
Right as the Rain
I've Got Beginner's Luck
Nice Work If You Can Get It
Let's Call the Whole Thing Off
Things Are Looking Up
Doin' What Comes Natur'lly
It Never Entered My Mind
My Heart Stood Still
More Than You Know
What a Difference a Day Made
I Get a Kick Out of You
Just One of Those Things
Anything Goes
I've Got You Under My Skin
Accentuate the Positive
Body and Soul
The Best Things in Life Are Free

Hortatory

Don't Blame Me
Don't Fence Me In
Don't Sit Under the Apple Tree
Don't Ever Leave Me
Don't Rain on My Parade
Do, Do, Do (What You Done,
   Done, Done Before)
Do Nothing Til You Hear
   From Me
Button Up Your Overcoat
Wrap Your Troubles in Dreams
Take Back Your Mink
Oh, Lady Be Good
Love Me or Leave Me
Say It Isn't So
Cry Me a River
Blame It on My Youth
Speak Low
Sing for Your Supper
Get Happy
Make Someone Happy
Put on a Happy Face
Clap Yo' Hands
Slap That Bass
Get Out of Town
Take the A Train
Fly Me to the Moon
Come Fly With Me
Hit the Road to Dreamland
Praise the Lord and Pass the
   Ammunition
Give It Back to the Indians
Use Your Imagination
Buckle Down, Winsocki!
Brush Up Your Shakespeare
Make It Another Old-Fashioned,
   Please
Call Me Irresponsible
Give Me the Simple Life
Try to Remember
Stay As Sweet As You Are
Willow Weep for Me

Blow, Gabriel, Blow
Beat Me, Daddy, Eight to the Bar
Get Thee Behind Me, Satan
Sit Down, You're Rocking
   the Boat!
Let Yourself Go
Pick Yourself Up
Look for the Silver Lining
Take Him
Just You Wait
Show Me
Squeeze Me

Questions

Who?
Why Do I Love You?
Why Was I Born?
Why Shouldn't I?
Why Can't You Behave?
Who Can I Turn To?
Who Cares?
Who Do You Love, I Hope?
Who Wants to Be a Millionaire?
How About You?
How About Me?
How Long Has This Been
   Going On?
How Deep Is the Ocean?
How's Chances?
How'd You Like to Spoon
   With Me?
How Are Things in Glocca
   Morra?
What Is There to Say?
What Is This Thing Called Love?
What Kind of Fool Am I?
What's the Use of Wonderin'?
What's Good About Goodbye?
What'll I Do?
Wouldn't It Be Loverly?
Could You Use Me?
Do I Love You, Do I?
Isn't It a Pity?
Isn't It Romantic?

Where's That Rainbow?
Have You Met Miss Jones?
Can I Forget You?
Shall We Dance?
Papa, Won't You Dance With Me?
Brother, Can You Spare a Dime?
Who's Afraid of the Big,
    Bad Wolf?
Well, Did You Evah?

Places

I Left My Heart in San Francisco
I've Got a Gal in Kalamazoo
Chattanooga Choo-Choo
Route 66
Memphis In June
Carolina in the Morning
Georgia on My Mind
Can't Get Indiana Off My Mind
Swanee
Stars Fell on Alabama
A Little Girl From Little Rock
On the Atchison, Topeka and the
    Santa Fe
Everything's Up to Date in
    Kansas City
Manhattan
New York, New York
Autumn in New York
I Love Paris
April in Paris
The Last Time I Saw Paris
A Foggy Day (in London Town)
A Nightingale Sang in
    Berkeley Square
The White Cliffs of Dover
Down Argentina Way
Moon of Manakoora
Oklahoma!
Camelot

Destinations

Alabammy Bound
Flying Down to Rio
On a Slow Boat to China
There's a Boat Dat's Leavin'
    Soon for New York
Goodbye, Mama, I'm Off to
    Yokohama
The Road to Morocco
Do You Know the Way to
    San José?

Real Estate

On the Street Where You Live
Sunny Side of the Street
Let's Take a Walk Around the Block
Way Out West (on West
    End Avenue)
Slumming on Park Avenue
Down in the Depths on the
    90th Floor
Penthouse Serenade
Forty-Second Street
Lullaby of Broadway
Chinatown, My Chinatown
I Cover the Waterfront
Boulevard of Broken Dreams
Standing on the Corner
The Boy Next Door
The Folks Who Live on the Hill
A Bungalow in Quogue

Finance

We're in the Money
Brother, Can You Spare a Dime?
I've Got Five Dollars
I Found a Million-Dollar Baby
    (in a Five-and-Ten-Cent Store)
Pennies From Heaven
Three Coins in the Fountain
Ten Cents a Dance
With Plenty of Money and You
Diamonds Are a Girl's
    Best Friend
The Best Things in Life Are Free

She

Laura
Tangerine
Sweet Sue
Sweet Lorraine
Sweet Georgia Brown
Sleepy Time Gal
Honeysuckle Rose
The Most Beautiful Girl in
   the World
The Hostess With the Mostes'
   on the Ball
The Girl From Ipanema
Little Girl Blue
Satin Doll
Lulu's Back in Town
Once in Love With Amy
Have You Met Miss Jones?
Mona Lisa
Lily Marlene
Baby Face
Melancholy Baby
The Girl That I Marry
Wait Till You See Her
A Gal in Calico
Hello, Dolly
Mame
Rosalie
Evelina
Samantha
Amapola
Margie
Nancy
Louise
Liza
Gigi

I and Me

I Found a Million-Dollar Baby
I Only Have Eyes for You
I Don't Want to Walk
   Without You
I Surrender, Dear

I Married an Angel
I Can't Give You Anything
   But Love
I Could Write a Book
I Guess I'll Have to Change
   My Plan
I Should Care
I Gotta Right to Sing the Blues
I Can't Get Started
I Wish I Were in Love Again
I'll Build a Stairway to Paradise
I'll Be Around
I'll Be Seeing You
I'll Walk Alone
I'll Never Smile Again
I'll Get By
I'll See You in My Dreams
I'll Remember April
I'm Old-Fashioned
I'm Confessin'
I'm in the Mood for Love
I'm Through With Love
I've Got a Crush on You
I've Got the World on a String
I've Got Five Dollars
I've Got it Bad and That
   Ain't Good
I've Got My Love to Keep
   Me Warm
I've Grown Accustomed to
   Her Face
What Kind of Fool Am I?
Who Can I Turn To?
Mean to Me
Me and My Shadow
But Not for Me
That's for Me
Lucky to Be Me
Don't Blame Me
They Didn't Believe Me
Everything Happens to Me
My Romance
My Old Flame

My Funny Valentine
My Foolish Heart
By Myself

Dreams
Dream
I'll See You in My Dreams
This Time the Dream's on Me
Out of My Dreams
I Had the Craziest Dream
I Can Dream, Can't I?
Dream a Little Dream of Me
Dream Dancing
Darn That Dream

Indecision
What'll I Do?
Maybe
I Can't Get Started
Who Can I Turn To?
Let's Call the Whole Thing Off

Conditional
If I Loved You
If I Had a Talking Picture of You
If I Only Had a Brain
If I Were a Bell
If Ever I Would Leave You
If I Should Lose You
Were Thine That Special Face
Wouldn't It Be Loverly?
S'posin'

Cardiology
Be Careful, It's My Heart
I Left My Heart at the Stage
   Door Canteen
I Left My Heart in San Francisco
My Heart Stood Still
Nobody's Heart Belongs to Me
With a Song in My Heart
My Foolish Heart

Flora and Fauna
I Talk to the Trees
Orchids in the Moonlight
The Heather on the Hill
Mountain Greenery
Apple Blossom Time
A Sleepin' Bee
Skylark
Bob White
Mister Meadowlark
Baltimore Oriole

10 Funniest Broadway Songs?
Little Tin Box. *Fiorello!* Sheldon Harnick

Gee, Officer Krupke! *West Side Story*. Stephen Sondheim

You Can't Get a Man With a Gun. *Annie Get Your Gun*. Irving Berlin

Always True to You in My Fashion. *Kiss Me, Kate*. Cole Porter

Adelaide's Lament. *Guys and Dolls*. Frank Loesser

Diamonds Are a Girl's Best Friend. *Gentlemen Prefer Blondes*. Leo Robin

I Wish I Were in Love Again. *Babes in Arms*. Lorenz Hart

A Hymn to Him (Why Can't a Woman Be More Like a Man?). *My Fair Lady*. Alan Jay Lerner

Captain Hook's Waltz. *Peter Pan*. Betty Comden and Adolph Green

A Woman's Prerogative. *St. Louis Woman*. Johnny Mercer

The 25 Most-Performed Songs and Musical Works of the 20th Century (in order of frequency). Compiled by the American Society of Authors, Composers and Publishers (ASCAP)

Happy Birthday to You. Mildred J. Hill and Patty Hill

Tea for Two. Vincent Youmans and Irving Caesar

Moon River. Henry Mancini and Johnny Mercer

Over the Rainbow. Harold Arlen and E. Y. Harburg

White Christmas. Irving Berlin

Hello, Dolly! Jerry Herman

As Time Goes By. Herman Hupfeld

Blue Moon. Richard Rodgers and Lorenz Hart

Rhapsody in Blue. George Gershwin

Night and Day. Cole Porter

Santa Claus Is Coming to Town. J. Fred Coots and Haven Gillespie

Misty. Errol Garner and Johnny Burke

Raindrops Keep Fallin' on My Head. Burt Bacharach and Hal David

Mack the Knife (theme from "The Threepenny Opera"). Kurt Weill and Mark Blitzstein

Unchained Melody. Alex North and Hy Zaret

The Christmas Song ("Chestnuts roasting"). Mel Tormé and Robert Wells

Sweet Georgia Brown. Ben Bernie, Kenneth Casey and Maceo Pinkard

Winter Wonderland. Felix Bernard and Richard B. Smith

I Left My Heart in San Francisco. Douglass Cross and George C. Corey, Jr.

I Only Have Eyes for You. Harry Warren and Al Dubin

I Got Rhythm. George and Ira Gershwin

The Way We Were. Marvin Hamlisch and Alan and Marilyn Bergman

Star Dust. Hoagy Carmichael and Mitchell Parish

I Could Have Danced All Night. Frederick Loewe and Alan Jay Lerner

That Old Black Magic. Harold Arlen and Johnny Mercer

Mildred and Patty Hill, the sisters who wrote "Happy Birthday to You," were teachers of kindergarten and Sunday school in Louisville, Kentucky, during the 1890s and were later associated with Columbia University in New York. Their song was originally called "Good Morning to You." With the addition of birthday lyrics it was copyrighted as "Happy Birthday to You" in 1935 and, according to ASCAP, has since been publicly sung hundreds of millions of times and extensively used in the theater, in movies and on television.

ACKNOWLEDGMENTS

For valuable editorial suggestions on the manuscript I'm grateful to John S. Rosenberg, Caroline Zinsser, David Godine, Chester Biscardi, Kathleen Landis and Warren Wechsler.

For other valued gifts of help and information I'm grateful to Gardner Botsford, Ted Chapin, Joe Derise, Fred Ebb, Allan Ecker, Rosemarie Gawelko, Hal Glatzer, Flora Griggs, Mary Cleere Haran, Harold Healy, Dick Hyman, John Kander, Sydney Leff, Walter Lord, Christine Moog, Gail Raab, Willie Ruff, Carl W. Scarbrough, Jim Steinblatt, Irwin Touster and Nancy Walworth.

For their generous help in my search for photographs I warmly thank Hoagy B. Carmichael, Betty Comden, Mike Dvorchak, Sheldon Harnick, Edward Jablonski, Gene Lees, Nick Markovich, David McKeown, Peter Mintun, Peter Rauch, Julia Riva, Rebecca Rosen, Barry Singer, Roberta Staats, Dave Stein, Margaret Styne, Joseph Weiss, Margaret Whiting and Vincent Youmans, Jr.

SOURCES AND NOTES

Stories about the great songwriters and their shows have circulated for so long and have been told in so many books that I no longer remember where I first heard what. I've written this book out of a lifetime of reading and listening to those stories and seeing the musicals and movies in which the songs were performed. For factual information about the songwriters I've consulted the sources cited below. The opinions about their work are my own.

But every discipline has its sacred texts, which shape the knowledge and the sensibility of its followers. Our bible is the composer Alec Wilder's *American Popular Song: The Great Innovators, 1900–1950* (Oxford University Press, 1972). Wilder examined the sheet music of some 17,000 songs, from which he selected 300 in which he felt that the composer had pushed into new territory or, at least, had "maintained the high level of sophisticated craftsmanship" that earlier innovators had established. His focus is not on the lyricists but on the composers, especially Berlin, Kern, Gershwin, Arlen, Rodgers and Porter. Written with deep knowledge and affection, the book can be endlessly revisited with a fresh sense of discovery.

My other good friend is Ira Gershwin's *Lyrics on Several Occasions* (Alfred A. Knopf, 1959; Limelight Editions, 1997). The book, which borrows the format of early English diarists like Samuel Pepys, is subtitled: "A Selection of Stage & Screen Lyrics Written for Sundry Situations; and Now Arranged in Arbitrary Categories.

To Which Have Been Added Many Informative Annotations & Disquisitions on Their Why & Wherefore, Their Whom-For, Their How; and Matters Associative. By Ira Gershwin, *Gent.*" In 21st-century English, it's a book containing 104 lyrics by Ira Gershwin, accompanied by explanatory comments written with humor and charm.

Two continuing bodies of work that I've long admired for their authority and rigor are *Gene Lees' Jazzletter* (PO Box 240, Ojai, CA 93024) and Stephen Holden's critical coverage of American popular song in the *New York Times*. Lees has been writing his newsletter about songwriters and jazz musicians since 1981, and many of its pieces have since found their way into his books.

Good biographies of the songwriters keep being written (see below). Lyric writers get their scholarly due in Philip Furia's *Poets of Tin Pan Alley: A History of America's Great Lyricists* (Oxford University Press, 1990).

Finally, my book couldn't have been written without *The Oxford Companion to Popular Music*, by Peter Gammond (Oxford University Press, 1991). I kept this 739-page volume within reach at all times and plundered it gratefully for titles, dates and biographical facts.

The papers of most of these songwriters are preserved in libraries and special collections, and I've listed those archives in my bibliography to help scholars on more specialized quests. For scholars interested in the relation of the songs to the musicals and movies in which they were performed, the broadest source is the New York Public Library for the Performing Arts, 40 Lincoln Center Plaza, New York, NY 10023. Or www.nypl.org/research/lpa/lpa.html

Specific acknowledgments follow.

Jerome Kern and Oscar Hammerstein II
The story of Ukulele Ike and Marilyn Miller is from Oscar Hammerstein's introduction to *The Jerome Kern Songbook: The Words and Music of 50 of His Best-Loved Songs* (Simon & Schuster, 1955).

Details of the first production of *Show Boat* are from "Some Words About 'Show Boat,'" by Miles Kreuger, and "Notes on 'Show Boat,'" by John McGlinn, both in the booklet accompanying McGlinn's 1988 recording of the original *Show Boat* with all its restorations (EMI-Angel 49108). The booklet also includes the complete libretto and lyrics. For further information, see "A Critic at Large: 'Show Boat' Crosses Over," by Ethan Mordden, the *New Yorker*, July 3, 1989.

Jerome Kern's papers are at the Library of Congress, Music Division, 101 Independence Avenue, SE, Washington, D.C. 20540-4710.

George and Ira Gershwin
Details about George Gershwin's early life and career are from *The Gershwins*, by Robert Kimball and Alfred Simon (Bonanza Books, 1973), a coffee-table book full of photographs and memorabilia of the Gershwin years. For further information, see *The Gershwin Years*, by Edward Jablonski and Lawrence D. Stewart (Doubleday & Company, 1958); *Gershwin: A Biography*, by Edward Jablonski (Doubleday & Company, 1988); and *Ira Gershwin: The Art of the Lyricist*, by Philip Furia (Oxford University Press, 1996).

The papers of the Gershwin brothers are at the Library of Congress and at the Ira and Leonore Gershwin Trusts, 101 Natoma Street, San Francisco, CA 94105.

Early Rodgers and Hart
Biographical details about the young Richard Rodgers and the early years of his collaboration with Lorenz Hart are from the biography *Richard Rodgers*, by David Ewen (Henry Holt and Company, 1957). Also see *Thou Swell, Thou Witty: The Life and Lyrics of Lorenz Hart*, edited and with a memoir by Dorothy Hart (Harper & Row, 1976).

Anatomy of the Popular Song
Ira Gershwin's explanation of what it takes to be a lyricist is from his *Lyrics on Several Occasions* (see above).

Vincent Youmans
The Vincent Youmans Collection is at the Library of Congress.

Harold Arlen
My article about Arlen, "Harold Arlen: The Secret Music Maker," ran in the May 1960 issue of *Harper's*. The definitive biography is Edward Jablonski's *Harold Arlen: Rhythm, Rainbow and Blues* (Northeastern University Press, 1996). An excellent documentary film, *Somewhere Over the Rainbow: Harold Arlen*, produced and directed by Don McGlynn, Myron Meisel and Joe Lauro, was presented on PBS television in 1999 and is now available on VCR (Deep C Productions, East Hampton, NY 11939). The film includes home movies of the young Arlen playing the piano during the Cotton Club years and enjoying the poolside life of Movieland with E. Y. Harburg and other Hollywood songwriters.

Andy Razaf
This chapter is indebted to two sources. One is *Black and Blue: The Life and Lyrics of Andy Razaf*, a thorough and interesting biography by Barry Singer (Schirmer Books, 1992). The other is the *Smithsonian Collection of American Recordings, American Songbook Series: Waller/Razaf*, especially the program notes by J. R. Taylor.

Cole Porter

My main source for details of Cole Porter's life was William Mc-Brien's *Cole Porter: A Biography* (Alfred A. Knopf, 1998), a biography of unusual sensitivity and depth—and the first, I believe, to assess Porter's work in the context of his homosexuality. Also see *Cole: Edited by Robert Kimball. A Biographical Essay by Brendan Gill* (Holt, Rinehart & Winston, 1971), an opulent coffee-table book that includes 200 Porter lyrics, chronologically arranged by show, plus hundreds of photographs, letters, manuscript pages and other memorabilia.

Cole Porter's archives are deposited mainly at the Cole Porter Musical and Literary Property Trusts, 1285 Avenue of the Americas, 31st floor, New York, NY 10019-6064, and at the Yale University Library, Historical Sound Recordings, Box 1603A Yale Station, New Haven, CT 06520.

Porgy and Bess

For a fuller account of the infiltration of African music into Eastern Europe and Russia, see the chapter "Venice" in my book *Willie and Dwike*, (Harper & Row, 1984; Paul Dry Books, 2000, paperback; retitled *Mitchell & Ruff*).

The story of Ben Harris and the sheet music cover of *Porgy and Bess* is told by Hal Glatzer in "Seen But Not Heard, Artists Helped Sell the Songs," the *New York Times*, August 23, 1998.

For another glimpse of George Gershwin's sensitivity to African Americans and their music, see Barry Singer's interview with the 85-year-old Anne Wiggins Brown, the original Bess, in the *New York Times*, March 29, 1998: "On Hearing Her Sing, Gershwin Made 'Porgy' 'Porgy and Bess.'" Brown recalls that as a 21-year-old graduate student at Juilliard, in 1933, she heard that Gershwin was writing an opera "about Negroes in South Carolina" and wrote him a letter. "Two days later his secretary called and said I should come down to his apartment and bring lots of music. I sang Brahms and Schubert and Massenet and even 'The Man I Love.' And then he said, 'Would you sing a Negro spiritual?' I was very much on the defensive at that age. I resented the fact that most white people thought that most black people should or only could sing spirituals. 'I am very sorry,' I said, 'but I haven't any of *that* music with me.' And then I broke out, 'Why is it that you people always expect black singers to sing spirituals?'

"He just looked at me. He didn't say or do anything at all; he didn't appear angry or disturbed. But I saw that he understood my reaction. And as soon as I saw that, my whole attitude just melted away and I wanted more than anything else to sing a spiritual for this man. I said, 'I can sing one spiritual without an accompaniment, if that's O.K. He told me it was. And I sang 'City Called Heaven.' It's a very plaintive, very melancholy spiritual. And I knew when it was finished that I had never sung it better in my life, because I was so emotionally involved at that moment.

"He was very quiet for some time. Finally he spoke: 'Wherever you go, you must sing that spiritual without accompaniment. It's the most beautiful spiritual I've ever heard.' And we hugged one another." That audition led to Brown's winning the part and to *Porgy*'s being renamed *Porgy and Bess* as Gershwin composed "more and more music" for her expanded role.

Writing for Fred Astaire: Irving Berlin

The best biography of the songwriter is *Irving Berlin: A Daughter's Memoir*, by Mary Ellin Barrett (Simon & Schuster, 1994). The author of several novels, Barrett brings to the story of her father's life the texture and insights of a novelist and the obvious love of a daughter. Also see *Irving Berlin, American Troubadour*, by Edward Jablonski (Henry Holt and Company, 1999).

Irving Berlin's papers are at the Library of Congress. Also see the Website www.irvingberlin.com.

Writing for Fred Astaire: Dorothy Fields

I'm indebted to Mary Cleere Haran for her article, "Dorothy Fields," in the *Village Voice*, June 12, 1993, especially for her point about Fields' sexual assertiveness. In the lyric of "Don't Blame Me," for example, Haran notes that Fields' persona is "forthright and self-assured, making the lyric just about as sexy as it can be. Never coy. Never hesitant. She gets right to the heart of the matter, unlike some of the boys, who could be ponderous (Hammerstein), verbose (Dietz) or flippant (Cole Porter). Which only reaffirms the age-old secret that men, not women, are really the prudes in this society."

My facts about Kay Swift, Ann Ronell and Dana Suesse were taken from the *American Masters* program, "Yours for a Song: The Women of Tin Pan Alley," broadcast on PBS television in New York on August 18, 1999.

Duke Ellington

I learned about the composer's early life and career from his book, *Music Is My Mistress*, by Edward Kennedy Ellington (Doubleday & Company, 1973). Other sources were "Ellington at 100: Reveling in Life's Majesty," by Wynton Marsalis, the *New York Times*, January 17, 1999, and "A Jazz of Their Own," by Strayhorn's biographer David

Hajdu, which describes the close bond between Ellington and Strayhorn, *Vanity Fair*, May 1999.

Hoagy Carmichael

Responding to an article of mine that mentioned the prevalence skies (buttermilk and otherwise) in his father's work, Hoagy B. Carmichael wrote me: "Dad often pointed out what was to him a 'buttermilk sky'—cloud formations that often cover the sky in tightly knit rows of small billows, like curdling milk. That formation must have had strong associations for him, going back to Indiana, because I have seen him point to the clouds often. 'Clouds,' 'sky,' 'stars' and certainly 'moon' are liberally sprinkled through many of the tunes. Where was the 'sun' in those early days in Indiana?"

He added: "You might enjoy having a look at Dad's first book, *The Star Dust Road*. You can get it in paperback from the Indiana University Press in Bloomington, Indiana. Like much of his music, it's a jazz piece, and it might put a few things about him in a slightly different light. He also wrote *Sometimes I Wonder*, published by Farrar, Straus & Giroux, but it is darn hard to find."

Hoagy Carmichael's papers are at the Archives of Traditional Music, 117 Morrison Hall, University of Indiana, Bloomington, IN 47405. The Website for the collection is www.dlib.indiana.edu/collections/hoagy/index.html.

Biographical facts about the lyricist Mitchell Parish are from the obituary by Stephen Holden in the *New York Times*, April 2, 1993.

Harry Warren

Much of what I needed to verify for this book I found without leaving home: by listening to old records, by reading the information on record jackets and sheet music covers, and by thumbing through the "songbooks" of various songwriters. Typical of that inelegant but useful genre is *The Great Songs of Harry Warren, from 42nd Street to Hollywood* (Warner Bros. Publications, Inc., 1989). The sheet-music-size book includes a brief biography by Warren's daughter, Cookie Warren Jones; the music and words of 58 of his songs, from "About a Quarter to Nine" to "Zing a Little Zong"; a chronological list of (presumably) all his 342 published songs—from "Rose of the Rio Grande" (1922) to "Just Call Me Sunny" (1981)—and of the 77 movies those songs were in, and some photographs of the composer with the likes of Kate Smith, Al Jolson and Busby Berkeley. It's just about all I need to know about Harry Warren, and it's all admirable.

For further research, consult Four Jay's Music Company, 6399 Wilshire Boulevard, Los Angeles, CA 90048, or the Website www.harrywarrenmusic.com.

E. Y. Harburg

Gene Lees' "Salute to a Squirrel," published in his *Jazzletter*, vol. 12, no. 8 (August 1993), is a shrewd analysis of the contrast between Harburg's poor boyhood and the privileged upbringing of the other major songwriters. "That Harburg alone in his crowd was not born to comfort," Lees writes, "goes far to explain his compassion for the common man and the deep difference between his work and that of every other Broadway lyricist. Alan Jay Lerner's occasional attempts to write musicals of social conscience, including *Love Life*, with Kurt Weill, are awkward and embarrassing. Lerner knew nothing of poverty and poor people . . . Harburg's shows have a bite and urgency that Lerner could not attain and that others on Broadway never even aspired to."

Also see Aljean Harmetz's *The Making of the Wizard of Oz* (Alfred A. Knopf, 1977). This enjoyable book about the complexities of producing one of America's favorite movies has a chapter describing how Harburg and Harold Arlen went about writing the score.

E. Y. Harburg's archives are at the Harburg Foundation, 225 Lafayette St., New York, NY 10012, and at the Yale University Library, Historical Sound Recordings, Box 1603A Yale Station, New Haven, CT 06520.

The Songs of World War II

Frank Loesser's advice on this patriotic genre is quoted in Paul Fussell's book, *Wartime* (Oxford University Press, 1989). Early in the war, Fussell writes, the American government encouraged the writing of songs that it thought would be good for morale, like "We're Going to Hang Out the Washing on the Siegfried Line" and "The Japs Don't Have a Chinaman's Chance." Loesser's extensive "Ballad of Rodger Young," which memorialized an infantryman who posthumously won the Medal of Honor for storming a Japanese machine-gun nest, "proved too embarrassing for either the troops or the more intelligent home folks to take to their hearts," Fussell says. "Sensing that some explanation of his behavior was called for, Loesser later commented on this kind of songwriting: 'You give [them] hope without facts; glory without blood. You give them a legend with the rough edges neatly trimmed.'"

Johnny Mercer

For an affectionate look back over Mercer's life and work, see *Our Huckleberry Friend: The Life, Times and Lyrics of Johnny Mercer*, collected and edited by Bob Bach and Ginger Mercer (Lyle Stuart, Inc., 1982), a grab bag of reminiscence, lyrics, photographs, letters and other memorabilia. Also see the songbook *Too Marvelous for Words* (Warner

Bros. Publications, Inc., 1985), the music and lyrics of 60 Mercer songs, from "Accentuate the Positive" to "You Were Never Lovelier."

Johnny Mercer's archives are at the William Russell Pullen Library, Special Collections Department, Georgia State University, 100 Decatur Street, SE, Atlanta, GA 30303-3081.

Made in Hollywood

Again I thank Aljean Harmetz. In her engaging book, *Round Up the Usual Suspects: The Making of 'Casablanca'—Bogart, Bergman and World War II* (Hyperion, 1992), Harmetz describes how Herman Hupfeld's "As Time Goes By" was exhumed for the movie *Casablanca* and woven through its musical score. Her book is rich in details about the Hollywood moviemaking process and about the historical accidents that gave *Casablanca* its emotional impact in the early days of the war, especially the casting in small but memorable roles of many actors who were recent refugees from Europe themselves.

The painful birth of David Raksin's "Laura" is described in "The Man Who Was Laura and the Golden Age of Film Music," by Ed Shanaphy, *Sheet Music Magazine*, January/February 1995.

Kurt Weill

Recalling the origins of his song "Tschaikowsky," Ira Gershwin writes in *Lyrics on Several Occasions*: "Not all of the 49 composers have been necessarily merely names to me. Rumshinsky, who wrote musical-comedy scores for the Yiddish theater, I met several times when I lived on Second Avenue; he was a pinochle-playing companion of my father's . . . Godowsky's son Leo, musician and inventor, married my sister."

Victor Mature's colorful obituary, by Aljean Harmetz, was in the *New York Times* on August 10, 1999.

Kurt Weill's primary archive in this country is the Kurt Weill Foundation and the Weill-Lenya Research Center, 7 East 20th Street, New York, NY 10003-1106. Or www.kwf.org.

Rodgers and Hammerstein

Oscar Hammerstein's account of how Richard Rodgers differed from other songwriters is from his introduction to *Lyrics*, by Oscar Hammerstein II (Simon & Schuster, 1949), in which he describes his own approach to the craft of lyric writing. The book also includes 71 of Hammerstein's lyrics.

Oscar Hammerstein's papers and Richard Rodgers' musical manuscripts and professional papers are at the Library of Congress. For details on the Rodgers & Hammerstein collaboration—performance information, background articles, song lists, etc.—see the Website www.rnh.com.

Singers of the Song

Gene Lees' *Singers and the Song II* (Oxford University Press, 1998), an expanded version of the book first published in 1987, examines the style and the methods—especially the phrasing—of many popular singers, including Ella Fitzgerald, Julius La Rosa, Peggy Lee, Johnny Mercer, Edith Piaf, Frank Sinatra and Jo Stafford. With an especially valuable chapter on the Brazilian composer and singer Antonio Carlos Jobim.

Jule Styne

The biographical details are mainly from the excellent obituary by Eleanor Blau in the *New York Times*, September 21, 1994.

Jule Styne's archive is at the Theater Arts Collection, Harry Ransom Humanities Research Center, University of Texas, PO Drawer 7219, Austin, TX 78713-7219. Or www.lib.utexas.edu/hrc/home.html

Frank Loesser

"Wall to Wall Frank Loesser," a 12-hour marathon of Loesser songs presented by Symphony Space, in New York, on March 29, 1999, hosted by Robert Kimball and Isaiah Sheffer, was a helpful archeological excavation of numbers that Loesser wrote for Hollywood movies in the 1930s and early 1940s, including "The Traffic Was Terrific," "No Ring on Her Finger," "Doing the Dishes," "Sand in My Shoes," "Kiss the Boys Goodbye" and "I'm Going North."

The details of Loesser's and Irving Actman's Universal contract are from a biography of Loesser by his daughter, Susan Loesser, *Most Remarkable Fella* (Donald I. Fine, Inc., 1993).

Frank Loesser's papers are at Frank Loesser Enterprises, 56 West 45th Street, New York, NY 10036.

Betty Comden and Adolph Green

The papers of Comden & Green are at the New York Public Library for the Performing Arts (see above) and at the Museum of the City of New York, Fifth Avenue and 103rd Street, New York, NY 10029.

Jimmy Van Heusen

Biographical facts are from the obituary by Stephen Holden in the *New York Times*, February 8, 1990.

The Jimmy Van Heusen Collection of Musical Works and Papers, 1920–1991, is at the UCLA Music Library Special Collections, Box 951490, Los Angeles, CA 90095-1490.

The biographical facts about Sammy Cahn are from the obituary by Stephen Holden in the *New York Times*, January 16, 1993. The story of Cahn's violin-playing boyhood is from *They're Playing

Our Song, by Max Wilk (Atheneum, 1973), an anecdotal book of interviews with 21 songwriters from Jerome Kern to Stephen Sondheim.

Alan Jay Lerner and Frederick Loewe

The Street Where I Live, by Alan Jay Lerner (Da Capo Press, 1994), was my source for the production history of *My Fair Lady.* Lerner minutely recalls the long and laborious conception, gestation and birth of three Lerner and Loewe shows: the musicals *My Fair Lady* and *Camelot* and the movie *Gigi.* Complete lyrics from all three shows are included.

John Kander and Fred Ebb (and others)

This last roundup doesn't include the important composer-lyricist team of Burt Bacharach and Hal David because they occupy a different niche. Although they did write one Broadway musical, *Promises, Promises* ("I'll Never Fall in Love Again"), their legacy is the string of tremendous individual hits they wrote during the 1960s, many of them introduced by Dionne Warwick. Bacharach's dynamic musical signature was something new in American popular song. Which is why his tunes still linger in the national memory: "Alfie," "Close to You," "What the World Needs Now Is Love," "Do You Know the Way to San José?", "I Say a Little Prayer," "Raindrops Keep Falling on My Head," "The Look of Love," "Reach Out for Me" and many more.

John Kander and Fred Ebb aren't the only working custodians of America's musical theater tradition. Many cabaret artists of a younger generation have become ardent preservationists, not only in the historical content of their acts but as scholars, writers and consultants. Some of the best are Karen Akers, Ann Hampton Callaway, Michael Feinstein, Mary Cleere Haran, Diana Krall, Kathleen Landis, Maureen McGovern, John Pizzarelli and Daryl Sherman.

Two of New York's cultural institutions have also embraced the tradition. One is Lincoln Center for the Performing Arts, whose *American Songbook* series, devoted to American standards, was launched in 1999 with homages to Harold Arlen, Richard Rodgers and Jimmy Van Heusen and is now a continuing component of Lincoln Center. Created by Nathan Leventhal, *American Songbook* is under the artistic direction of Jonathan Schwartz, long the dean of preservationists in his multiple roles as a radio host. The other institution is City Center, whose *Encores!* series, under the musical direction of Rob Fisher, has been producing revivals of American musicals in concert form since 1994. Some of the born-again shows have been Bock and Harnick's *Fiorello!,* Kern and Hammerstein's *Sweet Adeline,* Rodgers and Hart's *The Boys From Syracuse,* Arlen and Mercer's *St. Louis Woman* and Irving Berlin's *Louisiana Purchase.*

PICTURE ACKNOWLEDGMENTS

The sheet music covers are from my own collection, except for page 73 (the Andy Razaf estate); pp. 32 and 132 (Nancy Walworth); pp. 50 and 149 (Harold Healy); pp. 154 and 166 (Walter Lord), and page 174, the Kurt Weill Foundation. Credit pages for the photographs follow:

8, 16, 30, 130, 178, The Rodgers & Hammerstein Organization.

22 (top), 60, 102, 106, courtesy of Peter Rauch.

22 (bottom), 27, 58, 108, 114, 177, courtesy of Edward Jablonski.

65, photograph by Edward Jablonski.

48, 52, courtesy of Vincent Youmans, Jr.

66, 94, 97, 116, 129, 216, 228, Photofest.

70, 74, The Andy Razaf estate, courtesy of Barry Singer.

84, 91, 93, courtesy of the Cole Porter Musical and Literary Property Trusts.

98, courtesy of Kathleen Landis.

109, courtesy of Peter Mintun.

122, courtesy of Hoagy B. Carmichael.

136, 143, courtesy of Julia Riva.

144, 147, courtesy of the Harburg Foundation.

153, 198, 200, courtesy of Frank Loesser Enterprises.

156, photograph by Gene Lees. Courtesy of Gene Lees.

162, courtesy of Margaret Whiting.

170, photograph by Louise Dahl-Wolfe; the Staley-Wise Gallery.

192, 194, courtesy of Margaret Styne.

206, 208, courtesy of Betty Comden.

212, photograph by Rivka Katvan.

218, 220, 221, UCLA Music Library Special Collections.

234, courtesy of John Kander.

237, courtesy of Sheldon Harnick.

INDEX OF PEOPLE

INDEX OF MUSICALS AND MOVIES

INDEX OF SONG TITLES

PERMISSIONS

ABOUT THE
AUTHOR

William Zinsser is a writer, editor and teacher. He began his career on the *New York Herald Tribune* and has since written regularly for leading magazines. He taught writing at Yale, where he was master of Branford College, and now teaches at the New School, in New York, his home town, where he lives with his wife Caroline Zinsser.

BOOKS BY
WILLIAM ZINSSER

Any Old Place With You
Seen Any Good Movies Lately?
The City Dwellers
Weekend Guests
The Haircurl Papers
Pop Goes America
The Paradise Bit
The Lunacy Boom
On Writing Well
Writing with a Word Processor
Willie and Dwike
    (republished as *Mitchell & Ruff*)
Writing to Learn
Spring Training
American Places
Speaking of Journalism
Easy to Remember

AUDIO BOOKS BY
WILLIAM ZINSSER

On Writing Well
How to Write a Memoir

BOOKS EDITED BY
WILLIAM ZINSSER

Extraordinary Lives: The Art and Craft of American Biography
Inventing the Truth: The Art and Craft of Memoir
Spiritual Quests: The Art and Craft of Religious Writing
Paths of Resistance: The Art and Craft of the Political Novel
Worlds of Childhood: The Art and Craft of Writing for Children
They Went: The Art and Craft of Travel Writing
Going on Faith: Writing as a Spiritual Quest

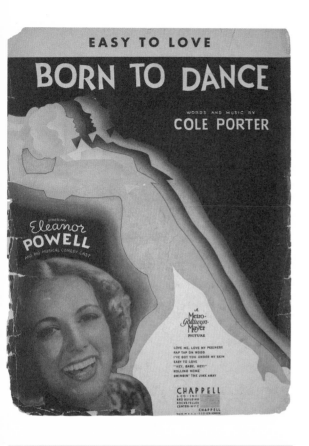

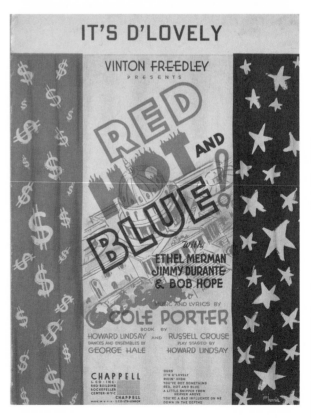